KENT COUNTY, DELAWARE LAND RECORDS

VOLUME 2
1702-1722

Mary Marshall Brewer

HERITAGE BOOKS
2008

HERITAGE BOOKS
AN IMPRINT OF HERITAGE BOOKS, INC.

Books, CDs, and more—Worldwide

For our listing of thousands of titles see our website
at
www.HeritageBooks.com

Published 2008 by
HERITAGE BOOKS, INC.
Publishing Division
100 Railroad Avenue #104
Westminster, Maryland 21157

Copyright © 1997 Mary Marshall Brewer

Other books by the author:

Kent County, Delaware Land Records. Volume 2: 1702-1722
Kent County, Delaware Land Records. Volume 3: 1723-1734
Kent County, Delaware Land Records. Volume 4: 1735-1743
Kent County, Delaware Land Records. Volume 5: 1742-1749
Kent County, Delaware Land Records. Volume 6: 1749-1756
Kent County, Delaware, Land Records. Volume 7: 1756-1764
Kent County, Delaware, Land Records. Volume 8: 1764-1768
Land Records of Sussex County, Delaware, 1681-1725
Land Records of Sussex County, Delaware: Various Dates: 1693-1698, 1715-1717, 1782-1792, 1802-1805
Land Records of Sussex County, Delaware, 1763-1769
Land Records of Sussex County, Delaware, 1753-1763

All rights reserved. No part of this book may be reproduced or transmitted in any form or by any means, electronic or mechanical, including photocopying, recording or by any information storage and retrieval system without written permission from the author, except for the inclusion of brief quotations in a review.

International Standard Book Number: 978-1-58549-404-0

INTRODUCTION[1]

Few records of the Swedish Colony (1638-1655) have survived. From 1655 to 1664 and from 1673 to 1674, the Dutch West India Company and the City of Amsterdam were proprietors of the land which became Delaware (ignoring claims by the Calverts of Maryland). The surviving records are held by the Archives of New York at Albany.

The Duke of York was proprietor from 1664 to 1673 and from 1674 to 1682. These land records are also held at Albany. *Original Land Titles in Delaware, commonly known as The Duke of York Record, 1646-1679*, was printed by order of the General Assembly of the State of Delaware (1899), reprinted by Family Line Publications in 1989.

Kent County, originally a part of Whorekill District (created in 1664), became an independent territory under the name of St. Jones County in 1680. In circa 1682, simultaneous with the transfer of government from the Duke of York, the name was changed to Kent County.

Subsequent to 1674, settlers (principally from Maryland) began to take up land in this area. On 13 April 1676, patents were issued to persons residing within the limits of Kent County, as follows:

William Stevens, *Yorke*, 600 acres.
William Ford, Ducke Creeke, 800 acres.
William Sharpe, Ducke Creeke, 500 acres.
John Morgan, Ducke Creeke, 300 acres.
William Simpson, *Simpson's Choice*, 400 acres.
John Briggs, *Aberdeane*, 400 acres.
Peter Baucom, 200 acres.
Thomas Philip, Jones' Creek, 600 acres.
Robert Francis, Jones' Creek, 400 acres.
Francis Neal, Jones Creek, 400 acres.
John Stevens, *Content*, Duck Creek, 1200 acres.
John Stevens, *London*, Little Creek, 1300 acres.

---

[1] Most of the information was obtained from J. Thomas Scharf, *History of Delaware, 1607-1888* (1888). Philadelphia: Richards, 2 vols. Reprinted by Family Line Publications, 1990.

Later the following patents were granted:

5 March 1678
>John Kiphaven and Peter Hanson, *Hopewell*, 413 acres, on north side of Murder Creek.

23 February 1678
>John Briggs, *Poplar Ridge*, 260 acres, above Jones' Creek adjoining Poplar Neck.

11 March 1678
>Robert Hart, Jr., *Pritchard's*, 600 acres, on north side of Misspan Creek.
>Orphan's Lot, 600 acres near *Pritchard's*.
>Cornelius Verhoofe, *New Sevenhaven*, 1218 acres, on north side of Misspan Creek, by Indian Bridge and Beaver Creek.

12 March 1678
>John Briggs and Mrs. Mary Phillips, *Kingston Upon Hull*, 450 acres, "where they now dwell," on the north side of Jones' Creek; a portion of it was formerly taken by George Whale in June 1671.

10 September 1679
>Peter Groenendike, *New Sevenhaven*, 400 acres, on north side of Murderkill Creek.

14 February 1680
>Thomas Garvin, *Garvin's*, 300 acres, on St. Jones' Creek, adjoining John Brinkloe.
>Thomas Clifford, 400 acres on St. Jones' Creek.

10 May 1680
>William Sherritt, *Sherritt's Choyce*, 116 acres, on south side of Duck Creek.

F. Edward Wright
Westminster, Maryland
1996

ABBREVIATIONS USED

a - acre
ackn - acknowledge(d)
adj - adjoining
adminr - administrator(s)
afsd - aforesaid
atty - attorney(s)
br - branch
co - county
cr - creek
dau - daughter(s)
decd - deceased
DEL - Delaware
e - east
Gent - Gentleman/Gentlemen
junr - junior
MD - Maryland
n - north
NJ - New Jersey
PA - Pennsylvania
Phila - Philadelphia
pt/o - part of
s - south
senr - senior
Suss - Sussex
tr - tract
w - west

Deed Record D Vol. 1

1. 25 Feb 1702. Quit Claim. JOHN BOWMAN of Kent Co PA & MARGRET his wife the only surviving dau & heir of BENONI BISHOP late of same co decd whereas OVEN GARVIE of same co and ELIZABETH his wife the eldest lawfull dau of said BENONI BISHOP decd then the wife of said OVEN GARVIE but now decd ... 13 Feb 1693 sold unto JOHN TOUNZEN of same co a parcell of land called INDIAN FIELDS being pt/o a tr of land called Tounzens Folly s side of Murther Cr beginning at the corner of SAMUELL MOTTS lands ... to corner of FRANCIS RENALLS ... 200 a. ... JOHN BOWMAN and MARGRET his wife ... for a competent sume of silver quitt claim unto JOHN TOUNZEN afsd tr of land ... Wit: JACOB EMERSON justice, OWEN GARVIE justice. Ackn 4 May 1703. (D:pg 1)

2. 10 Jun 1701. Deed. MATHEW MANLOVE of Kent Co PA for 24 pounds sold to JOHN CLARK of same co planter ... 200 a. being pt/o a tr of land called Mount Pleasant n side of Mispillion Cr ... Wit: WILLIAM ANNAND, JOHN FOSTER, NATHANIELL HUNN. Ackn 10 Feb 1702. (D:pg 2)

3. 18 Dec 1702. Deed. WILLIAM BRINCKLE of Kent Co PA weaver for 15 pounds sold to SAMUELL BURBERY of same co planter ... a tr of land being pt/o a tr of land heretofore belonging to JOHN BRINCKLOE of afsd co called Lisbon on Jones Cr otherways called Dover River beginning at the corner of land formerly belonging to THOMAS RODGIERS ... 77 a. ... Wit: WILLIAM ANNAND, STEPHEN SIMONS. Ackn 10 Feb 1702. (D:pg 3)

4. 3 Dec 1701. Deed. WILLIAM SHERER of Kent Co PA for 20 pounds sold to FRANCIS WESTWOOD (WETTSWOOD) of same co ... 100 a. on Parmains Br ... bounded by RICHARD TURNER's land formerly bought of WILLIAM SHERER ... being pt/o 900 a. in one patent belonging to said WILLIAM SHERER and where SHERER now dwelleth ... WILLIAM SHERER promise and agree with FRANCIS WESTWOOD that said WILLIAM SHERER stood seized of a good and absolute estate of inheritance of the afsd premises and shall be vested settled on and upon said FRANCIS WESTWOOD ... Wit: JOHN BRINCKLOE, THOMAS SHARP, EVAN JONES. Ackn 10 Feb 1702. (D:pg 4)

5. 15 Apr 1702. Deed. JOHN SMITH of Kent Co PA husbandman sold to JAMES FITZ GERALD of same co planter ... a tr of land called Short Island being pt/o a tr of land formerly belonging to JOHN BURTON n side of Dover River adj land formerly belonging to HENRY STEVENSON ... at line of JAMES CLAYTON's land ... 100 a. ... Wit: WM ANNAND,

SAMUELL BERRY, JOHN EVENS. Ackn 14 Apr 1702. (D:pg 6)

6. 1 Apr 1702. Receipt. WM ANNAND deputy received of TIMOTHY OCHARON of Kent Co PA full satisfaction of all judgments, bills, bonds, accounts, debts, dues and demands and I release and discharge said TIMOTHY from same ... (D:pg 7)

7. 28 Mar 1702. Marriage. JOHN BOWMAN and MARGARET BISHOP hath taken each other as husband and wife ... Wit: GEORGE ROBESON justice, JOHN WALKER, THOMAS BOWMAN, EDMOND NEEDHAM, WAITMAN SIPEL, GARRET SIPELL, ANNA ROBESON, SARAI ROBESON, DANILL NEEDHAM, ELIN ROBINSON, ELIZABETH COALI?, MARY MILLES. (D:pg 7)

8. 22 Jul 1701. Deed of Mortgage. ROBERT FRENCH of Kent Co PA merchant for 138 pounds silver sold to JOHN BURTON of same co carpenter and ELIZABETH his wife ... a tr of land being remainder of a grater tr of land called Burtons Delight adj se with land formerly sold by said JOHN BURTON to DANIELL JONES decd on the nw with the land of JOSEPH OSBORN on the sw with land of WALTER DICKENSON ... 180 a. ... JOHN BURTON to pay unto ROBERT FRENCH the afsd sum at one whole and entire payment at or upon 20 Dec 1705 ... Wit: GRIFF JONES, WILLIAM ANNAND. Ackn 9 Sep 1702. (D:pg 8)

9. 10 Feb 1701. Deed. OWEN GARVIE of Kent Co PA for 10 pounds sold to JOHN DUBROIS of same place ... a tr of land called Dubrois Purchase ne side of the Muddy Br of Jones Cr beginning at a corner oak standing a little distance from the KINGS's road and from THOMAS WILLSON's path ... 100 a. ... OWEN GARVIE appoint JOHN TOUNSEN of same co my atty to ackn this deed in open court ... Wit: JOHN TOUNSEND, RICHARD JACKSON, LYDDEA JACKSON. Ackn 14 Apr 1702 by JOHN TOUNSEND atty for OWEN GARVIE. (D:pg 9)

10. 10 Feb 1701. Deed. HENRY MOLESTON of Kent Co PA for 17 pounds sold to ROBERT BETTS of same co planter ... a tr of land n side of Mispillion Cr called Goosberry and is pt/o a 600 a. tr of land which said HENRY MOLESTON bought of DAVID POWELL ... bounded by REINIER WILLIAMS' land ... 153 a. ... Wit: WM WILLSON, WILLIAM BRINCKLE. Ackn 12 May 1702. (D:pg 10)

11. -- -- 1700. Deed. THOMAS SMITH of Maidenhead w NJ yeoman and SUSANNA his wife and JOSEPH SMITH of Jamaica in Queens Co upon Long Island alias Nassau yeoman and MARY his wife ... whereas STEPHEN PARRADEE of Kent Co yeoman 13 Sep 1698 did sell unto SAMUELL MATHEWS of Kent Co yeoman a tr of land pt/o a tr of land

called Execter containing 200 a. n side of Murtherkill ... and whereas JOHN DUBROIS of Kent Co 14 Sep 1698 did sell unto SAMUELL MATHEWS a tr of land called Paradees Pastime it being that tr of land STEPHEN SIMONS bought of RODGEIR SHURLEY called Execter and sold by said STEPHEN SIMONS to STEPHEN PARRADEE which is pt/o a tr of land THOMAS HEATHARD lived on called Ousbey ... 75 a. whereas SAMUELL MATHEWS above named decd without issue and interstate ... SUSANNA and MARY being sisters of the whole blood unto said SAMUEL for 48 pounds sold to EDMOND NEEDHAM of Kent Co PA yeoman the afsd parcells of land as they were sold to SAMUEL MATHEWS ... Wit: WILLIAM WARDELL. Ackn 12 May 1702 by THOMAS SKIDMORE atty to above named SMITH's. (D:pg 11)

12. 22 Jun 1702. Personally appeared in this office RICHARD GLOVER desired his sons age to be recorded, JOHN GLOVER son to RICHARD GLOVER and ELIZABETH his wife born in Kent Co PA and was three years old 27 Jan last. (D:pg 12)

13. 9 May 1702. Deed. ROBERT PORTER of Kent Co PA planter for 11 pounds sold to JAMES POTTER of same co planter ... a tr of land late in occupation of LAWRENCE PORTER decd being pt/o a grater tr of land called Simsons Choice n side of Little Cr beginning at the corner of SAMUEL BERRY's land ... 50 a. ... Wit: JOHN FOSTER, SAMUELL BERRY, MORACE SMITH. Ackn 12 May 1702. (D:pg 18)

14. 11 Dec 1700. Writ of Execution. ROBERT MCLEARE at a court held 9 Jul 1700 hath recovered against JAMES BROWN a debt of 76 pounds also 3 pounds 10 shillings 3 pence costs and charges ... RICHARD WILLSON justice commands WILLIAM WILLSON sheriff to make delivery at a reasonable vallue of the lands of JAMES BROWN unto ROBERT MCLEARE ... . (D:pg 14)

15. 31 Dec 1700. Inquisition. By virtue of [above] execution an inquisition was held by WILLIAM WILLSON sheriff of Kent Co PA ... seized 160 a. being the land whereon said JAMES BROWN dwelt upon ... se side of Murther Cr appraised to vallue of [above] debt by the jury of JOHN WALKER, JOHN FOSTER, THOMAS SKIDMORE, JOHN SMITH, JOHN ROBESON, GEORGE ROBESON, JOHN CLARK, JOHN TOUNSEND, MATHEW MANLOVE, ROBERT EDMONDSON, STEPHEN SIMONS, EDMOND NEEDHAM twelve good and lawful men ... (D:pg 14)

16. 1 Oct 1701. Deed. WILLIAM WILLSON sheriff of Kent Co PA for 90 pounds 1 shilling sold [above] tr of land belonging to JAMES BROWN at a public sale to GEORGE ROBINSON (ROBESON) of same co ... to

satisfy [above] judgment ... Wit: GRIFF JONES, JOHN BRADSHAW. Ackn 14 Apr 1702. (D:pg 14)

17. 10 Jul 1702. Deed. THOMAS SKIDMORE of Kent Co planter for 14 pounds silver sold to JOSEPH SKIDMORE of same co husbandman ... a tr of land called Fishers Delight being pt/o a greater tr of land called Dover Farms sw side of Dover River ... 92 a. heretofore in possession of ADAM FISHER of same co ... Wit: STEPHEN SIMONS, EZEKIELL NEEDHAM Senr, WILLIAM ANNAND. Ackn 12 Aug 1702. (D:pg 15)

18. 10 Aug 1702. Deed. EZEKIELL NEEDHAM Junr of Kent Co PA planter for a competent sum of silver money already payd sold to EZEKIELL NEEDHAM Senr of same co cordwainder ... a tr of land called Haminersmith being pt/o a tr of land formerly of THOMAS, HENRY & ROBERT BEDWELL and ADAM FISHER called Long Reach s side of Dover River beginning at the corner of land formerly belonging to EDMOND NEEDHAM ... along the line of HENRY BEDWELL late of same co decd ... 100 a. Wit: WILLIAM ANNAND, THOMAS SKIDMORE. Ackn 12 Aug 1702. (D:pg 17)

19. 10 Aug 1702. Deed. JOHN FLOURS (FLOWERS) of Kent Co PA planter for 16 pounds sold to EZEKIELL NEEDHAM Senr of same co cordwainder ... tr of land heretofore belonging to STEPHEN PARADEE of same co called Skidmores Folly n side of Murder Cr pt/o a tr of land formerly belonging to THOMAS HEWHAT called Ousbey ... 100 a. ... Wit: WILLIAM ANNAND, STEPHEN SIMONS. Ackn 12 Aug 1702. (D:pg 17)

20. 10 Jul 1702. Deed. CAPT JOHN BRINCKLOE of Kent Co PA for 71 pounds sold to BENJAMIN WHITE of same co husbandman ... a tr of land called Lisbon n side of Dover River ... bounded by land now belonging to SAMUELL BURBERY ... 400 a. ... Wit: WILLIAM ANNAND, WM WINSMORE. Ackn 12 Aug 1702. (D:pg 19)

21. 23 May 1702. Deed. SAMUELL BURDETT (BOURDET) of NY marriner executor of PETER BURDETT late of Newcastle merchant decd for 20 POUNDS sold to JOHN NACARRO of Kent Co PA ... a tr of land n side of Duck Cr being pt/o a tr of land that EVAN JONES now liveth on called Aberconaway ... to the line of a piece of land called CONVENTREE ... 120 a. ... SAMUELL BURDETT appoint my trusty and beloved friend EVAN JONES of Duck Cr to be my atty to ackn afsd deed in open court ... Wit: GEORGE PEACOCK, JOHN WALKER, JOHN BRADSHAW. Ackn -- Nov 1702 by EVAN JONES atty for SAMUELL BURDETT. (D:pg 20)

22. 9 Nov 1702. Deed. RACHELL HOSKINS widow and executrix of the

will of HENRY HOSKINS late of Kent Co PA decd for 17 pounds sold to EVAN JONES of same co planter ... a tr of land called Denby Town being pt/o a greater tr of land s side of Duck Cr formerly laid out for THOMAS WILLSON Senr and by deed of gift bearing date 12 Oct 1686 was given by him to his son THOMAS WILLSON Junr and by him sold to HENRY HOSKINS ... and by his will bearing date -- -- 1702 given to RACHELL HOSKINS ... 100 a. ... Wit: JOHN BRADSHAW, THOMAS BEDWELL. Ackn 12 Nov 1702. (D:pg 21)

23. 31 Oct 1702. Deed. WILLIAM MAXWELL of Kent Co PA planter eldest lawfull son of JAMES MAXWELL late of same co decd for 35 pounds sold to JOHN MAHON of same co planter ... tr of land whereupon JAMES MAXWELL in his life time did dwell called Berrys Range near and towards the head of Jones Cr ... bounded by a tr of land containing 100 a. purch by JAMES MAXWELL of WILLIAM BERRY ... 95 a. ... Wit: JOHN EVANS, JOHN NICKOL, GRIFF JONES. Ackn 12 Nov 1702. (D:pg 22)

24. 9 Nov 1702. Deed. HENRY PARMAIN (PERMAIN) of Kent Co PA for 19 pounds sold to RALPH PRIME of same co ... 100 a. on Duck Cr being pt/o a 600 a. tr of land said HENRY PARMAIN called Parmains Choice ... bounded by WILLIAM EDWARDS (200 a. which he formerly bought of said PARMAIN) ... . (D:pg 24)

25. 31 Nov 1702. Deed. JOHN BOWMAN & MARGRET his wife surviving dau of BENONI BISHOP decd for 60 pounds sold to ROBERT HUDSON of Kent Co PA ... 600 a. being pt/o a tr of land formerly belonging to BENONI BISHOP lying upon the heade of Murther Cr called Bishops Choice lately surveyed by JONAS GREENWOOD ... Wit: JOSEPH ASHBERRY, WILLIAM NICHOLLS, THOMAS WEAD, JONAS GREENWOOD. Ackn 13 May 1703. (D:pg 25)

26. 11 Apr 1703. Deed. MICHAELL DONAHOE (ODONOHOE) of Kent Co PA for 15 pounds sold to JOHN SLAUGHTER of same co ... 100 a. out of the tr of land said MICHAELL DONAHOE now dwelleth ... Wit: GEO LOWTHER, JOHN BRADSHAW. Ackn 10 May 1703. (D:pg 25)

27. 10 Aug 1703. Deed. JOHN RICHARDSON Senr of Kent Co PA planter for 80 pounds sold to WILLIAM RODENEY of same co merchant ... 200 a. being the uppermost pt/o a 600 a. tr of land called York which said JOHN RICHARDSON formerly purch from WILLIAM STEVENS of Talbet Co MD ... neare Little Cr beginning at the corner of SAMUELL BERRY's land and alsoe a corner of WILLIAM MORTON's land lately bought of JOHN and WILLIAM STEVENS of Dorchester Co MD ... Wit: GEO LOWTHER, JONAS GREENWOOD. Ackn 10 Aug 1703. (D:pg 27)

28. 10 Aug 1703. Deed. WILLIAM RODENEY of Kent Co PA adminr of THOMAS ATHOW decd for a competant sume of money to him in hand paid sold to JONAS GREENWOOD of same co ... a tr of land s side of Isaaks Br out of Dover River called Wemoire ... 344 a. which is pt/o a 500 a. tr of land which WILLIAM RODENEY took up by virtue of a warrant ... sold to WILLIAM DARVALL and whereas afsd THOMAS ATHOW decd in his lifetime at a court 8 Sep 1696 recovered against said WILLIAM DARVALL a debt ... and by execution 10 Feb 1697 against the lands of WILLIAM DARVALL, THOMAS ATHOW was awarded afsd tr of land ... Wit: JOHN BRADSHAW, GEO LOWTHER. Ackn 10 Aug 1703. (D:pg 28)

29. 10 Aug 1703. Deed. JOHN SLAUGHTER of Kent Co PA planter for 12 pounds sold to WILLIAM RODENEY of same co ... a tr of land being pt/o a tr of land whereon MICHAEL ODONAHOE now liveth which was alsoe pt/o a 1000 a. tr of land formerly granted to [blank] s side of Dover River ... 100 a. ... Wit: NEHEMIAH FIELD, JOHN BRADSHAW. Ackn 10 Aug 1703. (D:pg 29)

30. 11 Aug 1703. Deed. JONAS GREENWOOD of Kent Co PA for a competent sume of money to him in hand paid sold to WILLIAM RODENEY of same co ... a tr of land [same as #30] ... Wit: GEO LOWTHER, JOHN BRADSHAW. Ackn 11 Aug 1703. (D:pg 30)

31. 1 Aug 1703. This indenture between WILLIAM WILLSON high sheriff of Kent Co and JAMES COUTTS & HERCULES COUTTS of Newcastle Co merchants by virtue of a writ to JOHN BRINCKLOE justice the 17 Jul 1702 grounded upon a judgement obtained at a court held the twelfth. (D:pg 31)

32. 9 May 1704. Deed. BENJAMIN WHITE of Kent Co PA yeoman for 60 pounds sold to HENRY BARNES of same co joyner ... a tr of land being pt/o a tr of land formerly belonging to JOHN BRINCKLOE called Lisbon ne side of Jones Cr otherwise called Dover River ... a little above the land called The Forelanding ... to corner of land formerly belonging to WILLIAM BRINCKLE ... 200 a. ... Wit: THOMAS FRENCH, WILLIAM WINSMORE. Ackn 9 May 1704 unto WILLIAM ANNAND for HENRY BARNES. (D:pg 31)

33. 10 Oct 1704. Deed. HENRY BARNES of Kent Co PA joyner for 60 pounds sold to THOMAS FRENCH of same co felt maker ... [above] tr of land ... Wit: THOMAS BEDWEL, EVAN JONES, WILLIAM ANNAND. Ackn 14 Nov 1704. (D:pg 32)

34. 30 Jun 1703 in NY. Power of Atty. JACOB MAURITZ of NY City

mariner and JOHANES PROVOST of same place merchant appoint our trusty & well beloved friend ROBERT FRENCH of Newcastle merchant to be our atty to ask recover & receive all such debts which shall be due us whatsoever ... but especially all such monys to us belonging which shall be in custody of the heirs executors or adminr of GRIFFETH JONES late of St. Jones Co decd ... Wit: JOHN VANBINGH, RICHARD WAY, ANDRIES GRAVENRACH. Proved 6 Jul 1703 by PHILLIP FRENCH Esq mayor of NY City. By order of the mayor WILL SHARPAS Clerk. (D:pg 33)

35. 30 Dec 1706. Quit Claim. JOHN BURTON of Kent Co eldest lawfull son and heir of JOHN BURTON of same co carpenter decd ... whereas JOHN BURTON in his lifetime by deed bearing date 22 Jul 1701 for 138 pounds sold unto ROBERT FRENCH of same co merchant a tr of land called Burtons Delight being pt/o a greater tr of land adj on the se with land of CAPT JOHN BRINCKLOE and on ne with land formerly sold by said JOHN BURTON to DANIELL JONES decd and on the nw with lands of JOSEPH OSBORN and on sw with lands of WALTER DICKENSON ... 180 a. ... ROBERT FRENCH for 138 pounds to be paid in one whole and entire payment at or upon 20 Dec 1705 to resell afsd tr of land back to JOHN BURTON ... because of the failure of afsd payment and for 12 shillings JOHN BURTON quitt claims afsd tr of land unto ROBERT FRENCH ... Wit: JOHN HORSTEAD, ARTHUR MESTON. Ackn 11 Feb 1706. (D:pg 34)

36. 13 Feb 1706. Deed. ROBERT FRENCH of town and co of Newcastle merchant for 138 pounds sold to JOHN BRINCKLOE of Kent Co gentlemen ... [above] tr of land ... Wit: WILLIAM BRINCKLE, DA BOROIS. Ackn 11 Feb 1706. (D:pg 35)

37. 13 Nov 1706. Deed of Mortgage. THOMAS NICHOLS of Kent Co PA planter for 44 pounds sold to ROBERT FRENCH of Newcastle merchant ... tr of land where said NICHOLS now dwelleth 100 a. being bound to the ne, nw and sw with the land of ROBERT FRENCH formerly called Baneses Choice ... if THOMAS NICHOLS pays to ROBERT FRENCH at the landing called Forests Landing in Dover River 44 pounds in four equal payments yearly on the 2 Oct in every year with lawful interest thereof ... this present bargain and sale will be utterly void ... Wit: THOMAS BEDWELL, SAMUELL LOW. Ackn 11 Feb 1706. (D:pg 36)

38. 12 Feb 1706. Receipt. THOMAS NICKOLLAS received from ROBERT FRENCH [above] 44 pounds ... Wit: WILLIAM BRINCKLO, DANIELL NEEDHAM. (D:pg 37)

39. 11 Feb 1706. Deed. TIMOTHY THOROLD of Kent Co planter for 35

pounds 12 shillings sold to ROBERT FRENCH of Newcastle Co merchant ... a tr of land bounded to the nw with land of MICHALL DONAHOE, to sw with land formerly called Dundee to se and nw with land of ROBERT FRENCH formerly belonging to DANIELL NEEDHAM 80 a. ... Wit: SAMUELL BERRY, SAMUELL LOW. Ackn 11 Feb 1706. (D:pg 37)

40. 12 Feb 1706. Deed. DANIELL NEEDHAM of Kent Co planter for 7 pounds sold to ROBERT FRENCH of Newcastle merchant ... a tr of land s side of Dover River and n side of Isaacs Br being pt/o a tr of land called Long Reach ... corner of EZEKIELL NEEDHAM's land ... 100 a. ... Wit: WILLIAM TONGE, HENRY MOLESTON. Ackn 11 Feb 1706. (D:pg 38)

41. 11 Nov 1706. Deed. JOHN BRINCKLOE of Kent Co gentlemen in consideration of a tr of land lately in the occupation of JOHN BURTON Senr of same co decd adj to new plantation of said JOHN BRINCKLOE formerly mortgaged to ROBERT FRENCH of Newcastle Co merchant which mortgage expired 20 Dec last ... JOHN BRINCKLOE sold to ROBERT FRENCH merchant a tr of land which was formerly in occupation of FRANCIS HIRONS of Kent Co on Duck Cr ... 300 a. ... Wit: SAMUELL BURBERY, ARTHUR MESTON. Ackn by WILLIAM ANNAND atty for JOHN BRINCKLOE. (D:pg 39)

42. 13 Feb 1705. Deed. WILLIAM STEALE (STEILL) planter of Kent Co and FRANCES his wife for sume of [blank] sold to EDWARD BORROWES weaver of same co ... a tr of land s side of Dover River in the Murtherkill Hund beginning at the corner of JOHN SMITH's line ... 100 a. ... Wit: THOMAS SKIDMORE, NICOLAS NIXONE. Ackn 14 Aug 1705. (D:pg 40)

43. 12 Nov 1706. Deed of Mortgage. GEORGE MORGAN of Kent Co planter for 100 pounds sold to ROBERT FRENCH of Newcastle Co merchant ... a tr of land sw side of Little Cr ... bounded on nw with land of JOHN NICKOLSON and on the sw and se with land of ROBERT FRENCH formerly called Glovers Neck 207 a. ... if GEORGE MORGAN pays to ROBERT FRENCH 100 pounds in seven equall payments yearly on 11 Nov in every year with interest then this present sale to be utterly void ... Wit: DAVID DUNCAN, JAMES MORRIS. Ackn 11 Feb 1706. (D:pg 41)

44. 11 Feb 1706. Receipt. GEORGE MORGAN received [above] 100 pounds from ROBERT FRENCH ... Wit: JONAS GREENWOOD, JOHN CLAYTON. (D:pg 42)

45. 8 Feb 1706. Deed. JOHN FRENCH of Newcastle Co gentlemen executor of the will of WILLIAM MORTON late of Kent Co decd ...

whereas the said WILLIAM MORTON in his lifetime did contract with JASPER HARWOOD of Kent Co husbandman that JASPER would truely and faithfully serve him the said WILLIAM MORTON and doe and performe such worke and labour as he should imploy him in for a certain time of years and at the expiration thereof in consideration of his service WILLIAM MORTON would have given JASPER HARWOOD 50 a. of land ... sw of Duck Cr called Willsons Wild ... JOHN FRENCH doth ackn said service willfully done and performed pursuant to contract ... JOHN FRENCH confirms unto JASPER HARWOOD afsd tr of land ... JOHN FRENCH appoint WILLIAM ANNAND his atty to ackn these presents in open court ... Wit: HERCULES COUTTS, WILLIAM TONGE. Ackn 11 Feb 1707 by WILLIAM ANNAND atty for JOHN FRENCH. (D:pg 42)

46. 14 Feb 1706. Deed. JASPER HARWOOD of Kent Co husbandman for 13 pounds sold to RICHARD KING of same co yeoman ... [above] tr of land ... Wit: HENRY MOLESTON, WILLIAM TONGE. Ackn 20 Feb 1707. (D:pg 43)

47. 8 Aug 1704. Deed. EDMOND NEEDHAM of Kent Co PA for a valuable consideration in hand paid sold to DANIELL NEEDHAM of same co ... a small tr of land n side of Murther Cr adj land where said EDMOND now dwelleth which is pt/o a 1600 a. tr of land called Ousbey formerly in the possession of THOMAS HETHARS late of same co decd ... at the head line of STEPHEN SIMONS land ... paralining with land of RICHARD SHEWLY bought of EDMOND NEEDHAM ... 100 a. ... Wit: SAMUELL BROOKE, JONAS GREENWOOD. Ackn 8 Aug 1704. (D:pg 43)

48. 22 Jan 1705. Deed. JOHN WALKER taylor of Kent Co for 35 pounds sold to THOMAS SHARP of same co ... 151 a. s side of Duck Cr adj land where THOMAS ELLITS now dwelleth ... called Travellers Delight ... Wit: JONAS GREENWOOD, GEORGE HUDLESTON, THOMAS DUGDALE. Ackn 12 -- 1705. (D:pg 45)

49. 12 Mar 1704. Power of Atty. MARY SEELY of Great Yarmouth in the County of North in England widowe one of the dau of THOMAS ROUSE formerly of Southwold in Suss Co and afterwards of Kent Co PA joyner decd & JOHN DENNUS (DENNIS) of Great Yearmouth cordwinder & HANNAH his wife another of the dau of said THOMAS ROUSE ... appoint THOMAS EMINS of Great Yarmouth mariner & master our trusty and loveing friend to be our atty to ask demand and receive of JOSEPH BAKER of towne of Egmund in Chester Co PA and JOHN ROBINSON of Kent Co PA in execution of the will of above THOMAS ROUSE ... sums of money, goods, estate both personall & real to him duly oweing payable ... Wit: THOMAS HURY, ALLEXANDER BRUCE,

JOSEPH COLMAN mayor of Great Yarmouth. (D:pg 47)

50. 12 Mar 1704 at North Great Yarmouth. MARY SEELY of Great Yarmouth widdow and JOHN DENNIS of same place cordwainder & HANNA his wife and ANNE wife of JAMES GARINER of same place mariner and MARY wife of JOSEPH CARR of same place twister did personally appear before me JOSEPH COLEMAN Esq mayor & justice of the peace ... MARY SEELY and HANNAH DENNIS joyntly make oath that they are the naturall & lawfull dau of THOMAS ROUSE joyner ... and that they were baptised at Countham in same co as they find entered in a register book kept in the same town and that the sayd THOMAS ROUSE went from Southwold about 37 years since beyond seas to Barbadoes where he lived severall years & from thence went into PA & lived severall years & dyed about two years since in Kent Co ... that said MARY SEELY hath three children now liveing in good health which she had by her late husband THOMAS SEELY, THOMAS SEELY aged about 18, MARY SEELY aged about 18 & JOSEPH SEELY aged about 8 years which said children came alsoe this day before me ... Wit: THOMAS HURREY, ALLEXANDER BRUCE. (D:pg 47)

51. 8 Nov 1705. Power of Atty. THOMAS EMINS (EMMS) late of Great Yarmouth in England but now of Phila PA mariner ... by virtue of [above] letter of atty substitute SAMUEL CARPENTER of Phila merchant and WILLIAM HORN of same city smith as my atty on behalfe of MARY SEELY, JOHN DENNIS and HANNAH his wife ... Wit: DAVID LOYD, RICHARD HEATH. (D:pg 48)

52. 12 Feb 1705. Deed. FRANCIS HIRONS of Kent Co and FRANCES his wife for 150 pounds sold to JOHN BRINCKLOE of same co gentlemen ... a tr of land s side of Duck Cr formerly called Hillyards Adventure ... bounded by SIMON HIRONS Junr ... 300 a. ... Wit: WILLIAM RODENEY, WILLIAM ANNAND, CHARLES HILLYARD. Ackn 12 Feb 1705. (D:pg 50)

53. 13 May 1706. Deed. STEPHEN PARADDE of Kent Co planter for 90 pounds sold to WILLIAM RODENEY of same co merchant ... a tr of land called Paraddene being pt/o a tr of land called London which WILLIAM MORTON decd and the said WILLIAM RODENEY lately purch from JOHN STEVENS and WILLIAM STEVENS of Dorset Co MD n side of Little Cr ... to a line of JOHN RICHARDSON's land ... 120 a. same land which WILLIAM RODENEY and WILLIAM MORTON did sell unto said STEPHEN PARADDE 1 Sep 1699 ... Wit: ROBERT FRENCH, WILLIAM ANNAND. Ackn 14 May 1706. (D:pg 51)

54. 9 May 1704. Deed. SAMUEL BURBERY of Kent Co PA planter for

20 pounds sold to ROBERT FRENCH of Newcastle PA merchant ... a tr of land being pt/o a tr of land formerly belonging to JOHN BRINCKLOE called Lisbon ne side of Jones Cr otherways called Dover River beginning at the corner of land formerly belonging to THOMAS ROGERS ... 77 a. ... formerly in the possession of WILLIAM BRINCKLO ... Wit: WILLIAM MORTON, JONAS GREENWOOD. Ackn 9 May 1704. (D:pg 52)

55. 15 May 1706. Deed. HENRY MOLESTON of Kent Co PA for a competent sume of money paid sold to DANIELL SMITH of same co planter ... severall tr pt/o land both in the possession of WILLIAM BERRY decd called New Designe ne side of Dover River ... one beginning at the corner of the land of JOHN COURTNEY decd ... 50 a. called Countrie Land formerly sold by said WILLIAM BERRY unto WILLIAM MORTON decd and by him to SAMUELL BURBERY decd and by him to GRIFFITH JONES decd and the other beginning at the corner of SAMUELL BURBERY's land ... to MORTON's land ... to COURTNEY's land then down the br by BARTLET's ... 145 a. adj said 50 a. and is the same that was formerly sold from WILLIAM BERRY decd unto SIMON HIRONS and from him unto GRIFFITH JONES decd and for payment of said GRIFFITH JONES decd debts, DANIELL SMITH and ELIZABETH his wife late widdow and adminr to GRIFFITH JONES decd, sold to HENRY MOLESTON 13 May 1706 ... Wit: WILLIAM ANNAND, SAMUELL LOW. Ackn 15 May 1706. (D:pg 53)

56. 13 May 1706. Deed. DANIELL SMITH of Kent Co planter and ELIZABETH his wife adminr of GRIFFITH JONES late of same co gentlemen decd sold to HENRY MOLESTON of same co gentlemen [above] tr of land ... to pay considerable debts as yet unpaid ... Wit: WILLIAM RODENEY, WILLIAM ANNAND. Ackn 15 May 1706. (D:pg 54)

57. 10 Oct 1703. Deed. EVAN JONES of Kent Co PA planter for 25 pounds sold to JOHN WALKER of same co taylor ... a tr of land called Denhightoune s side of Duck Cr being pt/o a greater tr of land formerly laid out for THOMAS WILLSON Senr late of same co ... 100 a. ... Wit: JOHN BRINCKLOE, WILLIAM ANNAND. Ackn 9 Feb 1703. (D:pg 56)

58. 11 Feb 1703. Deed. RICHARD HAMBLY of New Castle Co PA blacksmith sone and heir of RICHARD HAMBLY late of same co decd ... whereas JOHN RICHARDSON Senr and MARY his wife of Little Cr in Kent Co PA by deed of sale 8 Mar 1692 between them and RICHARD HAMBLY decd millwright did convey a tr of land on both sides of Duck Cr called The Partnership ... 1800 a. for 18,000 pounds of tobacco with cask ... JOHN RICHARDSON recovered through judgments at court of Newcastle 14 Dec 1703 ... judgment became due and payable to ROBERT

FRENCH by virtue of an assignment from JOHN RICHARDSON ... RICHARD HAMBLY sold unto ROBERT FRENCH of same co merchant afsd tr of land to satisfy judgment ... Wit: ANDREW PATERSON, WILLIAM CARDIN. Ackn 18 May 1704 at New Castle. Ackn 8 Aug 1704 at Dover Kent Co by ARTHUR MESTON atty for RICHARD HAMBLY. (D:pg 57)

59. 1 Feb 1705. Agreement. SIMON HIRONS Junr of Kent Co PA planter and FRANCIS HIRONS of same co planter ... whereas they joyntly bought a tr of land called Hillyards Adventure s side of Duck Cr ... 600 a. for three score pounds ... agree to divide the afsd tr of land and no longer own joyntly ... Wit: JONAS GREENWOOD, WILLIAM ANNAND. Ackn 12 Feb 1705. (D:pg 59)

60. 10 Nov 1702. Deed. WILLIAM WINSMORE of Kent Co PA for 30 pounds sold to THOMAS WILLSONE of same co planter ... a tr of land called Dembytoun being pt/o a tr of land s side of Little Cr called Great Pipe Elme ... by Lewicks Br ... to corner of MATHEW WILLSON's land ... 50 a. ... Wit: WILLIAM ANNAND, SAMUELL BURBERY. Ackn 10 Feb 1702. (D:pg 60)

61. 15 May 1706. Deed. DANIELL (DANINELL) GOODIN of Kent Co cordwinder and ELIZABETH his wife relict and adminr of JOHN FLOWERS late of same co decd ... whereas JOHN FLOWERS at the time of his decease was indebted unto divers persons and left behind him severall young children to the nurture and education of said ELIZABETH ... at a court held 8 May 1705 by her petition, land belonging to JOHN FLOWERS decd be sold to pay debts ... for 54 pounds sold to ROBERT FRENCH of New Castle merchant ... a tr of land called Dundee which said JOHN bought of WILLIAM LAWRENCE and MICHALL WALTON both of Phila 9 May 1704 500 a. ... 150 a. being sold unto JOHN DAWSON of Talbot Co MD in the lifetime of JOHN FLOWERS ... alsoe 50 a. sold to DAVID MILL now in occupation of THOMAS NICKOLLS of Kent Co ... remainder 350 a. bounded with tr afsd ... the rent of 100 a. of land formerly sold unto MARY WINGATE now the wife of TIMOTHY THEROLD of Kent Co allreadie due and owing ... Wit: THOMAS FRENCH, JOHN CLARK. Ackn 14 May 1706. (D:pg 61)

62. -- -- 1702/3. Deed. JOHN SMITH of Kent Co PA planter for 28 pounds sold to WILLIAM STEELL of same co ... a tr of land called Steels Lot n side of Mother Cr and n side of Sarvis Br ... 100 a. ... Wit: JOHN FOSTER, ISACK TREELAND. Ackn 10 Feb --. (D:pg 63)

63. 11 Apr 1704. Deed. WILLIAM LAWRANCE of Phila taylor and MICHAEL WALTON of same place yeoman for 61 pounds sold to JOHN

FLOWERS of Kent Co planter ... a tr of land heretofore belonging to DANIELL TOAES of MD called Dundee ... Wit: WILLIAM MORTON, ARTHUR MESTON. Ackn 9 May 1704 by WILLIAM ANNAND atty for WILLIAM LAWRENCE and MICHAEL WALTON. (D:pg 64)

64. 9 May 1705. Deed. ISAAC FREELAND of Kent Co planter for 14 pounds sold to ROBERT FRENCH of Newcastle merchant ... two parcells of land called Isaac's Purchase being pt/o a tr of land called Longroath s side of Dover River and n side of Isaacs Br beginning at the corner of land formerly belonging to HENRY BEDWELL ... 88 a. the other beginning at the corner of EZEKIELL NEEDHAM's land ... 50 a. formerly in the possession of GABRIEL JONES ... Wit: GEORGE LOWTHER, THOMAS BEDWELL. Ackn 8 May 1705. (D:pg 65)

65. 6 May 1704. Deed. Whereas WILLIAM WILLSON high sheriffe of Kent Co by virtue of a writ by JOHN BRINCKLOE esq 17 Jul 1702 grounded upon a judgment obtained at Kent Co Court 12 May 1702 by JAMES and HERCULES COUTTS against THOMAS EVERETT late of Kent Co for a debt of 5 pounds 5 shillings 11 pence also 3 pounds 5 shillings 6 pence ... 1 Aug 1703 for afsd consideration sold unto JAMES and HERCULES COUTTS a tr of land called Highmans Ferry n side of Little Cr adj land called Welling Brook ... to corner of JOHN RICHARDSON's land ... 138 a. ... JAMES and HERCULES COUTTS both of New Castle merchants for 60 pounds sold to JOSHUA CLAYTON of Kent Co ... afsd tr of land ... Wit: JAMES ASKWE, WILLIAM TONGE. (D:pg 66)

66. 8 Dec 1699. Deed. SARAH EDMONDSON, JAMES EDMONDSON, WILLIAM EDMONDSON and THOMAS EDMONDSON of Talbot Co MD executors of the will of JOHN EDMONDSON late of same co decd ... whereas said JOHN EDMONDSON decd in his lifetime sold to HUGH HALL of Island of Barbadoes alsoe decd, for 50 pounds ... a tr of land 1800 a. n side of Duck Cr adj land of WILLIAM WILLSON ... to line of JOHN RENALLS ... surveyed 19 Jun 1681 by RICHARDSON unto WILLIAM RIDGWAY from St. Jones Court 10 Mar 1682 and by WILLIAM RIDGWAY and WILLIAM DIXON sold to JOHN EDMONDSON decd ... SARAH, JAMES, WILLIAM and THOMAS EDMONDSON assign unto HUGH HALL of Phila merchant and son of HUGH HALL decd afsd tr of land ... Wit: WILLIAM RODENEY, SARAH RODENEY. Ackn 9 Sep 1701 by JAMES and WILLIAM EDMONDSON. (D:pg 67)

67. 1 Apr 1704. Power of Atty. Whereas the within named SARAH EDMONDSON & THOMAS EDMONDSON could not conveniently be had to ackn [above] deed of sale in due time as they ought to have done

and said SARAH, JAMES and WILLIAM EDMONDSON being since decd ... THOMAS EDMONDSON only surviving executor to the estate of JOHN EDMONDSON decd do makeover the [above] deed unto HUGH HALL ... THOMAS EDMONDSON appoint my loving friends HENRY MOLLESTON and JONAS GREENWOOD to be my atty to ackn and deliver [above] deed in open court ... Wit: JOHN LANE, WILLIAM RODENEY. Proved 13 May 1707. (D:pg 69)

68. 11 Sep 1703. Power of Atty. JOHN MARTIN of Phila atty to and for the assignees of bankrupt awarded against WALTER DICKINSON Hall of Hertford in England now in records of Phila ... appoint my loving friend ROBERT FRENCH of New Castle merchant ... to take into possession and sell 900 a. near Jones belonging to WALTER DICKINSON ... Attest: JASPER YEATS, JAMES SANDELANDS. (D:pg 71)

69. 13 Dec 1706. Deed. EZEKIEL NEEDHAM Senr of Kent Co cordwainer for 20 pounds sold to NICHOLAS NIXON of same co blacksmith ... a tr of land called Skidmores Folly n side of Murther Cr ... being pt/o a tr of land formerly belonging to THOMAS HEWTHAT of same co decd called Ousbey ... 100 a. ... Wit: JONAS GREENWOOD, JOHN CLAYTON. Ackn 11 May 1706. (D:pg 72)

70. Sep 1708. Lease. JOSEPH GROWDON esq of Phila for 5 shillings leased to THOMAS SHARP of Kent Co yeoman ... a tr of land on sw br of Duck Cr ... br dividing it from land of JAMES STEEL ... 626 a. ... for one year ... Wit: SAMUELL PRESTON, RICHARD HEATH. Ackn 9 Nov 1708 by EVAN JONES atty to JOSEPH GROWDON. (D:pg 73)

71. 2 Sep 1708. Deed. JOSEPH GROWDON esq of Phila for 210 pounds sold to THOMAS SHARP of Kent Co yeoman ... [above] tr of land ... Wit: RICHARD HEATH, SAMUELL PRESTON. Ackn 9 Nov 1708 by EVAN JONES Atty to JOSEPH GROWDON. (D:pg 75)

72. 7 Oct 1708. Power of Atty. JOSEPH GROWDON appoints EVAN JONES as his atty to ackn in open court two leases & releases to THOMAS SHARP for 626 a. and to JAMES STEEL for 714 a. ... Wit: WILLIAM ANNAND clerk. (D:pg 75)

73. 1 Dec 1709. Deed. DANIELL NEEDHAM of Kent Co yeoman & ELIZABETH his wife relict and executrix of will of JOHN NICKOLSON late of same co decd for 50 pounds sold to JOSHUA CLAYTON of same co yeoman ... a tr of land on Little Cr called Northamtom ... to corner of GEORGE MORGAN's land ... 100 a. ... whereas JOHN NICKOLLSON by his will bequeath to afsd ELIZABETH his then wife afsd tr of land ... Wit: FRANCIS ALLEN, WILLIAM ANNAND. Ackn 14 Feb 1709. (D:pg 75)

74. 10 Dec 1709. Deed. JOSHUA CLAYTON of Kent Co yeoman for 50 pounds sold to DANIELL NEEDHAM of same co yeoman ... [above] tr of land ... Wit: FRANCIS ALLEN, WILLIAM ANNAND. Ackn 9 Feb 1709. (D:pg 76)

75. 9 Dec 1708. Deed. EVAN JONES of Kent Co gentlemen for 20 pounds sold to PHILLIP DENNY of same place ... a tr of land s side of Duck Cr ... 180 a. as by patent and survey 17 Jun 1707 ... Wit: MARK BARDON, JOHN BRADSHAW. (D:pg 77)

76. 14 Feb 1709. Deed. TIMOTHY HANSON & SUSANNA his wife one of the dau of WILLIAM FREELAND late of Phila decd for 150 pounds sold to ROBERT PORTER of Dover Hund Kent Co yeoman ... a tr of land n side of Little Cr beginning at the corner of JOHN STEVENS' land called London ... 158 a. by patent 5 Jul 1684 granted to JOHN RICHARDSON which 1 Aug 1685 he did give & grant to said WILLIAM FREELAND & SUSANNAH his wife which WILLIAM FREELAND by his will bearing date 23 Feb 1697 did bequeath to above named SUSANNA his dau ... Wit: SAMUELL BERRY justice of peace, HUMPHRY BARRAT, FRANCIS ALLEN. Ackn 9 May 1710. (D:pg 77)

77. 10 May 1710. Deed. ROBERT PORTER of Dover Hund Kent Co yeoman for 150 pounds sold to TIMOTHY HANSON of same place yeoman ... [above] tr of land ... Wit: SAMUELL BERRY, FRANCIS ALLEN, HUMPHREY BARRET. Ackn 10 May 1710. (D:pg 78)

78. 1 Aug 1710. Deed of Mortgage. JOHN BRINCKLOE of Dover Hund Kent Co & ELIZABETH his wife for love and goodwill and 100 pounds to be paid unto their dau ELIZABETH so soon as she shall arrive of full age or be maryed which first shall happen sold to THOMAS CRAWFORD of same place clerk & ELIZABETH his wife granddau of said JOHN & ELIZABETH ... a tr of land two miles above St. Jones Cr ... se side of a swamp which divideth this from a piece of land called Poplar Neck ... to line of ROBERT JONES' land ... 60 a. by patent bearing date 14 Aug 1678 by Sir EDMOND ANDREWS granted to JOHN BRIGGS who by assignment 23 Apr 1681 granted to HENRY STEVENSON who by indenture 19 Aug 1684 granted same to above named JOHN BRINCKLOE ... and whereas there is alsoe a tr of land called Brinckloe His Choice n side of Dover River beginning at the corner of the land of JOHN BRINCKLOE called Poplar Ridge ... to land of RICHARD BASSNETT ... 250 a. by patent bearing date 17 Jun 1693 granted to above named JOHN BRINCKLOE ... formerly granted to ARTHUR MESTON as butted and bounded in the deed ... THOMAS CRAWFORD and ELIZABETH shall not during the natural life of said JOHN BRINCKLOE and ELIZABETH his wife sell or dispose of the land

without their consent ... Wit: WILLIAM WINSMORE, FRANCIS ALLEN. Ackn 9 Aug 1710. (D:pg 79)

79. 9 Aug 1710. Bond. THOMAS CRAWFORD of Dover Hund Kent Co clerk & ELIZABETH his wife are bound unto JOHN BRINCKLOE esq and ELIZABETH his wife of same place for 200 pounds ... THOMAS CRAWFORD and ELIZABETH his wife shall not interrupt the above named JOHN BRINCKLOE & ELIZABETH his wife from the peaceable & quiett possession & enjoyment of one half pt/o [above] tr of land during the naturall life of said JOHN BRINCKLOE and ELIZABETH his wife and shall not dispose of said land without their consent ... Wit: WILLIAM WINSMORE, FRANCIS ALLEN. Ackn 9 Aug 1710. (D:pg 81)

80. 10 May 1710. Deed. By a certain act of assembly made at Annapolis MD 11 Nov 1709 THOMAS EDMONDSON of Talbot Co MD gentlemen was impowered to sell the lands left in the will of his decd father JOHN EDMONDSON for payment of his debts ... THOMAS EDMONDSON for 200 pounds sold to ROBERT GRUNDY (GROUNDY) of same co merchant ... halfe pt/o a tr of land called Wappen 1000 a. and alsoe a tr of land upon Murther Cr 300 a. and alsoe a tr of land on Murtherkill Cr 500 a. and alsoe a tr of land called Cambridge 100 a. and alsoe a tr of land called Doncaster 1025 a. and alsoe a tr of land sw br of Duck Cr 1200 a. and alsoe a tr of land called Grigges Purchase 1000 a. and alsoe a tr of land called Little Geneva 400 a. and alsoe a tr of land called New Line 600 a. and alsoe a tr of land called Skidmore 400 a. and alsoe a tr of land called Hodkins Choice 400 a. and alsoe a tr of land called Worester 350 a. and alsoe a tr of land called Ellsworth 900 a. alsoe two other tr of land one called High Hoak and the other The Hole lying in Newcastle Co and lastly any other lands belonging to JOHN EDMONDSON ... Wit: CHARLES HILLYARD, JOHN BRINKLO, SAMUELL BERRY. Ackn 9 May 1710. (D:pg 81)

81. 12 May 1708. Deed. THOMAS BEDWELL and ROBERT BEDWELL surviving sons & heirs of ROBERT BEDWELL late of Kent Co decd gentlemen for 5 pounds sold to MARY SHAW of same co widdow of THOS SHAW late of same co decd ... a tr of land being pt/o a greater tr of land on n side of Dover River called Longreach formerly belonging to GABRIELL JONES ... to corner of land formerly belonging to SAMUELL BURBERY ... 137 a. ... Wit: STEPHEN JACKSON, JOHN HUDSON. Ackn 12 May 1708. (D:pg 83)

82. 8 Aug 1710. Deed. JOHN FRENCH esqr of Newcastle for 300 pounds sold to RICHARD RICHARDSON of same co yeoman ... tr of land on Little Cr called St. Andrews ... at corner of land called Simsons Choice ... to corner of SAMUELL BERRY's land ... to land of WILLIAM

RODENEY decd ... 600 a. ... Wit: JOHN BRINCKLOE, CORNEESS EMPSON. Ackn 9 Aug 1710. (D:pg 84)

83. 9 Aug 1711. Deed. JOSHUA (JOSHUAI) TOMPKINS of Burlington Co in w NJ cordwainer surviving lawfull son & heir of ANTHONY TOMPKINS late of Kent Co gentlemen ... by pattent bearing date 26 Mar 1684 granted to FRANCIS WHITWELL decd a tr of land called Benefield s side of Duck Cr bounded by another tr of land of said FRANCIS WHITWELL's ... since FRANCIS WHITWELL died intestate and adminr of estate is WILLIAM BERRY and WILLIAM SOUTHEBE both of Kent Co and by their deed of sale 10 Jun 1686 did grant one halfe of said tr of land (in whole containing 1000 a.) unto GRIFFITH JONES of Phila merchant and by his deed of sale 22 Aug 1687 did grant unto ANTONY TOMPKINS father to said JOSHUA TOMPKINS halfe pt/o afsd land ... for 150 pounds sold to EVAN JONES ... lower halfe of said land next to the land called Whitewells Chance ... Wit: JOHN BRADSHAW, JAMES STEEL. Ackn 14 Aug 1711. (D:pg 85)

84. 10 Dec 1709. Deed. MARY SHAW of Kent Co widdow for 20 pounds sold to ROBERT FRENCH of Newcastle merchant ... a tr of land n side of Dover River called Longreach beginning at a corner of a pt/o said land called Longreach formerly belonging to GABRIELL JONES decd ... to corner of land formerly belonging to SAMUELL BURBERY ... 137 a. ... Wit: JONAS GREENWOOD, WILLIAM WINSMORE, WM ANNAND. Ackn 14 Feb 1709/10. (D:pg 87)

85. 10 Aug 1711. Deed. JOHN BERRY of Talbott Co MD cooper son and heir of WILLIAM BERRY late of Kent Co gentlemen decd son and heir of WM BERRY late of MD yeoman decd for 36 pounds sold to ROBERT FRENCH of Newcastle Co merchant ... a tr of land in Dover Hund bounded on nw side with land of JAMES MAXWELL decd and on se side with land called Porters Lodge belonging to said ROBERT FRENCH ... surveyed by EPHRIM HARMAN 400 a. and is pt/o a larger 1000 a. tr of land called Berrys Range by patent 26 Mar 1684 unto WILLIAM BERRY of MD decd and by right of inheritance descended to his son WILLIAM BERRY of Kent Co decd who dyed in possession thereof but now by right of inheritance is in occupation of his son JOHN BERRY ... Wit: JOHN BRINCKLOE, JAMES STEEL. Ackn 14 May 1712. (D:pg 88)

86. 10 Dec 1709. Deed. THOMAS WILLSON of Kent Co planter for 20 pounds sold to PHILEMON EMERSON of same co planter ... a tr of land being pt/o a tr of land called Denby Town s side of Duck Cr ... between the land of JOHN ELLICE and the land of RICHARD WHITHART ... 100 a. ... said premises were heretofore in possession of WILLIAM WILLSON decd ... Wit: WILLIAM ANNAND, JOHN BRADSHAW. (D:pg 89)

87. 10 Dec 1710. Deed. DANIELL NEEDHAM of Kent Co yeoman for 30 pounds sold to WILLIAM NEWELL of same co yeoman ... a tr of land n side of Murther Cr being pt/o a greater tr called Ousbey formerly belonging to THOMAS HEWTHAT late of Kent Co decd beginning at a corner of land formerly belonging to STEPHEN SIMONS decd ... paralinning with the land of JOHN REDMAN ... 100 a. Wit: WILLIAM ANNAND, ADAM FISHER. (D:pg 90)

88. 10 Oct 1711. Deed. RICHARD RICHARDSON of Kent Co yeoman for 20 pounds sold to JOHN CLAYTON of same co yeoman ... a tr of land being pt/o a greater tr called Sketndrews being in Little Cr Hund beginning at the corner of land called St. Andrews ... to line of land belonging to CAPT WILLIAM RODENEY decd called Taverton ... 50 a. ... Wit: JAMES STEEL, WILLIAM ANNAND. (D:pg 91)

89. 19 Nov 1711. Deed. MARY RICHARDSON of Kent Co widow and executrix of the will of JOHN RICHARDSON late of same co decd for 15 pounds sold to JOSHUA CLAYTON of same co yeoman ... pt/o a 1000 a. tr of land in Little Cr Hund called Wellingbrook by will of JOHN RICHARDSON bequeath to MARY RICHARDSON his wife one halfe pt/o said land ... beginning by the land said JOSHUA now lives ... to land purchased by ROBERT PORTER of said MARY RICHARDSON ... 24 a. ... Wit: RICHARD RICHARDSON, JOHN CLAYTON, WILLIAM ANNAND. Ackn 11 Nov 1715. (D:pg 92)

90. 15 Nov 1711. Deed. THOMAS NIXON and MARY his wife of Kent Co adminr of all goods and chattles of BENJAMIN BRADY late of the same co yeoman decd ... whereas BENJAMIN BRADY at the time of his death stood justly indebted to JOHN WELLS in the sume of 20 pounds 15 shillings 6 pence ... and dyed in possession of a tr of land called Chippenorton 800 a. ... whereas THOMAS NIXON intermarried with afsd MARY ... judgment against MARY BRADY adminr to sell so much of the land to satisfy debt and costs ... THOMAS NIXON and MARY his wife sold to JOHN WELLS of same place yeoman ... 150 a. in consideration of the afsd debt ... Wit: CHARLES HILLYARDS, THOMAS WITHERS. Ackn 16 Nov 1711. (D:pg 93)

91. 4 Feb 1711. Deed. ROBERT GRUNDY of Talbot Co MD merchant for 100 pounds sold to EDWARD SMOUT of Phila merchant ... halfe pt/o all the tr of land which was conveyed by THOMAS EDMONDSON to said ROBERT GRUNDY [same as #80] ... and EDWARD SMOUT doth constitute JAMES STEEL his atty to receive ackn of these presents in open court ... Wit: MARTHA STEEL, JOHN WOOTTERS, JAMES STEEL. (D:pg 94)

92. 10 May 1712. Deed. Whereas BENJAMIN GUMLEY late of Kent Co decd did by his will bequeath unto his son JOHN GUMLEY (GUMBLEY) of same co yeoman a tr of land s side of Duck Cr ... near line of WILLIAM GREEN late of Duck Cr decd ... to corner of FRANCIS WELLSWOOD ... to Permains Br ... provisoe in will that JOHN GUMBLY should dwell thereon during his naturall life or dispose of same to one of his brothers ... land between the said line and main cr conveyed to BENJAMIN GUMLEY his brother 1 May 1711 and BENJAMIN GUMLEY 6 May 1711 did sell unto said JOHN GUMLEY same tr of land ... JOHN GUMLEY for 116 pounds sold to SAMUELL TAYLOR of Phila afsd tr of land ... Wit: JOHN ROBESON, JAMES STEEL, WILLIAM PENNINGTON. Ackn 11 Nov 1712. (D:pg 96)

93. 10 May 1708. Deed. CHRISTOPHER MOORE of Talbot Co MD surviving son & heir of CHRISTOPHER MOORE late of Kent Co decd for 15 pounds sold to JOHN WILLSON of Talbot Co joyner ... a tr of land called Showforth on br of Murtherkill ... by Bishops Br to corner of land called Guilford ... parallel with ROBT PARVIS line ... 400 a. granted by warrant from Kent Co Court 17 Oct 1682 & surveyed 29 Nov 1683 unto CHRISTOPHER MOORE decd patent confirmed by JAMES CLAPOLE and ROBT TURNER commissioners 3 Nov 1684 unto CHRISTOPHER MOORE ... Wit: WILLIAM ANNAND, ROBT RIDDICK, WM MOORE. Ackn 11 May 1708. (D:pg 97)

94. 12 Nov 1712. Deed. SAMUELL HARRAWAY late of Duck Cr Hund Kent Co son and heir of WILLIAM HARRAWAY late of same place yeoman decd for 50 pounds sold to ROBERT FRENCH of New Castle Co merchant ... a tr of land in Duck Cr Hund ... by Hillyards Br ... along the land sold by said SAMUELL HARRAWAY to one ANDREW TEBOW ... 150 a. pt/o a 300 a. tr of land sold by JOHN HILLYARD late decd in his lifetime to afsd WILLIAM HARRAWAY decd in his lifetime ... Wit: THOMAS CRAWFORD, PHILLYS KERNEY. Ackn 12 Nov 1712. (D:pg 98)

95. 6 Aug 1709. Deed. THOMAS BEDWELL of Murderkill Hund Kent Co esqr sold to JOHN HALL of same place yeoman ... in consideration of said JOHN HALL's intermarriage with HANNAH his dau and for 10 shillings ... a tr of land s side of Dover River ... 175 a. ... Wit: JOHN BRINCKLOE, FRANCIS ALLEN. Ackn 12 Aug 1715. (D:pg 99)

96. 14 Apr 1715. Deed. GEORGE HART of Kent Co yeoman for 41 pounds 5 shillings sold to JAMES FITZGERRALD of same co yeoman ... a tr of land called Young Hall ne side of Dover River beginning at the corner of JOHN HART's land ... to line of DANIELL RODENEY's land ... 50 a. ... Wit: JOHN CLAYTON, THOMAS PARKE. Ackn 12 Aug 1715.

(D:pg 100)

97. 10 May 1715. Deed. JOHN FOSTER of Duck Cr Kent Co yeoman adminr of the estate of JOHN CHAUNT late of same co decd for 45 pounds sold to TIMOTHY HANSON of Little Cr same co yeoman ... two tr of land n side of Little Cr one of them beginning at the corner of land called Simsons Choise ... by line of JOHN CLAFFORD's land ... 40 a. the other tr ... to corner of THOMAS GENSELIN's land ... 50 a. ... Wit: JACOB TAYLOR, HUGH DERBOROW Junr. Ackn 12 Aug 1715. (D:pg 101)

98. 10 Aug 1715. Quitt Claim. WILLIAM HIRONS of Kent Co in consideration of 10 shillings to me paid by JOHN FRENCH executor of estate of WILLIAM MORTON late of same co decd ... quitt claime unto JOHN FRENCH gentlemen any part or parcell of estate of afsd WILLIAM MORTON ... Wit: JAMES STEEL, TIMOTHY HANSON, JAMES MOOR. Attest: WILLIAM RODENEY clerk. (D:pg 102)

99. 12 Aug 1715. Quitt Claim. Whereas the [above] release was granted to me JOHN FRENCH ... I quitt claim unto RICHARD RICHARDSON of Kent Co my full right and title hereof ... Wit: JOHN JOHNSON, JAMES STEEL. (D:pg 102)

100. 9 Aug 1714. Deed. SAMUELL TAYLOR of Duck Cr New Castle Co bolter for 200 pounds sold to MARY (MERCY) GREEN of Kent Co widdow ... a tr of land [same as #92] ... Wit: JOHN COOK, BEN SHURMER, ABSALON CUFF. Ackn 12 Aug 1715. (D:pg 103)

101. 15 Jun 1715. Deed. SAMUELL TAYLOR of Duck Cr New Castle Co bolter for 8 pounds sold to BENJAMIN SHURMER of the manner of Peith on the head of Duck Cr Kent Co gentlemen ... ye other part adj to a place laid out for a town called Salisbury beginning at the nw corner of the ground belonging to the meeting house of the people called Quaker ... adj to the lower pt/o a strip of land formerly granted to said BENJAMIN SHURMER by SAMUELL TAYLOR ... to corner of COWGILLS lott ... 8 a. ... another piece of ground on the head of Duck Cr ... by the Mill House ... to Greens Br ... 4 a. both pieces of land taken out of a tr of land 500 a. called Gravesend formerly belonging to MERCY GREEN and by her sold to SAMUELL TAYLOR 14 Aug 1714 ... Wit: JOHN PHILLIPS, WILLIAM WOODWARD, WILLIAM WILLS, ABSALOM CUFF. Ackn 12 Aug 1715 unto THOMAS HACKETT on behalfe of BENJAMIN SHURMER. Wit: HENRY TRACY, FRANCIS JONES, ABSALOM CUFF. (D:pg 105)

102. 4 Feb 1714. Deed. SAMUELL TAYLOR of Duck Cr New Castle Co

bolter for 12 pounds 10 shillings sold to BENJAMIN SHURMER of the head of Duck Cr Kent Co but late of England gentleman ... a tr of land near the head of Duck Cr (and cut of a tr of 520 a. called Graves End) ... 25 a. ... Wit: BENJAMIN ELLIS, SAMUELL GRIFFING, ABSALOM CUFF. Ackn 12 Aug 1715 unto THOMAS HACKETT for BENJAMIN SHURMER. Wit: HENRY TRACY, FRANCIS JONES, ABSALOM CUFF. (D:pg 107)

103. 14 Nov --. Deed. JOHN WELLS of Kent Co planter for 20 pounds sold to VINCENT EMERSON of same co gentlemen ... tr of land s side of Dover River being the major pt/o a 400 a. tr of land called Brinckloes Range ... to corner of WILLIAM BIGNELL's land ... 315 a. ... Wit: WILLIAM STARKEY, FRANCIS ALLEN. Ackn 9 Aug 1715. (D:pg 109)

104. 10 Aug 1715. Deed. THOMAS HILLIARD of Kent Co son and heir of JOHN HILLYARD of same place who was son and heir of JOHN HILLYARD late of White Hall same co decd for 20 pounds sold to ANDREW HAMILTON of same co gentlemen 600 a. ... whereas JOHN HILLYARD the grandfather in his lifetime was seized of 400 a. called White Hall and by his will devised the same to his son JOHN ... taken in execution of satisfaction of a debt recovered against the estate of said JOHN by GRIFFITH JONES ... GRIFFITH JONES sold land to the son JOHN HILLYARD ... 400 a. together with 200 a. of other lands adj same ... Wit: JOHN VANDERFORD. Ackn 10 Aug 1715. (D:pg 110)

105. 10 Aug 1715. Quitt Claim. THOMAS HILLYARD son and heir of JOHN HILLYARD late of Kent Co who was the son and heir of JOHN HILLYARD late of same co decd have quitt claimed unto JOSEPH JONES executor of the will of GRIFFITH JONES late of Phila decd all errors misentries whatsoever which have happened on the record on judgment obtained by GRIFFITH JONES against estate of said JOHN HILLYARD grandfather of me said THOMAS HILLYARD ... Attest: JOHN VANDERFORD. Ackn 10 Aug 1715. (D:pg 111)

106. 9 May 1715. Deed. JOHN CLAYTON Junr of Kent Co yeoman for 75 pounds sold to GEORGE HARTT of same co yeoman ... tr of land called New Brister ne side of Dover River beginning at corner being pt/o a tr of land called Bristers Delight ... at corner of JAMES FITZGERRALD's land ... along JOHN HARTT's land ... 100 a. ... Wit: JOHN HEARTT, THOMAS PARKE. Ackn 12 Aug 1715. (D:pg 112)

107. 8 Aug 1715. Deed. JOHN STEAVENS of Kent Co yeoman and ELIZABETH his wife for 18 pounds 15 shillings sold to JOHN MARUM of same place carpenter ... a tr of land called Maruns Delight being pt/o a tr called Little Pipe Elme on Little Cr ... bounded by a tr of land of

Edmunton ... 51 a. ... Wit: THOMAS CRAWFORD, HUGH DURBOROW Junr. Ackn 10 Aug 1715. (D:pg 113)

108. 10 Nov 1713. Deed. Whereas JOHN BURTON of Kent Co planter by deed 10 Feb 1684 did sell unto RICHARD MITCHELL of same place all that tr of land called Burtons Chance s side of Dover River ... beginning at Isaacks Br to Walters Br ... 100 a. ... whereas said MITCHELL dyed interstate and JOHN EDMONDSON and WILLIAM DIXON adminr 20 Feb 1686/7 assigned all rights to WILLIAM LAWRANCE of Phila merchant ... said WILLIAM LAWRANCE for [blank] pounds sold to JOHN CLAYTON Junr of Kent Co yeoman the afsd tr of land ... Wit: THOMAS CHALKLEY, JOHN CLAYTON Senr. Ackn 10 May 1715 by JOHN CLAYTON Senr on behalf of WILLIAM LAWRENCE. (D:pg 114)

109. 1 Feb 1713. Deed. ELIZABETH BEDWELL of Murderkill Hund Kent Co widdow relict of ROBERT BEDWELL late of same place yeoman decd one of the sons of ROBERT BEDWELL late of same co gentlemen decd ... whereas ROBERT BEDWELL the younger in his lifetime 1 Mar 1708 for 50 pounds did sell but not convey unto THOMAS BEDWELL of same co gentlemen a tr of land s side of Dover River ... 175 a. and is pt/o 500 a. whereof said ROBERT BEDWELL the elder dyed possessed of being pt/o a 1050 a. tr of land called Follyneck whereof the said ROBERT BEDWELL, JOHN GOODSON and SAMUELL CARPENTER commissioners 6 Mar 1690 granted to ROBERT BEDWELL in his lifetime patent 20 Aug 1679 resurveyed 10 Jan 1685 unto ROBERT BEDWELL being one of the sons of ROBERT BEDWELL decd and whereas ROBERT BEDWELL the younger late decd by will 4 Oct 1713 did appoint his well beloved wife ELIZABETH BEDWELL a party to these presents and to makeover in open court a good title to said 175 a. unto THOMAS BEDWELL ... Wit: WILLIAM RODENEY, JOHN HALL, FRANCIS ALLEN. Ackn 10 Aug 1715. (D:pg 115)

110. 2 Aug 1708. Deed. JOHN WILLSON of Talbot Co MD joyner for 20 pounds sold to DANIELL HUDSON of Kent Co planter ... a tr of land called Shewforth on Murther Cr at corner of Bishop's Br ... corner of land called Guilford ... parallel with ROBERT PARRISS's line ... 400 a. heretofore in possession of CHRISTOPHER MOORE ... JOHN WILLSON hereby impower VINCENT EMERSON esqr to be my atty to ackn and deliver deed in open court ... Wit: WILLIAM ANNAND, ABRAHAM TAYLOR. Ackn 12 Aug 1715 by VINCENT EMERSON Esqr as atty for JOHN WILLSON. (D:pg 117)

111. 8 Aug 1715. Deed. WILLIAM BURTON of Little Cr Kent Co labourer for 20 pounds sold to RICHARD NIXON of same place yeoman ... a tr of land called Mount Pleasant being pt/o a tr called Little Pipe

Elme s side of Little Cr beginning at head of a br of DANIELL JONES now SARAH RODENEY's land ... 100 a. ... Wit: THOMAS CRAWFORD, HUGH DURBEROW Junr. Ackn 10 Aug 1715. (D:pg 118)

112. 10 Aug 1714. Deed. JOHN WELLS of Kent Co yeoman for 17 pounds sold to HUMPHREY BARRETT of same co yeoman ... tr of land in Little Cr Hund on which said HUMPHREY BARRETT now dwelleth and is pt/o a tr of land called Chippinorton lately purch by said JOHN WELLS of THOMAS NIXON and MARY his wife relict and adminr of the estate of BENJAMIN BRADY decd ... s side of the road that goes from JONES to THOMAS EMERSON's plantation ... 58 a. ... Wit: SAMUELL BERRY, THOMAS FRENCH. Ackn 10 Aug 1715. (D:pg 119)

113. 12 Nov 1711. Deed. RICHARD RICHARDSON of Kent Co yeoman for 40 pounds sold to JABEZ JENKINS of same co weaver ... a tr of land near Little Cr being pt/o a tr of land called St. Andrews belonging to said RICHARD RICHARDSON beginning at a stake near the plantation of JOHN CLAYTON where ADAM LATHAN now dwells ... bounded by SAMUEL BERRY ... 114 a. ... Wit: JAMES MOIR, THOMAS WITHERS, JAMES STEEL. Ackn 13 May 1712. (D:pg 120)

114. 3 May 1725. Be it remembered that this day at the request of JABEZ JENKINS the grantee in [above] deed named, I have compared the original deed with this record thereof and do find that the last course and distance of the land was wholly omitted [and is corrected] ... (signed) BENJAMIN SHUMER regr clerk. (D:pg 121)

115. 14 Jun 1714. Power of Atty. WM LAWRANCE of Phila taylor appoint JOHN CLAYTON Senr of Kent Co to ackn in open court a deed of sale for 100 a. to JOHN CLAYTON Junr ... Wit: JAMES STEEL, JAMES BOYDEN. Proved 10 Jan 1714 by SAMUELL BERRY and TIMOTHY HANSON esqr justices of peace of Kent Co. (D:pg 122)

116. 8 Aug 1715. Power of Atty. BENJAMIN SHURMER of the manner of faith in Kent Co constitute my trusty friend THOMAS HACKET of same manner my atty to receive and ackn in open court two deeds of land of SAMUELL TAYLOR of Duck Cr ... Wit: JOHN PHILLIPS, JAMES MORRIS. (D:pg 122)

117. 8 Aug 1715. Deed. THOMAS BEDWELL of Kent Co gentlemen and HONOR his wife executrix of will of WILLIAM CLARK late of Lewis Town Suss Co esqr decd for 35 pounds sold to THOMAS NOCK of Kent Co ... a tr of land w side of St. Jones Cr alias Dover River by Tidbury Br ... 445 a. patent dated 2 Aug 1690 granted unto EZEKIEL NEEDHAM and by his deed 10 Sep 1690 conveyed unto WILLIAM CLARK decd ...

Wit: JAMES BAILY, SARAH BAILY. Ackn 9 Nov 1715 unto WM RODENEY atty for THOMAS NOCK. (D:pg 122)

118. 7 Nov 1715. Power of Atty. HONOR BEDWELL executrix of the will of WILLIAM CLARK of Lewis in Suss Co esqr late decd ... appoint my trusty friend WILLIAM RODENEY of Kent Co to be my atty to ackn [above] deed of sale ... Wit: JAMES BAILY, SARAH BAILY. Proved 7 Nov 1715 by JONATHAN BAILY justice of peace of Suss Co. (D:pg 123)

119. 10 Aug 1717. Deed. Whereas a tr of land s side of Murder Cr called Wms Fancy ... corner of JOHN MORONY's land ... 452 a. pt/o a 2000 a. tr of land called Fairfield granted to WM CLARK patent dated 29 May 1689 and sold by WM CLARK but not conveyed to JOSEPH ROWE ... and afterwards THOMAS BEDWELL & HONOR his wife relict & executrix of the will of afsd WM CLARK by indenture 15 Aug 1711 confirmed afsd tr of land unto DAVID ROWE (ROE) of Mispillion Hund Kent Co yeoman as son & heir of said JOSEPH ROWE decd ... for 45 pounds DAVID ROWE sold to WM BRINCKLE (BRINCKLEY) of same place gentlemen afsd tr of land ... Wit: TIMOTHY HANSON, WM WINSMORE. Ackn 10 Nov 1715. (D:pg 124)

120. 31 Jul 1713. Writt of Execution. VINCENT EMERSON esqr sherriffe of Kent Co ... with DANIELL RUTTY, MICHAEL LOBER, WILLIAM RODENEY, EDWARD WILLIAMS, JOHN NEWELL (NOWELL), DANIEL HUDSON, WILLIAM NOWELL, CHRISTOPHER JACKSON, RICHARD JACKSON, WILLIAM BARTER (BOOKSTED), JERIMIAH NICKERSON (NICKALSON) and JOHN SMITH jurors, good and lawful men ... went to ye land of New Seven Haven in Murtherkill Hund being lands in writt ... in presence of JOHN FISHER and ADAM FISHER ye younger & their next friend ADAM FISHER & CORNELIUS SULLIVANT and SARAH his wife ... land divided into two equal parts ... 223 a. delivered to JOHN FISHER and ADAM FISHER ye younger ... 223 a. delivered to CORNELIUS SULLIVANT & SARAH his wife ... . (D:pg 125)

121. 4 Nov 1715. Lease. JOSEPH JONES son and heir of GRIFF JONES late of Phila for 5 shillings lease to JAMES STEEL of Duck Cr Kent Co yeoman ... two tr of land one beginning at corner of HENRY STEVENS land ... 600 a. ... the other tr ... 1000 a. ... for one year ... Wit: ROBT MONTGOMRY, JAMES BOYDEN, A HAMILTON, ABRAHAM BICKLEY. Ackn 10 Nov 1715 by EVAN JONES esqr atty to JOSEPH JONES. (D:pg 126)

122. 5 Nov 1715. Deed. JOSEPH JONES son and heir of GRIFFITH JONES late of Phila decd for 50 pounds sold to JAMES STEEL of Duck

Cr Kent Co yeoman ... [above] parcells of land one patent 9 Dec 1690 the other 14 May 1687 unto GRIFFITH JONES ... by his will dated 4 Oct 1712 bequeaths unto said JOSEPH JONES his son and executor of his will, all his lands ... Wit: ROBERT MONTGOMRY, JAMES BOYDON, ANDREW HAMILTON, ABRAHAM BICKLEY. Ackn 10 Nov 1715 by EVAN JONES esqr atty to JOSEPH JONES. (D:pg 127)

123. 16 Sep 1715. Deed. SAMUEL BOURDET of NY city marriner surviving brother and executor of PETER BOURDET late of Kent Co decd for 10 pounds sold to JAMES STEEL of same co yeoman ... tr of land s side of Duck Cr ... bounded on the e by the land of late GEORGE SHARP ... 250 a. ... SAMUEL BOURDET appoint EVAN JONES of Kent Co yeoman his atty to ackn these presents in open court ... Wit: ANDREW HAMILTON, FR GONDWELL, F NASSON. Ackn 10 Nov 1715 by EVAN JONES esq atty for SAMUEL BOURDET. (D:pg 128)

124. 10 Feb 1713. Deed. HELENOR NACKARRA (ELINOR NICKARRA) of Kent Co widow and adminr of JOHN NACKARRA late of same co decd sold to EVAN JONES of same co yeoman ... JOHN NACKARRA in his lifetime and the time of his death [in debt] to severall person more than his personal estate could satisfy ... for 60 pounds due from estate of JOHN NACKARRA decd ELINOR NACKARRA sold to EVAN JONES ... a tr of land in Duck Cr Hund pt/o a tr of land belonging to EVAN JONES called Aberconday beginning at a corner of ISACK & ELISHA SNOW's ... to land called Coventree ... 120 a. ... Wit: JAMES STEEL, WILLIAM ANNAND. Ackn 10 Nov 1715. (D:pg 129)

125. 12 Nov 1712. Deed. JAMES GRIFFITH of Murtherkill Hund Kent Co yeoman sold to JOHN NEWELL of same place yeoman ... a tr of land where JAMES GRIFFITH lately lived called Weels Lott n side of Murtherkill Cr n side of Service Br ... 100 a. ... Wit: JOHN VANDERFORD, ISAAC MOIR, ISAAC SNOW. Ackn 10 Nov 1715. (D:pg 130)

126. 1 Oct 1712. Deed of Gift. GEORGE ROBISSON of Mispillion Hund Kent Co yeoman for love good will and affection give to my well beloved son SAMUEL ROBISSON ... a tr of land 111 a. pt/o a 200 a. tr by me purch of ABRAHAM SKIDMORE 20 May 1709 ... to first 89 a. of which was by the survey of MARY BETTS decd taken away and by her given and granted unto my dau ANN ROBISSON ... shall not be lawfull for said SAMUEL ROBISSON at any time before he arrive at the age of 25 years to sell or dispose of the land and if he should dye without issue before that time then same shall be to the only proper use of his sister CHARITY ROBISSON ... Wit: WILLIAM HIRONS, FRANCIS ALLEN. Ackn 10 Nov 1715. (D:pg 131)

127. 1 Oct 1712. Deed of Gift. GEORGE ROBISSON of Mispillion Hund Kent Co yeoman for love good will and affection give to my beloved son JOHN ROBISSON ... a tr of land whereon I now live se side of Murtherkill Cr 160 a. by me purch of WILLIAM WILLSON late sheriff 1 Oct 1701 ... and one more tr of land 50 a. adj to a tr of land by me formerly given to my son GEORGE ROBISSON ... it shall not be lawfull for said JOHN ROBISSON at any time before he arrives to the full age of 25 years to sell the land ... and if said JOHN shall dye without issue before that time then same shall be to the only proper use of his brother DANIELL ROBISSON ... Wit: WILLIAM HIRONS, FRANCIS ALLEN. Ackn 10 Nov 1715. (D:pg 132)

128. 14 Feb 1710. Deed of Gift. GEORGE ROBISSON of Mispillion Hund Kent Co yeoman for love good will and affection give to my son GEORGE ROBISSON Junr the younger one of the sons of said GEORGE ROBISSON ... plantation on Bacombrigg in Mispillion Hund 150 a. that he purch from JOHN BETTS decd ... together with 1 sorrel horse 3 years old, 4 cows and calves and 4 ewes and lambs and 1 plough horse called Cromwell which he bought of HENRY HALL ... it shall not be lawfull for GEORGE ROBISSON Junr to sell the 150 a. untill he arrive at the just age of 25 years without the lawful consent of his father GEORGE ROBISSON or his mother SARAH ROBISSON and if GEORGE ROBISSON Junr should dye without issue then the 150 a. shall be to the only proper use of his brother DANIEL ROBISSON ... and GEORGE ROBISSON Junr shall keep all the covenants and arguments made between his father GEORGE ROBISSON and WILLIAM DEMOCK planter that is, it shall not be lawfull for GEORGE ROBISSON the younger to buy or sell or make any contract or merchandize with any persons for any thing above the value of 5 shillings untill he shall arrive to the full age of twenty one years without the lawful consent of his father or his mother ... Wit: MARY ALLEN, FRANCIS ALLEN. Ackn 10 Nov 1715. (D:pg 133)

129. 2 Feb 1713. Deed. THOMAS BEDWELL of Murtherkill Hund Kent Co gentlemen and HONOUR his wife for 185 pounds sold to JOHN COE gentlemen of same place ... a tr of land s side of Dover River in Murtherkill Hund ... 550 a. pt/o a 1050 a. tr of land called Folly Neck and by WILLIAM MARKHAM, ROBERT TURNER, JOHN GOODSON and SAMUEL CARPENTER commissioners appointed by WILLIAM PENN proprietary by patent 6 Mar 1690 granted unto ROBERT BEDWELL father of THOMAS BEDWELL former patent granted by Govr EDMOND ANDROSS unto ROBERT BEDWELL 20 Aug 1679 resurveyed 10 Jan 1685 ... THOMAS BEDWELL being eldest son and heire of their father ROBERT BEDWELL decd did grant unto his brother ROBERT BEDWELL 175 a. who sold but did not convey back to THOMAS

BEDWELL and ROBERT BEDWELL since decd and by his will 4 Oct 1713 did appoint his well beloved wife ELIZABETH BEDWELL to make over in open court a good title for 175 a. unto THOMAS BEDWELL (1 Feb 1713 ELIZABETH BEDWELL did assign over unto THOMAS BEDWELL 175 a.) ... 175 a. and 375 a. remainder of said 550 a. ... Wit: WM RODENEY, JOHN HALL, FRANCIS ALLEN. Ackn 10 Nov 1715 unto WM RODENEY atty to HONOR BEDWELL. (D:pg 133)

130. 19 Sep 1715. Deed. EDWARD FRETWELL of Phila merchant for 5 shillings sold to JOSEPH WARRALL of Chester Co PA yeoman ... a tr of land sw br of Duck Cr ... by br which divides this land from the land now belonging to EVAN JONES ... 620 a. ... Wit: ANDREW HAMILTON, JOSEPH LAWRANCE, JOSEPH GRAINGER. Ackn 11 Nov 1715 by JAMES STEEL att to EDWARD FRETWELL. (D:pg 136)

131. 20 Sep 1715. Deed. Whereas WILLIAM PENN Governor by patent under his commissioners RICHARD HILL, ISAAC NORRIS and JAMES LOGAN 2 Aug 1715 did grant unto EDWARD FRETTWELL late of Wickersley in Co of York in Great Britain but now of Phila gentlemen a tr of land sw br of Duck Cr 620 a. ... EDWARD FRETWELL merchant for 120 pounds sold to JOSEPH WARRELL of Chester Co PA yeoman afsd tr of land ... EDWARD FRETTWELL hath made JAMES STEEL his atty to ackn these presents in open court ... Wit: AX HAMILTON, JOSEPH LAWRANCE, JOSEPH GRANGER. Ackn 10 Nov 1715 by JAMES STEEL atty for EDWARD FRETTWELL. (D:pg 137)

Deed Book E Vol 1

132. 28 Sep 1715. Bond of Conveyance. ABRAHAM BICKLEY of Phila merchant am bound to GEORGE NOWELL of Kent Co for 500 pounds ... ABRAHAM BICKLEY to convey 400 a. called KINGSTON UPON HULL ... unto GEORGE NOWELL ... Wit: JOHN FRENCH, ANTHONY HUSTONE, ANDRA HAMELTON. (E:pg 1)

133. 10 May 1715. Deed. JOHN STEVENS of Kent Co yeoman and ELIZABETH his wife for 42 pounds sold to RICHARD NIXSON of same co yeoman ... a tr of land called Nixons Delight on br of Little Cr ... along the line of STEPHEN PARRADEE's land ... along the line of THOMAS JOILLSON's land ... along line of JOHN MARON's land ... 110 a. ... Wit: THOMAS CRAWFORD, HUGH DURBOROUGH Junr. Ackn 12 Aug 1715. (E:pg 2)

134. 14 Jan 1712. Deed. EVAN JONES of Kent Co yeoman for 205 pounds sold to ISAAC SNOW and ELISHA SNOW both of same co

yeoman ... a tr of land n side of sw br of Duck Cr being the plantation where ISAAC SNOW and ELISHA SNOW now dwell beginning at a tr of land called Whitewells Chance ... along the line of a tr of land called Denifield now belonging to said EVAN JONES ... along the line of a tr of land called Coventry ... 199-1/2 a. ... Wit: WM ANNAND, THOMAS SHARP, JOHN FOSTER, JAMES STEEL. Ackn 12 Nov 1715. (E:pg 3)

135. 13 Aug 1715. Deed of Gift. EVAN JONES of Duck Cr Kent Co gentlemen for affection love and goodwill give to JOHN PAIN of same place planter and ELIZABETH his wife... a tr of land n side of sw br of Duck Cr beginning at the tr of land called Benyfield ... to line of land called Coventry ... 50 a. Wit: RICHARD SMITH, JAMES STEEL, JACOB TAYLOR. Ackn 10 Nov 1715. (E:pg 6)

136. 9 Dec 1708. Deed. EVAN JONES of Kent Co gentlemen for 20 pounds sold to PHILLIP DENNY of same co planter ... a tr of land s side of Duck Cr ... 180 a. patent bearing date 17 Jun 1707 ... Wit: MARK BARDEN, JOHN BRADSHAW. Ackn 10 Nov 1715. (E:pg 8)

137. 10 Feb 1714. Deed of Gift. THOMAS SHARP of Duck Cr Kent Co yeoman for affection and love give to my brother in law JOHN TILTON late of Suss Co but now of Duck Cr yeoman n side of sw br of Duck Cr ... by line of ABRAHAM BICKLEY's land ... 150 a. patent bearing date 3 Sep 1708 ... JOHN TILTON shall not at any time give or convey the said tr of land to any other person except it be to myself, my present wife or to some of my near relations and also I reserve out of said tr of land a passage for myself and said wife during our natural lives for the convenience of our servants, carts, horses and cattle through the e side ... Wit: EVAN JONES, ANDREW HAMILTON. Ackn 11 Nov 1715. (E:pg 10)

138. 10 Apr 1713. Deed. THOMAS BEDWELL, ROBERT BEDWELL and ADAM FISHER all of Kent Co gentlemen for 15 pounds sold to MARK BARDEN of same co carpenter ... a tr of land (patented to THOMAS BEDWELL and HENRY BEDWELL [his] brother and unto ROBERT BEDWELL and ADAM FISHER 1100 a.) called Long Reach in Murtherkill Hund on a br of Dover River ... to line formerly belonging to EZEKIEL NEEDHAM ... to corner of land formerly belonging to EDMOND NEEDHAM ... 100 a. ... HENRY BEDWELL is since decd without heirs ... Wit: FRANCIS ALLEN, WM ANNAND. Ackn 10 Nov 1715 by THOMAS BEDWELL and ELIZABETH BEDWELL relict of and executrix of ROBERT BEDWELL decd and ADAM FISHER. (E:pg 12)

139. 9 May 1709. Deed. JAMES FITZGERALD and KATHARINE his wife, JOHN STEVENS and ELIZABETH his wife, JOHN MARON and

MARY his wife all of Kent Co for 17 pounds sold to TIMOTHY OHARAN of same place ... 50 a. in Dover Hund being the plantation and pt/o the said land where HENRY STEVENS, the former husband of KATHARINE FITZGERALD died possessed with, being bounded by the lines of JOHN HALL and JAMES FITZGERALD ... it shall be lawfull for him said JAMES FITZGERALD and KATHARINE his wife from time to time during her natural life ... to enjoy one third pt/o above said 50 a. and 15 foot right up and down of one 50 foot tobacco house now standing and being upon said premises ... Wit: JONAS GREENWOOD, THOMAS WILLSON, STEPHEN PARRADEE. Ackn 10 Nov 1715. (E:pg 16)

140. 18 Aug 1713. Deed of Gift. JOHN BRADSHAW of Duck Cr Kent Co for love goodwill and affection give to my well beloved dau RACHEL BRADSHAW the now wife of JOHN HIGHAN of same co ... tr of land where RACHEL's husband JOHN HIGHAN hath a dwelling house frame being pt/o the tr of land I now dwell on, n side of sw br of Duck Cr called Bradshaws Chance ... Wit: HENRY MOOR, JONATHAN COLLINS. Ackn 10 Nov 1715. (E:pg 18)

141. 1 May 1711. Deed. STEPHEN PARRADEE of Kent Co yeoman and MARGRET his wife for 20 pounds sold to JOHN MARON of same co ... a tr of land lying in a fork of Little Cr being pt/o a tr of land purch by STEPHEN PARRADEE of RICHARD LEVICK beginning at the corner of land sold to THOMAS WILLSON ... 100 a. ... Wit: JOHN GUMLEY, BENJAMIN BOAK, WM ANNAND. Ackn 11 Nov 1715. (E:pg 20)

142. 10 Apr 1714. Deed. GEORGE HART of Kent Co yeoman and ANNA his wife for 37 pounds sold to THOMAS WELLS of same place yeoman ... 100 a. where GEORGE HART lately dwelt sw side of Jones Cr or Dover River and is pt/o a tr of land called Leason ... Wit: THOMAS CRAWFORD, GRIFFETH JONES. Ackn 11 Nov 1715. (E:pg 22)

143. 30 Dec 1710. Deed. RICHARD RICHARDSON of Kent Co for a competent sum of silver money sold to SAMUEL BERRY of same co gentlemen ... a tr of land in Little Cr pt/o a tr called Saint Andrews beginning at the line called Simsons Choice ... to corner of SAMUEL BERRY's land ... 50 a. which heretofore in occupation of JOHN FRENCH of New Castle ... Wit: ROBERT FRENCH, THOMAS CRAWFORD. Ackn 11 Nov 1715. (E:pg 24)

144. 13 Nov 1712. Deed. FRANCIS ALLEXANDER of Kent Co cordwainder for 52 pounds 10 shillings sold to JOHN MORGAN of same co planter ... a tr of land in Little Cr Hund pt/o a greater tr called Bettys Fortune ... w by a land surveyed for ABRAHAM FIELDS ... 120 a. ... heretofore in the possession of one JOHN FRENCH esqr and by his deed

bearing date 8 Aug 1710 conveyed unto FRANCIS ALEXANDER ... Wit: WM WINSMORE, WM ANNAND. Ackn 11 Apr 1715. (E:pg 27)

145. 12 Aug 1712. Quit Claim. Whereas GEORGE MARTIN in his lifetime ... did sell unto JOHN BRADSHAW of same co ... a tr of land n side of sw br of Duck Cr 300 a. called Bradshaws Chance in consideration of a tr of land that said JOHN BRADSHAW did grant to GEORGE MARTIN in his lifetime for payment of said 300 a. ... witness to bond was DAVID STRAWHIN and WALTER JONES both decd ... Feb 1684 GEORGE MARTIN did deliver possession of 300 a. and RICHARD MITCHELL and EVAN JONES signed as witnesses ... Know ye that GEORGE MARTIN, WILLIAM ANNAND and ELIZABETH ANNAND his wife all of Kent Co son and dau of GEORGE MARTIN late of same place decd ... quitt claim unto JOHN BRADSHAW afsd tr of land ... Wit: A HAMELTON, HOYIDIAH OFLEY?, WM HAWKEY. Ackn 12 Aug 1712. (E:pg 30)

146. 12 Nov 1711. Deed. FRANCIS RICHARDSON of Phila goldsmith and REBECA MURREY (MORRY) of same place widow for 27 pounds five shillings sold to JOHN ALLEY of Duck Cr Kent Co yeoman ... a tr of land patented 26 Mar 1684 unto FRANCIS WHITEWELL late of Kent Co decd ... called Kingston lying between Dawson's and Row's br ... side of Newton's br ... 360 a. ... whereas WILLIAM BERRY late of Kent Co decd adminr of estate of FRANCIS WHITEWELL by his deed bearing date 17 Mar 1687 granted unto FRANCIS RICHARDSON late of NY City merchant decd ... and by will bearing date 7 Jul 1688 said FRANCIS RICHARDSON decd the father did bequeath unto his son and dau FRANCIS and REBECA afsd tr of land ... FRANCIS and REBECA appoint EVAN JONES to be their atty to deliver this deed in open court ... Wit: JOSEPH THYIEN, HUMPHRY MORRY. Ackn 12 May 1713. (E:pg 31)

147. 12 May 1712. Deed. WILLIAM ANNAND of Kent Co gentlemen and GEORGE MARTIN of same co yeoman for 130 pounds sold to JOHN ALLEI of same co yeoman ... a tr of land (patent bearing date Aug 1685 granted unto FRANCIS RICHARDSON) s side of Duck Cr ... to corner of ALBERTSON's land ... 1500 a. ... and by his will FRANCIS RICHARDSON did bequeath said tr of land unto his son FRANCIS RICHARDSON and dau REBECCA who by their deed of sale 13 Dec 1712 did sell unto the said WILLIAM ANNAND and GEORGE MARTIN ... Wit: EVEN JONES, FRANCIS ALLIN, JAMES STEEL. Ackn 12 May 1713. (E:pg 33)

148. 9 Aug 1715. Deed. JAMES JACKSON of Kent Co yeoman and MARGET (MARGRET) his wife for 2 pounds sold to JOHN FOSTER of same co yeoman ... a tr of land s side of sw br of Duck Cr called Kingsale

... 70 a. being pt/o a tr of 750 a. formerly in the tenure of PATRICK WORD and afterwards confirmed by patent 4 May 1715 to JAMES JACKSON and MARGRIT his wife, dau of said PATRICK WORD ... with the said 70 a. executed by PATRICK WORD in his life time to URBANUS TOMPSON of same co decd bearing date 7 Sep 1696 and said URBANUS on 10 Feb 1700 sold same to JOHN FOSTER decd ... Wit: JAMES STEEL, SAMUEL BERRY. Ackn 11 Nov 1715. (E:pg 35)

149. 27 Sep 1715. Lease. ABRAHAM BICKLEY of Phila merchant for 5 shillings lease to GEORGE NOWELL of Kent Co ... a tr of land 450 a. called Kingston Upon Hull for one whole year ... Wit: JOHN FRENCH, ANTHONY HUSTON, A HAMELTON. Ackn 15 Feb 1715 by JAMES STEEL as atty to ABRAHAM BICKLEY. (E:pg 37)

150. 28 Sep 1715. Deed. Whereas WILLIAM FRAMTON and ELIZABETH his wife was seized of a tr of land called Kingston Upon Hull ne side of St. Jones Cr ... to line of ROBERT JONES ... 450 a. and the said WILLIAM and ELIZABETH dying intestate the said tr of land came to one THOMAS FRAMTON son and heir of said WILLIAM FRAMTON which THOMAS on 2 Jan 1712 sold to ABRAHAM BICKLEY ... ABRAHAM BICKLEY of Phila merchant for 200 pounds sold to GEORGE NOWELL of Kent Co yeoman afsd tr of land [same as #149] ... released from claims against MATTHEW GARDINER and WILLIAM BASSONETT and MARY PHILLIPP ... Wit: JOHN FRENCH, ANTHONEY HASTON, A HAMELTON. Ackn 15 Feb 1715 by JAMES STEEL atty for ABRAHAM BICKLEY. (E:pg 38)

151. 20 Jan 1715. Deed. TIMOTHY HANSON and JOSHUA CLAYTON Senr both of Little Cr Kent Co executors of will of ROBERT PORTER Senr of Murtherkill Hund Kent Co decd for 65 pounds sold to JOHN CLAYTON Senr of Little Cr ... 100 a. being pt/o a tr of land that MARY RICHARDSON executrix of the will of JOHN RICHARDSON Senr late of same co decd now dwelleth upon lying in Little Cr ... along the line that separates land of JOHN RICHARDSON Junr grandson to the above named JOHN RICHARDSON Senr decd from the land of said MARY RICHARDSON ... Wit: WM BRINCKLOW, RICHARD RICHARDSON, JAMES ELLIOT. Ackn 15 Feb 1715. (E:pg 40)

152. 8 Feb 1715. Deed. JOHN CLAYTON Senr of Little Cr Kent Co for 5 pounds sold to JOSHUA CLAYTON Senr of same place ... [above] tr of land ... Wit: WM BRINCKLOW, RICHARD RICHARDSON, JAMES MOIR. Ackn 15 Feb 1715. (E:pg 41)

153. 14 Feb 1715. Deed. MARK MANLOVE of Kent Co for 170 pounds sold to MATHEW MANLOVE of same co ... a tr of land called Strathcum

n side of Mispillion Cr ... 300 a. ... Wit: WILLIAM BRINCKLOW, ADAM FISHER. Ackn 15 Feb 1715. (E:pg 43)

154. 15 Feb 1715. Deed. WILLIAM HAWKEY of Duck Cr Kent Co yeoman for 5 pounds sold to JAMES STEEL of same place yeoman ... a tr of land on Duck Cr neck beginning in the line of a tr of land called Coventry ... in the line of other land belonging to said JAMES STEEL ... 11 a. ... Wit: EVEN JONES, GEORGE BOWES, T JANALLE. Ackn 15 Feb 1715. (E:pg 44)

155. 12 Feb 1715. Deed. JAMES JACKSON of Little Cr Hund Kent Co yeoman and MARGIT his wife for love and affection and 5 shillings sell to there brother WILLIAM KELLY ... a tr of land s side of Duck Cr ... to corner of tr of land formerly layd out to JOHN KELLY ... to Willson's Br ... to line of JOHN NELEY ... [blank] a. ... Wit: THOMAS CRAFORD, SAMUEL MANLOVE. Ackn 15 Feb 1715. (E:pg 45)

156. 20 Jan 1715. Quit Claim. HENRY PEARMAIN son and heir of HENRY PEARMAIN late of Duck Cr Kent Co decd for 5 pounds quitt claim unto JAMES STEEL of same place yeoman ... a tr of land formerly surveyed unto WILLIAM PICKERING bounded on the n with a br of Duck Cr and on the w with Gravely Run and on s VAXON land and on e with the land formerly granted by my said father unto GEORGE SHARP of same co ... and HENRY PEARMAIN appoint ANDREW HAMELTON esqr to be my atty to deliver these presents in open court ... Wit: D PEARCE, EVAN JONES. Ackn 15 Feb 1715 by ANDREW HAMILTON esqr for HENRY PEARMAIN. (E:pg 46)

157. 10 May 1712. JAMES MAXWILL of Kent Co planter younger son of JAMES MAXWILL late of Dover yeoman decd for 16 pounds sold to JOHN REIGESTER of same co carpenter ... whereas JAMES MAXWILL decd was in his lifetime and at the time of his death seized of a 350 a. tr of land in Dover Hund near the head of Dover River pt/o a greater tr called Berrys Range which said JAMES MAXWILL dyed intestate ... 81 a. ... Wit: SAMUEL BERRY, THOMAS PARKE, WILLIAM ANNAND. Ackn 15 Feb 1715. (E:pg 47)

158. 3 Jun 1715. Deed. SAMUELL TAYLER of Duck Cr New Castle Co bolter for 4 pounds sold to JOSEPH ENGLAND, JOHN COWGILL, CALEB OFFLEY and ABSOLOM CUFF yeoman all of same place ... a lott or piece of ground within the limits of a place laid out for a town called Sailsbury on the head of Duck Cr Kent Co ... at corner of the meeting house of the people called Quaker ... 2 a. ... Wit: JOHN WATERS, GEORGE THORP, FRANCIS JONES. Ackn 15 Feb 1715 by TIMOTHY HANSON atty to SAMUELL TAYLER. (E:pg 48)

159. 3 Jun 1715. Power of Atty. SAMUEL TAYLER do appoint TIMOTHY HANDSON of Kent Co to deliver [above] deed in open court ... Wit: CHARLES HARPER, HENRY PENEFF.

160. 8 Aug 17--. Deed. MARY RICHARDSON relict and executrix of JOHN RICHARDSON late of Kent Co decd ... whereas said JOHN RICHARDSON by his will bequeathed the one halfe of severall tr of land in particular the one half pt/o a tr of land called Willingbrook it being the home dwelling which she and said JOHN RICHARDSON both lived and dyed on Little Cr Hund ... 100 a. sold to ROBERT PORTER of same co planter afsd tr of land ... Wit: JONAS GREENWOOD, JOHN CLAYTON, EDMAND NEEDHAM, JOSEHUA CLAYTON, TIMOTHY HANDSON. Ackn 15 Feb 1716. (E:pg 50)

161. 10 Dec 1711. JOSHUA CLAYTON of Kent Co yeoman for [blank] pounds sold to DAVID MORGAN of same co yeoman ... a tr of land in Little Cr Hund pt/o a greater tr called Higham Ferry ... from cr to the plantation formerly belonging to RICHARD WILLSON decd ... to red oak standing in line of JOHN RICHARDSON's land ... 50 a. ... Wit: SAMUELL BERRY, WILLIAM BROWN. Ackn 15 Feb 1715. (E:pg 52)

162. 13 Feb 1711. Be it remembered that DAVID MORGAN is to clear all the overage of rents that is still due of the [above] mentioned land except what shall be all ready paid on the whole tr before said JOSHUA CLAYTON bought it (signed) DAVID MORGAN. Wit: SAMUELL BERRY, JOHN CLAYTON. (E:pg 53)

163. 16 Oct 1714. Deed. BENJAMIN SHURMER late of the city of Bristoll in Great Britain but now of Kent Co agent to WM DONNE, ABRAHAM LLOYD, CHARTER HARFORD, EDWARD LLOYD, CALEB LLOYD, GEORGE WHITEHEAD & RICHARD COOL of city of Bristoll ... whereas RICHARD HILL, ISAAC NORRIS & JAMES LOGAN commissioners of property to WM PENN esqr Governor in chief & agent to HENRY GOLDNIS of London ... received 78 pounds 12 shillings 6 pence paid by BENJAMIN SHURMER and certain articles bearing date 22 Sep last past executed between them ... have granted a tr of land being pt/o that mannor called Dukes or Proprietors Mannor ... 3125 a. ... to BENJAMIN SHURMER as agent for WM DONNE, ABRAHAM LLOYD, CHARTER HARFORD, EDWARD LLOYD, CALEB LLOYD, GEORGE WHITEHEAD & RICHARD COOL ... Wit: JONATHAN DICKINSON, JAMES LOGAN, JAMES STEEL, JAMES BOYDEN. Ackn 10 Mar 1716 by JAMES STEEL esqr atty to BENJAMIN SHURMER. (E:pg 54)

164. 18 Mar 1714. Be if remembered the [above] named BENJ

SHURMER gave livery & seizin of [above] mentioned 3125 a. unto THOMAS HACKETT agent to grantees WM DONNE, ABRAH LLOYD, CHA HARFORD, EDW LLOYD, CALEB LLOYD, GEO WHITEHEAD & RICHARD COOL for & in their behalf by delivering unto him turf & twig of said land ... Wit: JNO ELLIS, JOHN TAYLOR, HENRY TRACY, EDWARD LOWDEN. (E:pg 54)

165. 10 May 1716. ABRAHAM BICKLEY in open court of common pleas of Dover did on his solemn affirmation say that he see BENJAMIN SHURMER deliver & ackn [above] act of deed and that he see CHARLES ROAD signe as evidence thereto. Attest: WM RODENEY clerk. (E:pg 54)

166. 20 Dec 1715. Deed. THOMAS PARKE late of Murtherkill Hund Kent Co marriner and SARAH his wife for 75 pounds sold to NATHANIEL HALL of same place marriner ... a tr of land lying in Murtherkill Hund s side of Jones Cr called Shoemakers Hall ... near Isaac's Br ... by Walker's Br ... patent for 400 a. bearing date 26 Mar 1684 granted to ISAAC WEBB decd who dyed intestate whereas MARY WEBB relict of said ISAAC WEBB decd did sell 200 a. from said 400 a. to WM LAWRENCE & MICHEL WALTER ... whereas ROBERT WEBB son & heir of afsd ISAAC WEBB decd did sell to THOMAS PARKER 200 a. (afsd 200 a. only by MARY WEBB relict of ISAAC WEBB decd & mother of ROBERT WEBB sold excepted) and also 2 a. at ye end of ye mill down of THOMAS PARK also excepted ... and SARAH wife of THOMAS PARKE doth hereby freely and voluntarily quitt claim unto NATHAN HALL her right of dower ... Wit: ZAC SADDOCK, FUSTRUM? HODGES. Ackn 13 Feb 1715/6. (E:pg 55)

167. 14 Feb 1704. Deed. JOHN CLAYTON and JOSHUA CLAYTON of Little Cr Hund Kent Co yeoman for 35 pounds sold to NATHANIAL HALL of Monmouth Town in Co of Barnstable in New England merchant and MICHAEL STUART of Monmouth Town afsd ... tr of land s side of Dover River on s side of Walker's Br being half pt/o a tr of land of 400 a. called Shoemakers Hall formerly taken up by ISAAC WEBB and was then purch of THOMAS BEDWELL as atty to WILLIAM LAWRENCE and MICHAEL WALTON ... 200 a. ... Wit: JOHN BRADSHAW, JOHN FISHER, FRANCIS ALLEN. Ackn 13 Feb 1715/16. (E:pg 57)

168. 4 May 1711. Deed. DERICK KEYSAR the younger of Kent Co tanner and DEBORAH his wife executrix of the will of HERMAN OPDEGRAFTE late of same co decd and allso relict of the said decd ... whereas HERMAN OPDEGRAFTE decd in his lifetime was seized of a tr of land n side of Mispillion Cr on nw side of Swan Cr ... 300 a. ... and HERMAN OPDEGRAFTE decd by his will bearing date 13 Nov 1708 willed that his wife DEBORAH OPDEGRAFTE should have and enjoy his

estate both personall and reale and to dispose of same, pay his just debts and pay the children of him 12 pence as they should come at age ... and said DEBORAH is since intermarried with the afsd DERICK KEYSAR the younger ... DERICK KEYSAR the younger and DEBORAH his wife for 4 score pounds sold to JOHN TURNER of same co yeoman afsd tr of land ... Wit: WILLIAM BRINCKLE, ELIZABETH DOUGLAS. Ackn 13 Feb 1715 by ISAAC OPDEGRAVE as atty to DERICK KEYSAR and DEBORAH his wife. (E:pg 59)

169. 19 Sep 1715. Power of Atty. JOHN ROELOFF (ROLEFF) together with DEBORAH my wife relict and executors of DERICK KEYSER decd have appointed our trusty and well beloved friend ISAAC OPDEGRAVE son of HERMAN OPDEGRAVE decd our atty to ackn and deliver [above] deed unto JOHN TURNER ... Wit: THOMAS DUTTER, JOHN CAMBLE Junr. Proved 14 May 1716. (E:pg 63)

170. 13 Dec 1712. Deed. FRANCES RICHARDSON of Phila silver smith and REBACCA MURREY of same place widow, son and dau of FRANCES RICHARDSON late of NY merchant decd for 130 pounds sold to GEORGE MARTAIN of Kent Co yeoman and WILLIAM ANAND of same place gentlemen ... a tr of land s side of Duck Cr beginning at the corner of Woodstock Bower ... by Dawson's Br ... to corner of ALBERTSON's land ... 1500 a. ... FRANCES RICHARDSON and REBECCA MURREY made JAMES STEEL their atty to deliver this deed in open court ... Wit: WILLIAM HAMBLETON, THOMAS BARNES, MARY HAYWOOD. Ackn 12 May 1713. (E:pg 64)

171. 7 May 1716. Deed. GEORGE GREEN of Kent Co for a valuable consideration in hand sold to FRANCES VANNOY of same co yeoman ... 80 a. s side of sw br of Duck Cr being pt/o a tr of land called Betts Endeavour being formerly conveyed to CHRISTOPHER STANLEY and from him to SIMON HIRONS and from PERSES HIRONS executrix of SIMON HIRONS to GEORGE GREEN ... to corner of VINSON EMERSON's land ... in line of land called Chipennorton ... Wit: JOHN GREEN, RICHARD SMITH. Ackn 12 May 1716. (E:pg 66)

172. 1 May 1716. Deed. JAMES BOWMAN of Kent Co yeoman and MARY his wife joyntly for 120 pounds sold to THOMAS SKIDMORE of same co gentlemen ... a tr of land s side of Dover River ... 100 a. formerly called Whitewells Delight but now Dover Peer whereof FRANCES RICHARDSON Senr decd the father of FRANCES RICHARDSON Junr died seized and after his decease descended to FRANCES RICHARDSON son and heir and afterwards he did sell 300 a. to one STEPHEN SYMONS father of afsd MARY wife of JAMES BOWMAN which STEPHEN SYMONS in his life time on 29 Dec 1708 did make his will

and did bequeath to dau MARY 100 a. out of that tr of land called The Mill Nick bounded by JOHN SMITH's br ... Wit: WILLIAM RODENEY, JAMES MOIES. Ackn 12 May 1716. (E:pg 69)

173. 21 Jun 1716. Appointment. JACOB TAYLOR surveyor generall of PA ... nominate and appoint RICHARD SMITH to be deputy surveyor of Kent Co ... . (E:pg 72)

174. 3 May 1714. Deed. JOHN BOWERS of Kent Co yeoman for 18 pounds sold to JAMES MARTAIN of same co husbandman ... 150 a. ... by land of OWEN WILLIAMS ... Wit: HENRY JOYCE, JOHN JOHNSON, WILLIAM RODENEY. Ackn 12 May 1716. (E:pg 73)

175. 14 May 1716. NATHANIEL HALL received of WILLIAM RODENEY, WM BRINCLE, THO SKIDMORE 234 pounds full consideration of money due on a obligatory past bearing date 3 Feb 1715 and is alsoe in full of all other bills, bonds, debts ... Wit: DANIEL STANDISHE. (E:pg 75)

176. 15 May 1716. Be it remembered before me JOHN HALL esqr justice of ye peace for Kent Co ... JOHN ROWLAND did see the above named NATHANIEL HALL sign and deliver above instrument of writing ... . (E:pg 75)

177. 23 Sep 1715. Deed. SAMUEL TAYLOR of Duck Cr of New Castle Co bolter for 3 pounds 10 shillings sold to CHARLES HARPER of Kent Co taylor ... a tr of land laying within the limits of a place layed out for a town called Salisbury on the head of Duck Cr ... at corner stake w of said CHARLES HARPER's now dwelling house ... also another piece of land ... Wit: HENRY TRACY, ABSALOM CUFF. Ackn 12 May 1716. (E:pg 76)

178. Power of Atty. SAMUEL TAYLOR appoint TIMOTHY HANSON to deliver [above] deed to CHARLES HARPER ... Wit: HENRY TRACY, ABSALOM CUFF. Proved 30 Jul 1716. (E:pg 79)

179. 13 Aug 1712. Deed. ABRAHAM SKIDMORE of Kent Co for 21 pounds sold to ZACKERIAH GOFFER of same place ... a tr of land called Ruhmans Woorth se side of Motherkill Cr ... I have not already sold and made over land in open court to ZACHARIAH GOFFER and GEORGE ROBERTSON of same co ... Wit: FRANCIS ALEXANDER, ROBERT BECK. Ackn 12 May 1716. (E:pg 80)

180. 9 May 1716. Deed. FRANCIS WHITWELL late of Kent Co decd did take up a tr of land on side of sw br of Duck Cr called Brookhoss 400 a. patent granted by EDMUND ANDROS esqr Governor of NY dated Jan

1675 ... and since conveyed to WILLIAM BERRY and from him to SIMON HIRONS decd ... now WILLIAM HIRONS and PEIRSES HIRONS widow and son of SIMON HIRONS late decd of Kent Co joyntly for a valuable consideration in hand paid sold to JAMES POTTER of same co yeoman ... 100 a. being pt/o the afsd tr ... beginning at Fowels Point and at w end of plantation formerly belonging to RICHARD WILLSON ... Wit: JOHN CLAYTON, JAMES MORE, NATHANIEL PENOCK. Ackn 12 May 1716. (E:pg 82)

181. 10 May 1712. Deed. ROBERT WEBB son and heir of ISAAC WEBB late of Murtherkill Hund Kent Co yeoman decd for 50 pounds sold to THOMAS PARKE of same place mariner ... a tr of land in Murtherkill Hund s side of Jones Cr called Shoemakers Hall beginning at the mouth of Isaacs Br ... on Walkers Br ... 400 a. patent bearing date 26 Mar 1684 by WILLIAM PENN Proprietor granted to WILLIAM WEBB decd who died intestate and whereas MARY the mother of said ROBERT WEBB by deed did grant him 200 a. and WILLIAM LARRANCE and MICHEL WILLSON by same deed ... and 200 a. belonging to his mother ... Wit: TIMOTHY HANSON, SPENCER ALEXANDER. Ackn 13 May 1712. (E:pg 85)

182. 23 Oct 1711. Deed. THOMAS BURRAS of Burlinton Co in NY weaver for 37 pounds 10 shillings sold to JAMES GRIFFETH of Kent Co husbandman and MERCY his wife ... a tr of land called Sleeps Lot n side of Sarvis Br of Murtherkill Cr ... 100 a. ... Wit: DANIEL MORREY, ELIZABETH FORBY, JAMES LOCKHAIT. Ackn 12 May 1716. (E:pg 87)

183. 26 Oct 1710. Power of Atty. THOMAS BURRAS appoint ADAM FISHER of Kent Co to deliver [above] deed unto JAMES GRIFFETH and his wife ... Attest: THOMAS SKIMORE. (E:pg 89)

184. 20 May 1713. Deed. ELENOR ROBERTSON wife of JOHN ROBERTSON of Kent Co dau and coheir of THOMAS HEWTHATE of same co yeoman decd whereas said THOMAS HEWTHATE in his lifetime was seized of a tr of land pt/o a greater tr on Mutherkill Cr called Ousby and by his will did give and bequeath his land to his son RALPH HEWTHAT and failing him said RALPH heirs the said land to be equally divided among his four daus, PRISALA EDMONDS wife of ROBERT EDMONDS, ANNE NEEDUM wife of EDMOND NEEDUM and the said ELENOR ROBERTSON wife of JOHN ROBERTSON and MELLECENT BEDWELL wife of THOMAS BEDWELL and whereas said RALPH HEWTHAT is since decd without heirs of his body begotten the said lands were by the will vested in the said PRISALLA, ANNE, ELENOR and MELLECENT and whereas the said JOHN ROBERTSON and ELENOR his wife by deed bearing date 11 Jun 1700 did sell unto SAMUEL

BROOKS of same co all that tr of land said HEWTHATE died possessed of called Hopewell on Murtherkill Cr ... along STEPHEN SIMON's land ... 75 a. ... whereas at a Court of Common Pleas at Dover -- May 1712 by a writt, sheriff assigned to ELENER ROBERTSON as her pt/o the inheritance of the father said THOMAS HEWTHATE the 75 a. ... Wit: JOHN FORSTER, WILLIAM BRINCKLE. Ackn 12 May 1716. (E:pg 89)

185. 21 Mar 1715. Deed. SAMUEL TAYLOR of Newcastle Co for 430 pounds sold to JOHN SWIFT of Phila ... a tr of land near the head of Duck Cr pt/o a tr of 1000 a. formerly taken up by WILLIAM GREEN late of Duck Cr decd and cut off by him from the whole tr and called Graves End afterwards sold by him to FRANCES BARNEY of Cecle Co MD and said BARNEY bearing date 8 Dec 1691 sold to EBENERER BLACKTOIN of same co decd and by EBENERER son and herr to afsd EBENERER bearing date 15 Aug 1711 sold unto MERCY GREEN widow of above said WILLIAM GREEN decd who bearing date 14 Aug 1714 sold the same to SAMUEL TAYLOR ... beginning at a small bridge at Kings Road at Greene Br ... 528 a. ... Wit: HENRY TRACY, ABSALLUM CUFF. Ackn 12 May 1716. (E:pg 92)

186. Power of Atty. SAMUEL TAYLOR appoint TIMOTHY HANSON to be my atty to deliver the [above] covenance to JOHN SWIFT ... Wit: HENRY TRACY, ABSOLOM CUFF. (E:pg 96)

187. 1 May 1716. Deed. JOHN MILLS of Mispillan Hund Kent Co planter son and heir of JOHN MILLS late of same co decd for 14 pounds sold to OWEN GARVEY of same co planter ... a tr of land (pt/o 500 a. tr of land patent granted by WILLIAM PENN esqr Governor of PA bearing date 5 Jul 1684 unto EDWARD PRINER ... EDWARD PRINER by deed bearing date 14 Jun 1692 conveyed afsd tr of land to JOHN MILLS the father) ... s side of Motherkill Cr ... by land of WILLIAM BRINCKLOE ... to land of EDMUND BIBBY ... 114 a. ... Wit: JAMES STEEL, JOHN BRINCKLOE. Ackn 12 May 1716. (E:pg 96)

188. 4 Jun 1708. Deed of Gift. JOHN CLARKE of Kent Co for goodwill, love and affection give to my dear and loveing wife ELIZABETH CLARKE ... the plantation that I now live upon with 200 a. during the time of her natural life ... Wit: JOHN THROPP, MARKE MANLOVE. Ackn 12 Aug 1716. (E:pg 99)

189. 10 May 1713. Deed. MARY RICHARDSON executrix of the will of JOHN RICHARDSON late of Kent Co decd and adminr of goods and chattels of MICHEL SYMKINS decd ... whereas MICHELL SYMKINS was indebted unto JOHN RICHARDSON for 9000 pounds of tobacco and sundry other sumes of money for which said JOHN in his lifetime

obtained several judgements against the estate of said MICHEL SYMKINS decd and are yet unpayed ... there was granted unto said MARY RICHARDSON letters of administration upon estate of MICHEL SYMKINS and there was no personal estate to be found ... court granted judgement to sell lands of the decd for payment of the just debts ... MARY RICHARDSON for 100 pounds sold to JOSEPH WORRELL of Chester Co yeoman ... a tr of land called Livinford n side of Western Br, North Br of Duck Cr ... Wit: ANDREW HAMLETON, WILLIAM HIRONS. Ackn 12 May 1716. (E:pg 100)

190. 15 Feb 1715. Deed. WILLIAM MANLOVE of Little Cr Hund Kent Co yeoman son of WILLIAM MANLOVE late of Mispillion Hund in same co decd ... by virtue of a patent under hand of WILLIAM MARKHAM, ROBERT TURNER and JOHN GOODSON commissioners of WILLIAM PENN esqr Proprietor of PA bearing date 29 Mar 1694 ... WILLIAM MANLOVE the father in his lifetime became seized of a tr of land on Mispilian Hund afsd ... intersects the line of JOHN CURTES land ... bounding with land called Swampborn ... 400 a. ... WILLIAM MANLOVE did by his will bequeath unto his son WILLIAM MANLOVE all of afsd tr of land ... WILLIAM MANLOVE the son for 50 pounds sold afsd tr of land to JOHN CLARK of Mispelan Hund same co yeoman ... Wit: JOHN COE, JAMES STEEL. Ackn 11 May 1716. (E:pg 104)

191. 7 May 1711. Deed. GRIFFETH HUGHS & ANNE his wife of Kent Co for 10 pounds sold to JOHN SIPPLE of same co ... 50 a. n side of a fork of Murtherkill Cr ... in the line of RICHARD WELLS land ... Wit: NATHANIEL HUNN, JOHN REYNOLLS, JONAS GREENWOOD. Post script: JOHN SIPPLE shall have a cart way of 30 foot wide through the said land ... Wit: NATHANIAL HUNN, JOHN RENOLLS, JONAS GREENWOOD. Ackn 15 May 1711. (E:pg 106)

192. 20 Jul 1711. Deed. WILLIAM HILLIARD son of JOHN HILLIARD decd for [blank] pounds sold to CHRISTOPHER SIPPLE of Kent Co ... a tr of land 50 a. being pt/o a tr called Edmondsons Choice being conveyed unto JACOB EMERSON by ROBERT EDMONDSON bearing date 29 Nov 1684 and by said JACOB to JOSEPH [?] on 10 Jun 1690 ... on side of a br of Murderkill that runs between the land of BENONY BISHOP called St. Collom & the land of THOMAS ROUSE beginning at a corner of JACOB EMERSON's land ... Wit: THOMAS BEDWELL, REYNEAR WILLIAMS. Ackn 14 May 1711. (E:pg 108)

193. 3 May 1714. Deed. TIMOTHY HANSON of Kent Co yeoman and SUSANNAH his wife for 200 pounds sold to JOHN BOWERS of same co yeoman ... a tr of land in Mispillion Hund by Bawcomb Brigg Cr ... to br dividing this and land of LUKE MANLOVE ... 303 a. ... Wit: VINEEN

EMERSON, JAMES STEEL, WILLIAM RODENEY. Ackn 12 May 1716. (E:pg 110)

194. 5 May 1716. Deed. JOHN MILLS of Mispillion Hund Kent Co planter son of JOHN MILLS decd for 16 pounds sold to JOHN CRIPPEN ... a tr of land pt/o patent [same as #187] ... beginning by Murther Cr and from thence by PETER BRINCKLOE's land ... by the line of JOHN BOWERS ... to br which divides this land from EDMUND BIBBY's land ... 316 a. ... Wit: JOHN BRINCKLOE, JAMES STEEL. Ackn 12 May 1716. (E:pg 113)

195. 10 Sep 1708. Deed. WILLIAM REYNOLDS of Kent Co son and heir of JOHN REYNOLDS yeoman decd late of same co and JOHN REYNOLDS of same co another of the sons of the said JOHN REYNOLDS decd for 50 pounds sold to JOHN REES and OWEN DAVID both of Phila husbandman ... a tr of land called Fox Hall between two br of Great Duck Cr ... 500 a. which was granted unto JOHN REYNOLDS the father in his life time by a patent bearing date 26 Mar 1684 ... Wit: WILLIAM GREEN, WILLIAM WELLS. Ackn 12 May 1716. (E:pg 116)

196. 30 Jan 1711. Deed. GEORGE NOWELL of Kent Co yeoman for 22 pounds sold to ALEXANDER DONELSON of same co planter ... a tr of land called New Aberdeen being pt/o a tr formerly called Kingston Upon Hull ne side of Dover River ... by land called Town Point ... 50 a. ... Wit: THOMAS FRENCH, THOMAS CRAFORD. Ackn 12 May 1716. (E:pg 119)

197. 1 May 1710. Deed. JAMES FITGARREL of Kent Co and CATHRINE his wife for [blank] pounds sold to FRANCES EASTGATE of same co yeoman ... a tr of land 50 a. being halfe pt/o 100 a. formerly purch by HENRY STEPHENS decd of JOHN BURTON n side of Dover River ... bindeth on land of RICHARD LEVICK formerly belonging to PETER PARADDEE ... bounded by land FRANCES FITGARRELL bought of JOHN SMITH ... said premises was heretofore in tenure of TIMOTHY THOROLD decd or lately in tenure of said FRANCES EASTGATE and since in tenure of said JAMES EASTGATE ... Wit: THOMAS CRAFORD, SAMUELL BERRY, FRANCES ALLEXANDER. Ackn 12 May 1716. (E:pg 121)

198. 2 Feb 1711. Quit Claim. Whereas PHEBE MORGAN executrix of the will of DAVID MORGAN decd by indenture bearing date 12 Dec 1693 did grant unto GEORGE HART decd the tr of land called Leesen sw side of Jones Cr beginning at the corner of JOHN SHEPHARD's land ... 100 a. ... GEORGE HART by his will bequeathed afsd tr of land to his son GEORGE HART ... DAVID MORGAN son and heir of DAVID MORGAN

late of Kent Co yeoman decd for 45 shillings quitt claims afsd tr of land unto GEORGE HART son and heir of GEORGE HART late of same co decd ... Wit: WILLIAM DYER, FRANCES ALEXANDER. Ackn 12 May 1716. (E:pg 124)

199. 3 May 1714. Deed. TIMOTHY HANSON of Kent Co and SUSANAH his wife for 10 pounds sold to LUKE MANLOVE of same co yeoman ... a tr of land in Mispilion Hund beginning at the Bawcomb Brigg Cr ... by the land and plantation whereon the said LUKE MANLOVE now dwells ... binding with the land of JOHN BOWERS ... 140 a. ... Wit: VINSON EMERSON, JAMES STEEL. Ackn 12 May 1716. (E:pg 126)

200. Deed. CHRISTOPHER STANDLY decd by his will bearing date 11 May 1708 did bequeath unto MARY his wife all his plantation in Kent Co to sell at her pleasure ... said MARY is now intermarried with CHARLES RAMSEY ... for 12 pounds CHARLES RAMSEY and MARY his wife executrix of the will of CHRISTOPHER STANDLY sold to VINCENT EMERSON gentlemen a tr of land s side of sw br of Duck Cr called Betts Endeavour whereon CHRISTOPHER STANDLY dwells beginning at a corner of 50 a. of land SIMON HIRONS formerly purch of said STANDLY ... 50 a. ... Wit: GABRIEL LETCHAM, WILLIAM BRINCKLE. Ackn 12 May 1716 by JAMES STEEL atty to CHARLES RAMSEY & MARY RAMSEY. (E:pg 128)

201. -- -- 1716. Power of Atty. CHARLES RAMSEY and MARY RAMSEY of Cecil Co MD have appointed JAMES STEEL of Kent Co to be our atty to make over in open court [above] deed ... Wit: GABRIEL LATEHAM. Proved 12 May 1716. (E:pg 131)

202. 12 Dec 1706. Deed. RICHARD HALL and WILLIAM TIPPEN both of Talbot Co MD planters for 20 pounds sold to JOHN WELLS of Kent Co ... a tr of land on w side of Jones Cr otherways called Dover River called Brinckloes Range beginning at the corner of land belonging to DANIEL JONES decd called Denby ... 483 a. which premises were of late in the tenure of RICHARD HALL late of Talbot Co MD decd & by the said RICHARD HALL in his will bearing date 29 Apr 1704 bequeathed to his son the above named RICHARD HALL and the above named WILLIAM TIPPEN ... Wit: JONAS GREENWOOD, JOHN NICKLSON. Ackn 12 -- 1716. (E:pg 132)

203. 11 May 1716. Bond of Conveyance. EPHERAM EMERSON of Kent Co yeoman am bound unto JOHN HALL esqr of Kent Co for 1000 pounds ... EPHERAM EMERSON and MARY his wife to makeover unto JOHN HALL a tr of land called Willsons Choice s side of sw br of Duck Cr 300 a. and alsoe another tr of land called Willsons Purchase being pt/o a tr

called Bets Endeavour s side of sw br of Duck Cr ... Wit: JOHN JOHNSON, THOMAS EMERSON, WILLIAM STURKEY. (E:pg 134)

204. 10 May 1716. Bond of Conveyance. THOMAS EMERSON of Kent Co am bound unto JOHN HALL esqr for 450 pounds ... THOMAS EMERSON to make over a tr of land called Willsons Choice [same as above] ... Wit: JOHN JOHNSON, WILLIAM STURKEY, EPHERAM EMERSON. (E:pg 136)

205. 1 May 1710. Quit Claim. JOHN REESE of Duck Cr Hund quitt claim unto OWEN DAVID of same place ... 305 a. pt/o a 510 a. tr of land on Gravely River bought by OWEN DAVID and JOHN REESE of REYNOLDS called Foxhall ... Wit: ROBERT DRAUGHTON, FRANCIS HIRONS, BENJAMIN GUMBEY. (E:pg 137)

206. 15 Aug 1711. Deed. THOMAS BEDWELL of Kent Co and HONOUR his wife executrix of the will of WM CLARKE late of Lewistown Suss Co esqr decd sold to DAVID ROW son and heir of JOSEPH ROW late of Phila merchant decd ... whereas JOSEPH ROW decd in his lifetime paid to afsd WILLIAM CLARKE 200 pounds ... THOMAS BEDWELL and HONOUR his wife convey unto DAVID ROW a tr of land s side of Mother Cr called Fairfield ... w side of Jew Cr ... to Virgin Brook ... 2000 a. patent bearing date 29 May 1689 granted to WILLIAM CLARKE decd ... Wit: THOMAS CRAFORD, JAMES STEELL, FRANCES ALLEN. Ackn 16 Aug 1716. (E:pg 138)

207. 10 Nov 1710. Deed. JOHN CLARK of Kent Co yeoman for 9 pounds sold to JOHN MORRIS of same co weaver ... a tr of land n side of Mispilion Cr n side of Fishing Cr ... 100 a. ... Wit: JOHN REYNOLDS, JOHN REDMAN. Ackn 12 May 1716. (E:pg 141)

208. -- May 1710. Quit Claim. OWEN DAVID of Kent Co quitt claim unto JOHN REECE a tr of land [same as #205] ... Wit: ROBERT DROUGHTON, FRANCES HIRONS, BENJAMIN GUMBEY. Ackn 12 May 1716. (E:pg 143)

209. -- May 1710. Assignment. JOHN ROW of Kent Co and OWEN DAVID of same co did purch a tr of land of [blank] REYNOLDS son of JOHN REYNOLDS late of Duck Cr Hund decd 500 a. surveyed and divided between JOHN ROW and OWEN DAVID by GEORGE DA? surveyor of New Castle Co ... whoever had lower part down the br should pay unto him that had the upper part 6 pounds because the lower most part was best which said JOHN RECE consented to pay unto OWEN DAVID to improve the lower part where the plantation of JOHN ROW now is, but it is that the said JOHN ROW being very sickly and could not

43

follow his laborer as at other times and haven a great charge of children could not have complyed with ye payment of said money according to agreement ... JOHN ROW assign unto OWEN DAVID 50 a. to comply with agreement ... Wit: ROBERT DRANGHTON, FRANCES HIRONS, BENJAMIN GUMBEY. Ackn -- May 1716. (E:pg 144)

210. 13 May 1713. Deed. JOHN MARTIN of Kent Co for 15 pounds sold to CHARLES MARIN of same co ... parcell of land called Roodin being pt/o a tr of land called Edvinton ... 50 a. ... Wit: JOHN HARTE, JOHN HAVOIER? Ackn 12 May 1716. (E:pg 146)

211. 1 Feb 1706. Deed. THOMAS NICKOLS of Kent Co planter for 18 pounds sold to FERDINANDO ODOCKARTIE planter ... a tr of land s side of Dover River on ISAAC WEBB's br being pt/o a tr of land called Downdee ... 50 a. ... Wit: WILLIAM BRINKLE, SAMUEL BURREY. Ackn 12 May 1716. (E:pg 148)

212. 9 Apr 1706. Deed. RINEER WILLIAMS Senr of Kent Co for a valuable consideration in hand paid sold to WILLIAM MOLESTONE a tr of land n side of Mispilion Cr ... 400 a. ... Wit: AARON WILLIAMS, ROBERT BETTS, SAMUELL ROWLAND. Ackn 12 May 1716. (E:pg 150)

213. 3 Feb 1713. Deed. Whereas PATRICK WORD in his life time by his deed bearing date 13 Sep 1692 did assign unto his then son in law THOMAS DWYER and MARY his wife a tr of land pt/o a greater tr called Kingsgil s side of sw br of Duck Cr beginning at the corner by JOHN KELPERS br ... 100 a. ... whereas THOMAS DWYER is since decd without heirs and the MARY was afterwards intermarried with TUNAS TOBIAS who is allso decd without heirs and now MARY is intermarried to JOHN SEAT ... the said JOHN SEAT of Little Cr Hund Kent Co yeoman and Mary his wife the lawful dau of PATRICK WORD late of same place for [blank] pounds sold afsd tr of land to SAMUEL MANLOVE of same place yeoman ... Wit: JAMES JACKSON, JOHN FORSTER. Ackn 12 May 1716. (E:pg 152)

214. 10 Nov 1703. Deed. SAMUEL WEBSTER and RACHEL his wife of Suss Co PA and ROBERT BEETS and ELIZABETH his wife of Kent Co for 10 pounds sold to JOHN CLARK of Kent Co ... 300 a. being pt/o a tr called Mount Pleasant n side of Mispilion Cr by Fishing Br being a parcel of land given to RACHEL and ELIZABETH by their father MARK MANLOVE ... Wit: SAMUEL LOVE, MATHEW MANLOVE. Ackn 11 Nov 1703. (E:pg 154)

215. 10 Apr 1709. Deed. ABRAHAM SKIDMORE of Kent Co for 20

pounds sold to ZACARIAH GOFORTH of same place ... 96 a. being pt/o a tr layed out for THOMAS SKIDMORE decd called Richmanworth se side of Mother Cr ... to corner of GEORGE ROBERTSON's land ... Wit: BENJAMIN WHITE, MICHEL ODUNUKER. Ackn 12 May 1716. (E:pg 157)

216. 10 Aug 1712. Deed. WALTER HAMBLETON of Kent Co for 27 pounds sold to THOMAS JESTER of same place ... 300 a. being pt/o a tr of land formerly layed out for ROGER MANLOVE called Manloves Platt at the head of Strunkill Cr beginning at the land of COPPERS ... in the line of RICHARD WILLIAMS ... Wit: THOMAS WITHERS, JOHN BRADSHAW. Ackn 12 Aug 1712. (E:pg 159)

217. 10 Dec 1713. Deed. Whereas one WILLIAM FREEMAN late of Kent Co husbandman dyed intestate without heirs and was in his life time solely seized of one plantation with 446 a. called New Seven Haven on Murther Cr in Murtherkill Hund ... and at a court held 12 May last past CORNELIUS SWILLIVANT and SARAH his wife were summoned to answer unto JOHN FISHER and ADAM FISHER the younger who being under age ... wherefore JOHN and ADAM and CORNELIUS and SARAH in the right of inheritance of WILLIAM FREEMAN brother to SARAH and uncle to JOHN and ADAM whose heirs they are ... at court held 11 Aug last past 12 good men divided land into two equall parts ... 223 a. assigned to JOHN FISHER and ADAM FISHER the younger ... 220 a. assigned to CORNELIUS SWILLIVANT and SARAH his wife ... CORNELIUS SWILLIVANT and SARAH his wife both of Kent Co for 100 pounds sold afsd 220 a. to WILLIAM ANNAND of same place ... Wit: THOMAS FRENCH, JOHN REYNALLS, ?FMAN SIPPLE. Ackn 13 Feb 1713. (E:pg 162)

218. 24 Dec 1713. Deed. WILLIAM ANNAND of Kent Co for 100 pounds sold to CORNELIUS SULLIVAN (SWILLIVANT) of same co husbandman ... [above] tr of land ... Wit: THOMAS FRENCH, JOHN REYNOLLS, WATEMAN SIPPLE. Ackn 13 Feb 1713. (E:pg 166)

219. -- -- 1706. Deed. JOHN ALBERSON of New Dover and JOHN MANFORD of Queene Co both of Island Nassaw NY for 375 pounds sold to JOHN ALLEE of Hackingsack in Esea Co in Nova Coseasia yeoman ... tr of land patent bearing date 26 Mar 1684 granted unto JOHN DAWSON of Kent Co PA planter 600 a. called Woodstock Bower n side of sw br of Duck Cr ... JOHN DAWSON transferred his land by deed of sale bearing date 16 Dec 1684 unto said JOHN ALBERSON and JOHN MANFORD ... (signed) JOHN ALBERSON, JOHN MANFORD, AYDA MANFORD, JOHN LALLOI. Wit: JEREMIAH CARNNIFF, JOHN COURDEME. Ackn 15 Aug 1706. (E:pg 171)

220. 5 Mar 1706. Power of Atty. JOHN ALBERSON and JOHN MANFORD both of the Island Nassaw NY appoint EVAN JONES and TUNIS TOBIAS our atty to deliver [above] deed in open court ... Wit: HENRY FILKIN Justice, GARRET STOLLGOFF Justice. Proved 5 Mar 1706/7. (E:pg 171)

221. 27 Jul 1716. Deed. THOMAS HILLYARD of Kent Co yeoman for valluable consideration in hand paid sold to CHARLES HILLYARD same place gentlemen ... a tr of land called The Exchange formerly surveyed for JOHN HILLYARD on s side of sw br of Duck Cr ... only excepted 100 a. out of the s side of the tr on which his now dwelling house stands ... Wit: RICHARD SMITH, FAFADIAH OFFLEY. Ackn 15 Aug 1716. Wit: WILLIAM RODENEY Clerk. (E:pg 172)

222. 17 May 1716. Deed. ELISABETH ANNAND of Murtherkill Hund Kent Co widow, dau of GEORGE MARTAIN of Duck Cr late decd for good will, love and affection and for 30 pounds sell to my well beloved brother GEORGE MARTAIN of same place ... a tr of land that said GEORGE MARTAIN now lives upon in Duck Cr Hund called Gloster ... Wit: THOMAS SHARP, JOHN TILTON, JOHN BRADSHAW. Ackn 15 Aug 1716. (E:pg 175)

223. 16 Aug 1716. Deed. FRANCIS VANNOY and KATHRINE his wife of Kent Co for a valuable consideration in hand payd sold to GEORGE GREEN of same co ... 80 a. s side of sw br of Duck Cr being pt/o of a tr of land called Bets Endeavour which was formerly conveyed to CRISTOPHER STANDLY and from him to SIMON HIRONS and from PERSES HIRONS executrix to SIMON HIRONS decd to GEORGE GREEN and from him to FRANCIS VANNOY ... to corner of RICHARD WILLSON decd ... to corner of VINSON EMERSON ... by line of land called Chipenorton ... Wit: HUGH DERBUROW, JOHN WELLS. Ackn 15 Aug 1716. (E:pg 177)

224. 12 Feb 1706. Deed. RICHARD SHURLEY and REBACCAH his wife of Kent Co in consideration of 170 a. of land [see #225] sold to JOHN HALL Mispilion Hund same co ... a tr of land n side of Motherkill Cr in the fork of Service Br being pt/o a tr formerly taken up for THOMAS HETHERD ... 105 a. ... Wit: NICKLOS MAXON, THOMAS BEDWELL. Ackn 15 Aug 1716. (E:pg 179)

225. 12 Feb 1706. Deed. JOHN HALL of Kent Co PA in consideration of 105 a. of land [see #224] sold to RICHARD SHURLEY of same place ... pt/o a tr of land called Forsters Purchase and now called Shurleys Purchase n side of Bocombrick Cr beginning at the corner of GEORGE ROBERTSON's land ... 170 a. surveyed 8 Feb 1689 ... (signed) JOHN

HALL, ANNE HALL. Wit: NICHOLAS MAXON, THOMAS BEDWELL. Ackn 15 Aug 1707. (E:pg 182)

226. 10 Jul 1716. Deed. EPHERAM EMERSON of Dover Hund Kent Co and MARY his wife the said MARY being the surviving heiress of RICHARD WILLSON late of same co decd, for 85 pounds sold to WILLIAM MANLOVE of Little Cr Hund same co yeoman ... a tr of land patent bearing date 13 Apr 1690 under hands of WILLIAM MARKHAM, ROBERT TURNER, JOHN GOODSON and SAMUEL CARPENTER commissioners granted unto RICHARD WILLSON s side of sw br of Duck Cr by Mudy Br ... to corner of land formerly layed out for WILLIAM JACOKS ... 300 a. ... whereas said RICHARD WILLSON in his life time being lawfully seized of said tr of land did make his will and did bequeath the afsd tr of land unto his two daus ELIZABETH and MARY and ELIZABETH died since without issue the tr of land lawfully descended to MARY wife of EPHERAM EMERSON ... Wit: JOHN FORSTER, JAMES STEEL, JOHN HALL. Ackn 15 Aug 1716. (E:pg 184)

227. 13 Aug 1716. Deed. STEPHEN HARGROW (HEARGROW) of Kent Co yeoman for 10 pounds sold to SIMON HIRONS of same place yeoman ... tr of land (warrant bearing date 20 Jul 1716 to take up 200 a.) ... w side of Hillyard's Br ... to corner of JOHN NEWTON's land ... to line of land called Mill Range ... to land called The Exchange ... 180 a. ... Wit: RICHARD SMITH, JOHN PAIN. Ackn 15 Aug 1716. (E:pg 187)

228. 12 Aug 1716. Deed. JOHN NEWTON of Kent Co yeoman for 10 pounds sold to RICHARD SMITH of same place yeoman ... a tr of land 200 a. s side of sw br of Little Duck Cr surveyed and layed out to said JOHN NEWTON 27 Jun 1716 by warrant dated 21 Jun 1716 ... about a mile above SIMON HIRONS house ... on Hillyard's Br ... to corner of land called The Partenership or Mill Range formerly taken up by WHITWELL and RICHARDSON ... Wit: DAVID HAILER, RUTH RODENEY. Ackn 15 Aug 1716. (E:pg 189)

229. 14 Aug 1716. Power of Atty. JOHN NEWTON of Kent Co appoint WILLIAM RODENEY to be my atty to ackn [above] deed in open court ... Wit: STEPHEN HARGROW, DAVID HAILER. Proved 15 Aug 1716. (E:pg 190)

230. 15 Aug 1716. Deed. DANIEL RUTTY of Kent Co yeoman for a vallewable consideration in hand payed sold to SAMUEL WILLSON of same place yeoman ... a tr of land 400 a. called The Golden Thicket surveyed for DANIEL RUTTY by virtue of a warrant of an order from WILLIAM CLARK generall surveyor 10 Mar 1686 patent dated 1 Feb 1678 beginning at the nw br of Motherkill Cr ... Wit: SIMON HIRONS,

HENRY TRACY. Ackn 15 Aug 1716. (E:pg 191)

231. 1 Aug 1716. Deed. WILLIAM RODNEY of Kent Co yeoman for 28 pounds sold to ISAIAH WHITEHEAD carpenter ... a tr of land called Dover Farms s side of Dover River ... by line of WILLIAM DERIVALL's land ... 800 a. made up of several parcels of land following ... 400 a. granted by pattent to HUBER FRANCES, 200 a. granted by an order from the court at St. Jones 21 Mar 1684 to JOHN BURTON ... whereas EDMOND GIBBSON decd did in his life time purch of HUBERD FRANCES 400 a. and of JOHN BURTON 200 a. and devised the same by his will to his brother FRANCES GIBBSON ... was resurveyed and found to have 695 a. and afterwards was conveyed by FRANCES GIBBSON to WILLIAM RODENEY decd father of afsd WILLIAM RODENEY and 50 a. more purch by WILLIAM RODNEY of JAMES MAXWELL and 100 a. granted by virtue of a warrant and layed out to WILLIAM RODENEY and all parcels resurveyed in one tr were found to contain 800 a. confirmation of pattent bearing date 17 Oct 1701 ... WILLIAM RODENEY did make out his will 1 May 1708 and did bequeath unto my eldest sons WILLIAM RODENEY and THOMAS RODENEY all that tr of land called Dover Farms s side of Dover River 840 a. to be equally divided between them ... when son WILLIAM shall attain the age of 21 ... Wit: NICHOLAS MAXON, THOMAS SKIDMORE. Ackn 15 Aug 1716. (E:pg 193)

232. 1 Aug 1716. Deed. JOHN BOWERS of Kent Co yeoman for 10 pounds allready paid by OWEN WILLIAMS in his life time, sold to MARY WILLIAMS and ALECE WILLIAMS daus and coheirs of OWEN WILLIAMS late of same co decd ... a tr of land on Mispilion Hund beginning at the head of Bocombrigg Cr ... to land of JAMES MARTAIN ... 150 a. ... KATHRINE WILLIAMS relict of OWEN WILLIAMS and mother to MARY and ALECE shall peaceably and quietly occupie and enjoy the afsd land ... Wit: JOHN JOHNSON, GRIFF JONES. Ackn 15 Aug 1716. (E:pg 197)

233. 15 Aug 1716. Deed. JOHN REYNOLS and MARY REYNOLS (REYNALLS) of Kent Co ... whereas DANIEL BROWN of same co decd did in his will bequeath unto MARY REYNOLS then the wife of WILLIAM TOMSON since decd now the lawfull wife of JOHN REYNOLS 100 a. in these words I give and bequeath unto my dau in law MARY THOMSON 100 a. being the farm which I formerly promised her and is pt/o a tr of land I live upon at the lower end ... for 50 pounds JOHN REYNOLS and MARY his wife sold to WAITMAN SIPLE of same co ... afsd 100 a. ... Wit: GRIFF JONES, MARK MANLOVE. Ackn 16 Aug 1716. (E:pg 201)

234. 8 May 1711. Deed. SOLOMON SMITH of Kent Co planter for 28 pounds sold to JONATHAN STURGESS of Summerset Co MD planter ... a tr of land called Aberdeen n side of Dover River alias Jones Cr ... 100 a. ... Wit: FRANCES ALEN, ARTHUR MESTON. Ackn 16 Aug 1716. (E:pg 203)

235. 26 Jun 1710. Deed. FRANCES RICHARDSON of Phila goldsmith son and heir of FRANCES RICHARDSON late of NY City merchant decd and ELIZABETH RICHARDSON the wife of said FRANCES the son ... whereas by an indenture bearing date 15 Jun 1686 made between HENRY JOHNSON and ELENOR his wife and DANIEL RUTTY all of Kent Co on the one part and FRANCES RICHARDSON the father on the other part did convey unto FRANCES RICHARDSON the father 400 a. being one halfe of 800 a. called The Plains w side of Dover River ... FRANCES RICHARDSON the father being in his life time lawfully seized of the land made his will dated 7 Jul 1688 and did give one third of his estate unto his wife REBECAH RICHARDSON and the other two thirds unto his children FRANCES, REBECKA and JOHN ... JOHN is since decd, REBECCA the elder is decd ... FRANCES RICHARDSON as the eldest son is now seized of two equal full parts of said land ... FRANCES RICHARDSON and ELIZABETH his wife for 30 pounds sold to JAMES BROOKES the younger of Kent Co afsd tr of land ... FRANCES and ELIZABETH have made THOMAS SKIDMORE their atty to deliver their pt/o these presents in open court ... Wit: RICHARD HEATH, PHILLIP KERNEY. Ackn 16 Aug 1716. (E:pg 206)

236. 10 Aug 1716. Deed. JOHN LISENBEY son and heir of HENRY LISENBEY late of Kent Co decd for a valuable sume of money sold to HENRY LISENBEY of same place yeoman ... a tr of land s side of Murther Cr ... 200 a. formerly taken up by virtue of a warrant to HENRY LISENBEY decd father to said JOHN LISENBEY ... Wit: RICHARD SMITH, WM RODENEY. Ackn 16 Aug 1716. (E:pg 209)

237. 9 May 1713. Deed. SOLOMON SMITH, MORRIS SMITH and JOHN MORGAN of Kent Co PA for bonds of 30 pounds sold to JONATHAN STURGES of same co ... a tr of land called Aberdeen n side of Dover River ... by land that said SOLOMON sold to said JONATHAN STURGES ... 101 a. ... Wit: WILLIAM STARKEY, THOMAS ADAMS. Ackn 16 Aug 1716. (E:pg 212)

238. 9 May 1716. Deed. BENJAMIN RAYNOLDS (RANDOLS) of Kent Co for [blank] pounds sold to SAMUELL WATTKINGS of same co ... a tr of land called Wattkings Dear Purchase being pt/o a tr called The Indian Fields nw br of Murther Cr beginning at Piney Br ... 50 a. ... Wit: NICHOLAS MAXON, JOHN SIPLE. Ackn 16 Aug 1716. (E:pg 214)

239. 20 Sep 1716. Marriage. JOHN FORSTER (FOSTER) and ANNE LUSHER both of Kent Co were lawfully published ... did take each other to be man and wife ... Wit: EVAN JONES Justice, CHARLES HILLYARD Justice, JOHN HALL Justice, VINCENT EMERSON, MARK MANLOVE, WM MANLOVE, SAMUELL MANLOVE, ISAAC SNOW, LANCELOT LEWIS, JOHN PAIN, JAMES JACKSON, SAMUELL GLOVER, RICHARD SMITH, NATH AMPLUGH, JACOB AMPLUGH, JOHN POUNDS, ELIZ EMERSON, SARAH SHARP. (E:pg 215)

240. -- Nov 1716. Deed. GEORGE MORGAN of Kent Co yeoman for 130 pounds sold to JOHN REYNOLDS of same place yeoman ... a plantation and tr of land in Dover Hund composed of sundry small tr being ye plantation and pt/o the tr of land said GEORGE MORGAN now lives upon of which 60 a. was formerly purch of RICHARD GLOVER called Crooked Billett by deed dated 17 May 1690 and 50 a. being purch of THOMAS EVERETT 25 Sep 1688 and 100 a. bought of JOHN CHANTT called Crookhill 8 May -- all which joyned into one 210 a. tr called Reynolds Farm ... to corner of land formerly belonging to RICHARD GLOVER ... to fence dividing it from GEORGE MORGAN's son WILLIAM ... 100 a. ... Wit: JOHN BRADSHAW, JOHN FORSTER. Ackn 14 Nov 1716. (E:pg 216)

241. 14 Nov 1716. Deed. JOHN REYNOLDS of Kent Co for 40 pounds sold to GEORGE MORGAN of same place yeoman ... a tr of land called School House n side of Dover River ... to corner of land belonging to CAPT WILLIAM RODENEY ... to clear ground of JOHN REYNOLDS ... 200 a. ... Wit: JOHN FORSTER, JOHN BRADSHAW, JOHN REYNOLDS. Ackn 14 Nov 1716. (E:pg 219)

242. 14 Nov 1716. Deed. GEORGE MORGAN of Kent Co for [blank] pounds sold to WILLIAM MORGAN of same place yeoman ... a tr of land composed of sundry small tr [same as #240] ... in Dover Hund beginning at the fence that divides between this land, WILLIAM MORGAN's plantation, and GEORGE MORGAN's plantation ... 100 a. ... Wit: JOHN CLAYTON, JOHN STEAVENS. Ackn 14 Nov 1716. (E:pg 221)

243. 19 Aug 1716. Deed. BENJAMIN SHURMER late of the City of Bristoll in Great Britain but now Kent Co for 20 pounds 10 shillings sold to WILLIAM DONNE, ABRAHAM LOYD (LOYED), CHARLES HARFORD (HERFORD), EDWARD LOYD (LOYED), CELEB LOYED, GEORGE WHITEHEAD and RICHARD COOL of City of Bristoll merchants ... two parcells of land he bought of SAMUEL TAYLOR of Duck Cr New Castle Co 25 a. bearing date 4 Feb 1714 ... and 12 a. bearing date 15 Jun 1715 ... Wit: BENJAMIN ELLIS, SAMUEL GRIFFING. Ackn 10 May 1716 by JAMES STEEL esqr atty for

BENJAMIN SHURMER. (E:pg 225)

244. 26 Oct 1716. Deed. Whereas a tr of land in Dover Hund called Kingston Upon Hull which tr of land was granted to JOHN BRIGS and MARY PHILLIPS by patent dated 14 Aug 1678 450 a. ... [page torn] was afterwards in the occupation of STEPHEN NOWELL of same co decd but by some imperfection in the conveyance the said land came by decent unto THOMAS FRAMPTON son and heir of [?] FRAMPTON decd who amongst other lands did sell and convey land unto ABRAHAM BICKLEY 1 Jan 1712 ... ABRAHAM BICKLEY conveyed unto GEORGE NOWELL son and heir of said STEPHEN NOWELL decd 27 Sep 1715 ... GEORGE NOWELL of Kent Co for [blank] pounds sold to NATHANIEL HUN of same co 64 a. ... adj land called The Town Point ... Wit: DANIEL RODENEY, RICHARD SMITH. Ackn 14 Nov 1716. (E:pg 230)

245. 20 Oct 1716. Deed. WILLIAM HERN (HEARN) of Phila smith and atty to HANNAH DENNIS and MARY SEELY dau of THOMAS ROUSE late of Kent Co decd and JOHN DENNIS husband of HANNAH DENNIS of England for 75 pounds sold to NICHOLAS NIXON of Kent Co yeoman ... a tr of land called Hatherds Adventure n side of Murther Cr near the head ... 300 a. with 150 a. land next adj being the one half of a tr called Edmonds Chance ... WILLIAM HERN appoint loving friend THOMAS SKIDMORE of Kent Co to ackn this deed in open court ... Wit: JOHN CLARK, ROBERT CLATON, JAMES BRADSHAW. Ackn 15 Nov 1716 by THOMAS SKIDMORE atty to WILLIAM HERN. (E:pg 234)

246. 10 Oct 1716. Deed. TIMOTHY HANSON of Kent Co yeoman and JOSHUA CLAYTON of same co yeoman executors of the will of ROBERT PORTER late of same co decd ... whereas ROBERT PORTER in his lifetime stood lawfully seized of a tr of land n side of Little Cr beginning at a corner of JOHN CLIFFORD's land ... 50 a. ... ROBERT PORTER made his will 17 Feb 1714 ... for 15 pounds TIMOTHY HANSON and JOSHUA CLAYTON sell afsd tr of land to BENJAMAN BARRAT of same co taylor ... Wit: WM RODENEY, DANIEL RODENEY. Ackn 15 Nov 1716. (E:pg 237)

247. 13 Nov 1716. Deed. GEORGE GREEN of Kent Co farmer and RACHELL his wife for 40 pounds sold to JOHN HALL of same place gentlemen ... a tr of land s side of sw br of Duck Cr called Betts Endeavour granted by pattent to JOHN BETTS in 1684 400 a. conveyed to RICHARD WILLIAMS and from RICHARD WILLIAMS to CHRISTOPHER STANDLY ... said STANDLY being since decd said land in occupation of CHRISTOPHER STANDLY his son who made an alienation of 50 a. to SIMON HIRONS decd ... CHRISTOPHER STANDLY son since also decd and MARY STANDLY his wife being

appointed executrix was since intermarried to CHARLES RUMSEY and on 20 May 1712 did convey land to GEORGE GREEN ... afterwards GEORGE GREEN conveyed to FRANCIS VANNOY and KATHERIN his wife and they conveyed to GEORGE GREEN 16 May 1716 ... a tr of land pt/o afsd tr of land ... at the s corner of FRANCIS VANNOY's land and on the line of JOHN HALL's land ... 50 a. and 50 a. more belonging to VINCENT EMERSON ... Wit: WILLIAM COE, GRIFFITH JOANES esqr. Ackn 15 Nov 1716. (E:pg 238)

248. 14 Nov 1716. Deed. JOHN BERRY of Talbot Co MD planter sold to ROBERT GORDON of Phila merchant ... a tr of land s side of Dover River called Cypress Neck ... bound on the w with the land formerly THOMAS WILLIAMS' ... 400 a. ... Wit: JOHN COE, HUGH DURBORROW, THOMAS FRENCH. Ackn 15 Nov 1716. (E:pg 241)

249. 12 Nov 1716. Deed. EPHRAIM EMERSON and MARY his wife of Kent Co for 100 pounds sold to JOHN HALL esqr ... a tr of land in Little Cr Hund called Wilsons Choise 300 a. patent dated 26 Mar 1682 unto RICHARD WILSON ... beginning at the corner of JOHN BETTS ... to line of SIMON HIRONS' land ... to line of JOHN STEVENS ... near Whetstone Br ... to mouth of Green Br ... and also 50 a. purch by RICHARD WILSON of CHRISTOPHER STANDLY 13 Mar 1694 ... being pt/o a parcell called Betts Endeavour ... in possession of RICHARD WILLSON in his lifetime and in his will did give unto his two daus ELIZABETH and MARY and ELIZABETH being since decd said land came by decent to MARY who intermarried with EPHRAIM EMERSON ... Wit: JOHN THOMPSON, RICHARD JACKSON, RICHARD SMITH. Ackn 15 Nov 1716 by RICHARD SMITH atty to EPHRAIM EMERSON and MARY his wife. (E:pg 243)

250. 15 Nov 1716. Power of Atty. EPHRAIM EMERSON and MARY his wife appoint our friend RICHARD SMITH to be our atty to ackn [above] deed of sale in open court ... Proved 15 Nov 1716. Attest: WILLIAM RODENEY clerk and recorded by DANIELL RODENEY recorder. (E:pg 245)

251. 1 May 1711. Deed. JOHN FRENCH of New Castle esqr for 100 pounds sold to JOHN MAHON of Kent Co yeoman ... a tr of land n side of Little Cr called Bettyes Fortune the two parcells of land pt/o said Bettyes Fortune heretofore sold to ABRAHAM FEILDS and FRANCIS ALLEXANDER ... which said tr of land formerly belonged to WILLIAM MORTON late of Kent Co decd ... to corner of land formerly belonging to WILLIAM STEAVENS ... to line of WILLIAM SIMPSON ... 500 a. ... Wit: WILLIAM ANNAND, MICHAELL ODONAHOE. Ackn 15 Nov 1716 by WILLIAM ANNAND atty for JOHN FRENCH esqr. (E:pg 246)

252. 23 Oct 1716. Power of Atty. CHRISTOPHER STANLY of New Castle appoint my trusty and loveing friend VINCENT EMERSON my atty to assign over unto GEORGE GREEN a tr of land being pt/o a tr called Betts Endeavour in open court ... Wit: SAMUELL ARYRES, ELIZABETH THOMPSON, JOHN CAWDRY. Proved 15 Nov 1716. Attest: WILLIAM RODENEY clerk and recorded by DANIELL RODENEY. (E:pg 248)

253. 15 Nov 1716. Deed. JAMES FITZJERALD Senr of Kent Co planter for 80 pounds sold to JAMES FITZJERALD Junr of same place farmer ... a tr of land called Short Island being pt/o a tr formerly belonging to JOHN BURTON of same co decd n side of Dover River adj land formerly belonging to HENRY STEVENSON ... by line of JOHN CLAYTON now GEORGE HART's land ... 100 a. ... Wit: THOMAS PARKE, JOHN BRADSHAW, HENRY HART. Ackn 15 Nov 1716. (E:pg 249)

254. 25 Apr 1709. Deed. JOHN SAUNDERS and ELIZABETH his wife eldest surviving dau of THOMAS PETERSON late of Kent Co decd for 50 pounds sold to MARY RICHARDSON executrix of the will of JOHN RICHARDSON late of same co ... 400 a. being pt/o a 600 a. tr of land n side of sw br of Duck Cr ... to land formerly belonging to JOHN RENNALLS ... JOHN SAUNDERS and ELIZABETH his wife appoint their trusty friends JOHN BRADSHAW and WILLIAM ANNAND to be their atty to ackn deed of sale in open court ... Wit: JOHN WILSON, WILLIAM ANNAND. Ackn 11 May 1709 by WILLIAM ANNAND and JOHN BRADSHAW and ELIZABETH his wife for JOHN SAUNDERS and ELIZABETH his wife unto MARY RICHARDSON. (E:pg 252)

255. 7 Feb 1716. Deed. JAMES BALL of Kent Co yeoman for 50 pounds sold to JOHN COOK of same co yeoman ... a tr of land on western br of Duck Cr n side of Pearmain Br now called Gravelly Run being pt/o a greater 900 a. tr of land granted by patent to WILLIAM SHERRER and resurveyed 3 Dec 1701 by WILLIAM SHERRER unto FRANCIS WETTSWOOD by deed ... FRANCIS in his life time did make his will and did bequeath his said land unto JAMES BALL ... bounded by land formerly purch of said SHERRER by RICHARD TURNER ... 100 a. ... JAMES BALL appoint ABSOLOM CUFF my atty to deliver these presents in open court ... Wit: ABSOLOM CUFF, JABER JINKINS. Ackn 15 Feb 1716 by ABSOLOM CUFF atty for JAMES BALL. (E:pg 254)

256. 7 Feb 1716. Deed. PERCES and WILLIAM HIRONS widow and son of SIMON HIRONS late of Kent Co decd for 40 pounds sold to JAMES POTTER of same co yeoman ... a tr of land called Brookshear formerly taken up by FRANCIS WHITWELL patent dated at Yorke Jan 167- and 10 Dec 1685 conveyed to SIMON HIRONS decd by WILLIAM BERRY

and WILLIAM SOUTHEBE adminr of the estate of FRANCIS
WHITWELL and SIMON HIRONS in his lifetime did make his will and
did give 50 a. out of the 400 a. called Brookshear on s side of RICHARD
WILSON's plantation to be by his executrix sold for the payment of his
debts and the other 50 a. of the same tr out of the pt/o WILLIAM
HIRONS ... near Chippennorton line ... to corner of JOHN HALL's land
... 100 a. ... Wit: SIMON HIRONS, ROBERT HIRONS, DAVID
MORGAN, NATHANIEL ROACH. Ackn 15 Feb 1716. (E:pg 256)

257. 30 Dec 1716. Deed. PHILEMON EMERSON of Duck Cr Kent Co
planter & ELIZABETH his wife for 40 pounds sold to SAMUELL
FREEMAN of same place planter ... a parcell of land on s side of sw br of
Duck Cr ... to line of RICHARD WHITEHART ... 100 a. being pt/o a large
tr called Denbetown patent bearing date 5 Oct 1685 unto THOMAS
WILSON then of Kent Co but since decd who in his life time by deed 18
Feb 1686 conveyed land unto his son THOMAS WILSON ... THOMAS
WILSON conveyed same unto PHILEMON EMERSON ... Wit: JOHN
COE, TIMOTHY HANSON, JAMES STEEL. Ackn 15 Feb 1716. (E:pg
258)

258. 10 Oct 1716. Deed. JAMES STEEL of Duck Cr Kent Co yeoman and
MARTHA his wife for 115 pounds sold to JOHN COOK of same place
yeoman ... a tr of land patent under the hands of RICHARD HILL,
ISAAC NORRIS and JAMES LOGAN commissioners bearing date 10 Aug
last granted and confirmed unto JAMES STEEL a tr of land on the
western br of Duck Cr ... to land now of NATHANIEL HUMPLUGH ...
350 a. ... Wit: BENJAMAN SHURMER, JOHN PHILLPS. Ackn 15 Feb
1716. (E:pg 260)

259. 6 Feb 1716. Deed. THOMAS WALKER of Kent Co yeoman for 21
pounds sold to ELISHA SNOW of same place yeoman ... a tr of land s
side of sw br of Duck Cr being pt/o a 100 a. tr formerly laid for THOMAS
WILLSON called Denby Town and since conveyed by deed to EVIN
JONES ... 1702 RACHEL HOSKINGS executrix of HENRY HOSKINGS
and since conveyed from the said EVIN JONES to JOHN WALKER by
deed dated 10 Oct 1703 and said JOHN WALKER decd seized in actual
possession of same did make his will and did give his dwelling plantation
and land to be equally divided between his two sons RICHARD and
THOMAS WALKER which division was made 4 Feb 1716 ... the eastern
pt/o said land being the pt/o said THOMAS ... 53 a. ... Wit: ISAAC
SNOW, DAVID VICKERER. Ackn 15 Feb 1716. (E:pg 263)

260. 25 Apr 1716. Deed. SAMUELL TAYLOR of Duck Cr New Castle Co
bolter for 1 pound sold to GEORGE GRAHAM same place taylor ... a lott
or piece of ground in a place layed out for a town called Salisbury on the

head of Duck Cr ... to corner of WILLIAM HACKETT's lott ... GEORGE GRAHAM to pay 6 pence yearly and every year for ever hereafter on 23 Dec ... Wit: SAMUELL GRIFTING, ABSOLOM CUFF. (E:pg 264)

261. 16 Dec 1716. Quit Claim. JOHN SWIFT of Phila gentlemen quitt claim unto GEORGE GRAHAM ... [above] lott of land ... Wit: SAMUEL GRIFING, ABSOLOM CUFF. Ackn 14 Feb --. (E:pg 266)

262. 7 Feb 1716. Deed. PERSES, WILLIAM and JOHN HIRONS all of Kent Co for 160 pounds sold to SIMON HIRONS of same place yeoman ... two tr of land commonly the dwelling plantation of SIMON HIRONS [see #256] ... did make his will and did bequeath plantation and tr of land to be divided between his two sons WILLIAM AND JOHN, WILLIAM to have the north part ... JOHN the south part ... Wit: JAMES POTTER, ROBERT HIRONS. Ackn 14 Feb 1716/7. (E:pg 266)

263. 11 Feb 1716. Power of Atty. PERCES HIRONS and JOHN HIRONS both of Kent Co appoint our trusty and well beloved friend SAMUEL BERRY of same place to ackn [above] two deeds of sale in open court ... Wit: NATHANIEL ROCH, BARBERRY QUILLEN. (E:pg 268)

264. 25 Oct 1716. Deed. SAMUEL TAYLOR of Duck Cr New Castle Co bolter for 2 pounds 3 shillings sold to JOHN PHILLIPS of Lee Manner of Hrith on the head of Duck Cr Kent Co yeoman ... a lott laid out for a town called Salisbury on the head of Duck Cr ... at corner of CHARLES HARPER's lott ... JOHN PHILLIPS to pay SAMUEL TAYLOR 1 shilling yearly and every year hereafter on 23 Dec ... Wit: ABSOLOM CUFF, THOMAS HACKETT. Ackn 14 Feb 1716. (E:pg 269)

265. 15 Dec 1716. Quit Claim. JOHN SWIFT of Phila gentlemen quitt claim unto JOHN PHILLIPS the [above] lott of land ... Wit: ABSOLOM CUFF, THOMAS HAWKETT. Ackn 14 Feb 1716. (E:pg 270)

266. 14 Feb 1716. Power of Atty. SAMUEL TAYLOR and JOHN SWIFT appoint THOMAS HACKETT of Kent Co merchant our atty to deliver [above] deed in open court ... Wit: WILLIAM HAWKEY, ABSOLOM CUFF. Proved. Attest: WM RODENEY clerk. Proved 14 Feb 1716/7. (E:pg 271)

267. 10 Nov 1716. Deed of Mortgage. SAMUEL TAYLOR of Duck Cr Kent Co bolter for two pounds sold to CORNELIS TOBITT of Luel(?) Co MD yeoman ... a lott laid out for a town called Salisbury on head of Duck Cr beginning at the corner of CHARLES HARPER's lott ... CORNELIS TOBITT to pay SAMUEL TAYLOR 6 pence yearly on 23 Dec for ever ... Wit: SAMUEL GRIFING, ABSOLOM CUFF. Ackn 14 Feb 1716/7. (E:pg

271)

268. 16 Dec 1716. Quit Claim. JOHN SWIFT of Phila gentlemen quit claim unto CORNELIS TOBITT the [above] lott of land ... Wit: ABSOLOM CUFF, SAMUELL GRIFING. Received 1 pound consideration money from CORNELIS TOBITT. (E:pg 273)

269. 9 Feb 1712. Deed. WILLIAM REYNOLDS of Duck Cr Hund Kent Co planter sold for 3 pounds 10 shillings to EVAN JOANES Junr of same co planter and stone mason ... a parcell of land n side of sw br of Duck Cr being pt/o the land where JOHN REYNOLDS the father lives and adj to land formerly sold to JAMES THOMAS and lying on the western side ... 70 a. ... Wit: JONAS GREENWOOD, ISAAC SNOW. Ackn 14 Feb 1716/7. (E:pg 274)

270. 1 Feb 1716. Deed. JOHN JACKSON of Kent Co yeoman for 11 pounds sold to JOHN BRYANT of same place yeoman ... a tr of land s side of Hour Glass Marsh ... 200 a. ... surveyed by RICHARD SMITH deputy surveyor ... Wit: GEORGE ROBINSON, WILLIAM RODENEY. Ackn 14 Feb 1716/7. (E:pg 276)

271. 26 Mar 1682 at Phila. Confirmation of Patent. Whereas a tr of land called Willsons Choice s side of sw br of Duck Cr ... corner of JOHN BETTS ... in line of SIMON HIRONS ... to line of JOHN STEVENS ... 300 a. patent dated 15 Jun 1679 and surveyed 23 Jun 1679 to RICHARD WILLSON ... WILLIAM PENN Governor of PA confirms patent unto RICHARD WILLSON ... . (E:pg 277)

272. 14 Nov 1710. Deed. JOHN HALL of Murtherkill Hund Kent co yeoman for 50 pounds sold to JOHN REDMAN of same place bricklaer ... a tr of land in Murtherkill Hund ... 105 a. and hath been purch severally by THOMAS HEATHERS, EDMOND NEEDHAM and ANNA his wife, RICHARD SHURLEY & EZEKIEL NEEDHAM decd but now in the tenure of JOHN HALL ... Wit: JOHN WALKER, FRANCIS ALLEN. Ackn 16 Nov 1710. (E:pg 278)

273. 18 Dec 1710. Deed. SAMUEL TAYLER of Duck Cr New Castle Co bolter for 1 pound paid by WILLIAM HACKET sold to EDWARD CLUFF of Duck Cr Kent Co smith ... a piece of ground in a place layed out for a town called Salisbury on the head of Duck Cr ... beginning at the corner of SAMUEL TAYLER his lott ... 1/2 a. ... EDWARD CLUFF to pay SAMUEL TAYLER 6 pence on 23 Dec every year for ever ... Wit: HENRY JONES, GEORGE GRAHAM, ABSALUM CUFF. Ackn 14 May 1717. (E:pg 279)

274. Quit Claim. JOHN SWIFT of Phila gentlemen quit claime unto EDWARD CLUFF ... [above] lott of land ... Wit: ABSALAM CUFF, HENRY JONES. (E:pg 282)

275. 1 Jan 1716. Deed. MARK MANLOVE (MANLOV) of Mispillian Hund Kent Co yeoman for 60 pounds sold to HENRY HALL of same place yeoman ... a tr of land called Mount Pleasent n side of Mispillian Cr by Beaver Dam Br ... by Fishing Br ... 212 a. ... (412 a. of land and 88 a. of marsh adj to said land was granted by order of St. Jones Court 20 Sep 1680 and surveyed 13 Jan following to WILLIAM CLARK and confirmed by patent 26 Mar 1684 ... WILLIAM CLARK sold to GRIFFITH JONES late of Phila decd merchant ... GRIFFITH JONES 10 Sep 1694 sold unto MARK MANLOVE late of Kent Co decd father of afsd MARK MANLOVE ... MARK MANLOVE on 24 Nov 1694 did make his will and bequeathed afsd tr of land, now being leased to JOHN CLARK, to son MARK ... MARK MANLOVE the younger sold unto ROBERT BETTS of Kent Co 200 a. of said land) ... Wit: WILLIAM MALONEY, ZACHIRIAS GOFFORTH, SAMUELL COLEMAN. Ackn 15 May 1717. (E:pg 284)

276. 28 Apr 1717. Deed. SAMUEL TAYLER of Duck Cr New Castle Co bolter for 1 pound sold to JOSEPH WELLDON of the forest in New Castle Co yeoman ... lott of ground being within place laid out for a town called Salesbery on Duck Cr at corner of JOHN WILLIAMSON ... JOSEPH WELLDON to pay SAMUEL TAYLER 1 shilling on 23 Dec yearly for ever ... Wit: JOHN PARSON, ABSALOM CUFF. Ackn 15 May 1717. (E:pg 286)

277. 5 May 1717. Receipt. SAMUEL TAYLER received 1 pound consideration money and received 10 shillings from JOSEPH WELLDON which I do hereby ackn to be in full satisfaction of [above] and do hereby discharge him from said annual rents for ever ... Wit: FRANCES JONES, BENJAMIN HIRSON. (E:pg 288)

278. 9 May 1717. Deed. WILLIAM RODENEY son and heir of WILLIAM RODENEY late of Kent Co decd for a certain sume of money in hand payed sold to ROBERT & JAMES BEDWELL sons and coheirs of ROBERT BEDWELL late of Kent Co decd ... a tr of land called Wedmore wherewith the said WILLIAM RODENEY decd did in his life time sell unto [page torn] by deed dated 14 Feb 1717 but not fully executed ... therefore WILLIAM RODENEY son conveys unto ROBERT & JAMES BEDWELL the afsd tr of land ... by Isaac's Br ... 254 a. ... Wit: DANIELL RODENEY, JOHN HALL. Ackn 15 May 1717. (E:pg 289)

279. 9 Feb 1716. Deed. SAMUEL TAYLER of Duck Cr New Castle Co bolter for 1 pound sold to GEORGE GRAHAM of Duck Cr Kent Co ... a

lott in the place layd out for a town called Saulesbury on head of Duck Cr beginning at another lott formerly granted to said GEORGE GRAHAM ... 1/4 a. ... [page torn] ... Wit: ABSALOM CUFF, HENRY JONES. Ackn 15 May 1717. SAMUEL TAYLER received of GEORGE GRAHAM 1 pound 1 shilling it being the consideration money within mentioned. (E:pg 291)

280. 15 May 1717. Quit Claim. JOHN SWIFT of Phila quit claim unto GEORGE GRAYHAM the [above] lott of land ... Wit: HENRY JONES, EDWARD CLUFF, ABSALOM CUFF. (E:pg 293)

281. 19 Feb 1716. Deed. SAMUEL TAYLER of Duck Cr Newcastle Co bolter for 1 pound sold to BENJAMIN SHURMER of Manor of Frith in Kent Co ... a lott being in a place laid out for a town called Salesbury on the head of Duck Cr beginning at ABSOLAM CUFF's lott ... to lott of HENRY JONES ... to lott formerly belonging to CHARLES HARPER ... BENJAMIN SHURMER to pay to SAMUEL TAYLER 6 pence on 23 Dec yearly every year hereafter ... Wit: JAMES STEEL, ABSALAM CUFF. Ackn 15 -- 1717. SAMUEL TAYLER received 1 pound from BENJAMIN SHURMER it being the consideration money within mentioned. (E:pg 294)

282. 15 -- 1717. Receipt. SAMUEL TAYLER received of BENJAMIN SHURMER 5 shillings which I hereby ackn to be in full satisfaction for the [above] mentioned 6 pence and I hereby discharge him from said annual rents ... Wit: FRANCES JONES, BENJAMIN HIXSON. (E:pg 296)

283. 15 May 1717. Deed. THOMAS WELLS of Kent Co eldest son of JAMES WELLS of same co decd for 50 pounds sold to MARK MANLOV Senr of same co ... a tr of land called Farmer Elsworth n side of Mother Cr ... 900 a. surveyed 20 Aug 1684 ... Wit: SAMUELL BERY, HUGH DURBOROW. Ackn 15 May 1712. (E:pg 297)

284. 12 Nov 1716. Deed. Whereas a tr of land patent bearing date 26 Mar 1684 unto JOHN BETTS of Kent Co called John Betts Endeavor ... 400 a. ... JOHN BETTS and RICHARD WILLIAMS by deed of sale bearing date 20 Aug 1685 did sell to CHRISTOPHER STANLEY of Kent Co the afsd tr of land and whereas CHRISTOPHER STANLEY died intestate the said tr of land descended to the eldest son CHRISTOPHER STANLEY who also dying left his wife MARY sole executrix of his will and gave her the afsd tr of land except a part which was sold for the payment of his debts and bringing up of his children as by the said will. But said tr of land remained unsold and in the possession of the executrix until the eldest son of CHRISTOPHER STANLEY last aforementioned who is allso

named CHRISTOPHER STANLEY became to the age of 21. The executrix married CHARLES RUMSY and they together with her son by their deed of sail bearing date 20 May 1712 did for 102 pounds 10 shillings sell to GEORGE GREEN then of Phila afsd tr of land ... as CHRISTOPHER STANLEY was not 21 sale was not good ... CHRISTOPHER STANLEY of New Castle Co cordwiner now conveys unto GEORGE GREEN of Kent Co yeoman tr of land sw side of Duck Cr excepting three parcels all ready sold, 50 a. sold to RICHARD WILLSON, 50 a. sold to SIMON HIRONS, 50 a. sold to VINCENT EMERSON ... Wit: THOMAS ADAMS, HUGH DURBOVOW. Ackn 15 May 1717. (E:pg 299)

285. 10 Sep 1717. Deed. JOHN FRENCH of Newcastle Co gentlemen for 135 pounds sold to JOHN BRINCKLOE of Dover Hund Kent Co gentlemen ... a tr of land patent signed by RICHARD HILL, ISAAC NORRIS & JAMES LOGAN bearing date 20 Sep 1715 unto JOHN FRENCH called The Cave ... 588 a. ... pattent recorded in Phila in Pattent Book A Vol 5 page 173 ... JOHN FRENCH appoint TIMOTHY HANSON & RICHARD RICHARDSON of Kent Co yeoman his atty to ackn and deliver deed in open court ... Wit: JOHN COOK, GEORGE MARTIN, JAMES STEEL. Ackn 14 May 1718. (E:pg 304)

286. 10 Nov 1717. Deed. ROBERT GRUNDY of Talbot Co MD gentlemen in consideration of his bond drawn payable to the said THOMAS EDMONDSON for the sume of 500 pounds sold to THOMAS EDMONDSON of same place ... one full halfe of all the land in a deed made by him the said THOMAS EDMONDSON unto him the said ROBERT GRUNDY bearing date 10 May 1710 ... and allso for one full third pt/o all the estate reall and personall that is due to him either in Newcastle Co, Kent Co or Suss Co doth return and make back againe all the right title that said ROBERT GRUNDY may be saide to have to any of the lands ... (signed) ANDREW CALDWELL atty for ROBERT GRUNDY. Wit: MICHAEL LOWBER, PHILLIP MORGAN, JOHN BERRY. (E:pg 306)

287. 25 -- 1717 at Great Yarmouth. Be it known that before us THOMAS LEGRIRE esqr mayor and justice of the peace for the Burgh of Great Yarmouth in County of Norfolk? in Great Britain and THOMAS ROYALL gentlemen notary ... personally appeared HANNAH DENNIS and MARY SEELY both of Great Yarmouth widows, the two daus and coheirs of THOMAS ROUSE late of Kent Co PA joyner decd and ABRAHAM TODD of Great Yarmouth tayler and MARY his wife aged 28 years and upwards, and THOMAS SEELY of Great Yarmouth aged 30 years and upwards which said MARY TODD and THOMAS SEELY are two of the children of MARY SEELY. The said HANNAH DENNIS has no children surviving.

They appoint ISAAC SEELY of Great Yarmouth mariner aged 21 years and upwards of small (statue?) swarthy complexion and wearing his own black hair ... their atty ... to demand and take possession of all lands late of said THOMAS ROUSE of which he died possessed (other than what the said HANNAH DENNIS and MARY SEELY have sold before in PA and Island of Barbados or in any other place) ... and demand all sums of money owing to estate ... . (E:pg 307)

288. 8 Mar 1715 at Talbot Co MD. Deposition. CALEB ISGATE of Talbot Co MD aged 74 years concerning his knowledge of ELLEANOR ELLENSWORTH wife of HUGH MODEUAMOTT of ? co her being the legitimate dau of WILLIAM ELLENSWORTH and SARAH his wife of St. Jones PA decd ... declares that about 27 years ague & upward and severall other times before, WILLIAM ELLENSWORTH came to his house in Talbot Co MD where then the said ELLEANOR resided and being (?) was maintained and brought up and did often (say?) in the presence and hearing of this deponent declare the said ELLEANOR was his legitimate child and born of SARAH his wife at Peach Blossom ... (signed) THOMAS ROBINS justice, JOHN BUTTEN justice. (E:pg 310)

289. 8 Mar 1715 at Talbot Co MD. Deposition. ABIGAIL WISE of Talbot Co MD widow aged 72 years did declare the very same things as [above] ... having heard the afsd WILLIAM ELLENSWORTH say the same words at the said house and other places calling her his child and dau ... (signed) THOMAS ROBINS, JOHN BULLER justices. (E:pg 310)

290. Deed of Gift. GEORGE ROBISSON of Kent Co a tr of land s side of Dover River called Whitewells Delight where said GEORGE ROBISSON now dwelleth 774 a. ... for love good will and affection give to my well beloved children LAWRENCE ROBISSON, DANIEL ROBISSON and CHARITY ROBISSON ... land to be divided ... tr of land with limitation of myself and my wife SARAH ROBISSON to live our natural lives in and upon 100 a. adj unto Smiths Br to my dau CHARITY ROBISSON ... son LAWRENCE ROBISSON to have the upper side ... son DANIELL ROBISSON to have the lower side ... [page torn] ... given them after they attain 30 years of age ... Wit: HENRY FOYRE?, JOHN CLARK. Ackn 13 Nov 1717. (E:pg 311)

291. 26 Mar 1684 at Phila. Confirmation of Patent. Whereas a tr of land called Benefeild s side of sw br of Duck Cr ... to Frenchman's Br ... 1000 a. granted by a warrant from Suss Co Court [date blank] surveyed 30 May 1680 to FRANCIS WHITWELL ... WILLIAM PENN Governor of PA confirms patent unto FRANCIS WHITWELL ... signed by order PATRICK ROBINSON deputy. (E:pg 313)

292. 10 Jun 1685. Deed. WILLIAM BERRY of Kent Co PA adminr appointed to the estate of FRANCIS WHITWELL decd for 30 pounds due by said WHITWELL to GRIFFITH JONES ... do sell unto GRIFFITH JONES equal half of [above] lands ... (signed) WM BERRY, WM SOUTHBY. Wit: JAMES THOMAS, SAMUELL BULLER. Signed, sealed & delivered by WM SOUTHBY ... Wit: ABRAHAM WILLROE?, WILLIAM ROYDON. (E:pg 314)

293. 20 Mar 1685. Deed. CHARLES PICKERING of New Castle PA have a just right and title unto 500 a. on sw br of Duck Cr being half of 1000 a. that was FRANCIS WHITWELL's adj to the land that now is JOSEPH GROWDEN's which he purch of said WHITWELL and allso 200 a. which was WILLIAM FREEMAN's adj to same with a house ... together with four breeding sows with their increase ... I have sold unto RALPH FRETWELL of Barbados esqr for 100 pounds afsd 700 a. ... Wit: JOHN EDMONDSON, [?]. WM BERRY & WM SOUTHBY as adminr of FRANCIS WHITWELL ackn satisfaction with [above] agreement ... Wit: JOHN EDMONSON, THOMAS HARBOTT. (E:pg 314)

294. 25 -- 1717. Deed. BENJAMIN SHURMER of Duck Cr Kent co yeoman and SARAH his wife for 40 pounds sold to WILLIAM PARSON of Duck Cr New Castle Co husbandman ... a tr of land called Surgan on Western Br or Gravelly Run of Duck Cr by virtue of a warrant dated 25 Feb 1714 laid out for and by BENJAMIN by a special commission to him given for that purpose from JACOB TAYLOR surveyor general 8 Mar 1716 ... to corner of land called [?] formerly taken up by one RIDGWAY ... to eastern line of the Mannor of Feith ... 200 a. ... Wit: THOMAS HARBOTT, ROBERT DIFFY, JOHN MIFLING Ackn 13 Feb 1718/9. (E:pg 315)

295. 1 Nov 1718. Deed. JOHN PHILLIPS of Duck Cr New Castle Co merchant and HANAH his wife for 30 pounds sold to JOHN STOOPS of Salisbury Kent Co ... a piece of ground in the town of Salisbury on the head of Duck Cr ... beginning at a lott already belonging to said JOHN STOOPS ... to Greene Br ... to edge of main street ... 1 a. ... JOHN PHILLIPS and HANAH his wife appoint BENJAMIN SHURMER of Kent Co gentlemen to be their atty to deliver these presents in open court ... Wit: JOHN HACKETT, ABSALOM CUFF. (E:pg 318)

296. 5 Feb 1717. Deed. Whereas RICHARD HILL, ISAAC NORRIS & JAMES LOGAN commissioners bearing date 4 May 1715 confirmed unto JAMES JACKSON of Duck Cr Kent Co yeoman & MARGARETT his wife a tr of land s side of the sw br of Duck Cr beginning at the corner of JOHN HOSTER's land called Alloms Cabbins ... to THOMAS WILSON's br ... by JOHN KELLY's land called Galloway ... 750 a. patent recorded

in Book A Vol 5 page 109 ... JAMES JACKSON and MARGARETT his wife for 200 pounds sold to JAMES STEEL of same place yeoman afsd tr of land ... excepting out of said tr a parcell 70 a. formerly sold from the e side to JOHN HOSTER & also 140 a. sold from the s end to SAMUEL MANLOVE & a small parcell being on Wilsons Br granted to [page torn] ... Wit: JOHN FOSTER, ANN FOSTER, GEORGE HORTON. Ackn 12 Feb 1717. (E:pg 321)

297. 5 Feb 1717/8. Deed. JAMES STEEL of Duck Cr Kent Co yeoman for 50 pounds sold to JAMES JACKSON of same place yeoman and MARGARET his wife ... a parcell of land s side of sw br of Duck Cr beginning at the mouth of Ellinsworth's Br ... to other land of JAMES STEEL ... 200 a. being pt/o a tr called Herrybridge ... Wit: JOHN FOSTER, GEORGE HORTON, ANN FOSTER. Ackn 12 Feb 1717. (E:pg 323)

298. 13 May 1717. Deed. GEORGE MARTIN of Duck Cr Kent Co for 50 pounds sold to SAMUEL POUNDS of Newcastle Co ... a tr of land n side of sw br of Duck Cr in the fork of the Black Princes Br ... 100 a. ... Wit: JAMES STEEL, RICHARD EMPSON. Ackn 14 Aug 1717. (E:pg 324)

299. 20 May 1712. Deed. CHARLES RUMSEY of Kent Co MD and MARY his wife executrix of the will of CHRISTOPHER STANLY late of New Castle decd and CHRISTOPHER STANLEY eldest son of said CHRISTOPHER STANLEY for 102 pounds sold to GEORGE GREEN of Phila yeoman ... a tr of land patent 25 Mar 1684 unto JOHN BETTS of Kent Co called John Betts Endeavour s side of sw br of Duck Cr [see #284] ... Wit: JOHN WATERS, JAMES STEEL. Ackn 15 Aug 1712 by JAMES STEEL atty for CHARLES RUMSEY and MARY his wife. (E:pg 327)

300. 26 Nov 1713. Quit Claim. FRANCIS RICHARDSON of Phila silver smith quit claim unto GEORGE MARTIN of Duck Cr Kent Co yeoman all manor of actions, suits, bills, bonds, debts sums of money, judgments and demands whatsoever ... Wit: JOHN HARPER, JO. LAWRENCE. (E:pg 331)

301. 1 Feb 1717. Power of Atty. MARY EDMONSON wife of THOMAS EDMONSON of Talbut Co MD appoint my trusty and well beloved friend ANDREW CALDWELL of Kent Co to be my atty ... to deliver and ackn in open court any deed or conveyance for any tr of land that my said atty warrant for to doing ... Wit: JOHN BERY, MARMADUKE PENWELL, FR(ANCIS?) PETIPHER? Proved 15 Feb 1717. (E:pg 331)

302. 20 Apr 1708. Deed. ROBERT PARVISS surviving son and heir of

ROBERT PARVISS late of Kent Co, New Castle Co and Suss Co decd for 25 pounds sold to JOHN WILSON of Talbut Co MD ... a tr of land called Gilford n side of Murther Cr in fork of Bishops Br ... 600 a. by virtue of a warrant from Kent Co Court bearing date 17 Oct 1682 layed out for said ROBERT PARVISS decd ... Wit: WILLIAM ANNAND, WILLIAM ENOIR? Ackn 11 May 1708 by VINCENT EMERSON atty to ROBERT PARVISS. (E:pg 332)

303. 30 Apr 1708. Power of Atty. ROBERT PARVISS appoint my trusty and well beloved friend VINCENT EMERSON of Kent Co to be my atty to deliver [above] deed of sale in open court ... Wit: WILLIAM ANNAND, WILLIAM ENOIR? Proved 30 Apr 1708. (E:pg 333)

304. 8 Jan 1717/8. Deed. Whereas by deed of sale 15 Feb 1715/6 JOSHUA CLAYTON of Kent Co yeoman did sell unto DAVID MORGAN of same place planter and SARAH his wife a tr of land where said DAVID MORGAN now livith ... by the path which goes from Little Cr to the plantation formerly belonging to RICHARD WILSON decd ... to line of JOHN RICHARDSON's ... 50 a. being pt/o a tr of land called Higham Ferry ... DAVID MORGAN and SARAH his wife for 20 pounds sold back to JOSHUA CLAYTON afsd tr of land ... Wit: HENRY JOYCE, HUGH DURBOROW. Ackn 10 Feb 1717. (E:pg 335)

305. 10 Feb 1717/8. Deed. JOSHUA CLAYTON of Little Cr Hund Kent Co yeoman and SARAH his wife for 20 pounds sold to DAVID MORGAN of same place planter ... a tr of land DAVID MORGAN now dwells upon ... to line of JAMES POTTER ... to corner of land called Willingbrook formerly laid out for JOHN RICHARDSON decd ... to land that did belong to ROBERT PORTER decd ... 50 a. ... Wit: HENRY JOYCE, HUGH DURBOROW. Ackn 13 Feb 1717. (E:pg 336)

306. 1 Mar 1718. Deed. Whereas NICHOLAS NIXON of Kent Co blacksmith in Court of Common Pleas held 14 Aug recovered a judgement for [blank] sum ... it was ordered that JOHN LUCAS and REBECCA his wife adminr of JAMES BROOKS late of Kent Co yeoman decd sell the lands of the decd ... in consideration of the afsd judgement JOHN LUCAS and REBECCA his wife sold unto NICHOLAS NIXON ... five third pt/o of tr of land in Murtherkill Hund 400 a. being pt/o a 800 a. tr called The Plains ... (signed) JOHN LUCAS, REBECCA BROOKS. Wit: THOMAS CRAWFORD, WM RODENEY. Ackn 13 May 1717/8. (E:pg 338)

307. 13 May 1716. Deed. NATHANIEL ROCH of Little Cr Hund Kent Co planter and DEBORAH his wife & dau of JOHN WILSON decd for 28 pounds sold to THOMAS ALLTON of same place planter ... a tr of land (patent bearing date 1 Oct 1685 unto THOMAS WILSON 1200 a. called

Denby Town s side of sw br of Duck Cr, the lower pt/o that neck now called Whitehart Neck and said THOMAS WILSON by deed of gift bearing date 18 Feb 1686 did give unto his son JOHN WILSON 350 a. being pt/o afsd tr and said JOHN WILSON dying without disposing of the said 350 a. and all his children dying in their minority without issue except one dau named DEBORAH the 350 a. descended into the possession of DEBORAH and she is now the wife of NATHANIEL ROCH) ... to line of SAMUEL WHITEHART ... 95 a. ... Wit: RICHARD WHITEHART, HUGH DURBOROW. Ackn 16 May 1716. (E:pg 340)

308. 14 May 1718. Deed. RICHARD WHITEHART of Little Cr Hund Kent Co yeoman for 10 pounds sold to SAMUEL FREEMAN of same place yeoman ... a piece of land in Little Cr Hund being pt/o that piece said RICHARD WHITEHART now dwelleth beginning at the corner of the land of JOHN WALKER decd ... to land of SAMUEL FREEMAN afsd ... 20 a. ... Wit: HUGH DURBOROW, NATHANIEL ROCH. Ackn 16 May 1718. (E:pg 342)

309. 10 May 1713. Memorandum. WILLIAM STARKEY went upon a tr of land s side of Dover River between the land the court house is built upon and the land sold by WILLIAM SOUTHEBE to EDWARD STARKEY 400 a. according to a plott made by JONAS GREENWOOD surveyor and did deliver possession to EPHRAIM EMERSON in behalf of him the said EPHRAIM and MARY his wife and THOMAS EMERSON and ELIZABETH his wife according to a judgment ... at a Court of Common Pleas held 12 May ... Wit: JONATHAN STURGIS, ISAAC FREELAND, HENRY SHAW. Recorded 31 Jul 1719. (E:pg 345)

310. 1 Mar 1714. Articles of Agreement. WILLIAM DONNE iron monger, CHARLES HARFORD, EDWARD LLOYD, ABRAHAM and RICHARD COOLI merchants, CALIB LLOYD grorer, GEORGE WHITHEAD tobacconist all of the City of Bristoll and ROBERT VEFFEY of the Parish Lindington in the Ille of Axolimi the Co of Linroth husbandman ... whereas the parties above named together with several other persons have agreed to be copartners, adventures and joynt traders together with workman and servants into America for planting and importing ... ROBERT VEFFEY to serve as treasurer & committee in America for 4 years ... will be provided with meat, drink, washing and lodging and payed the yearly sum of 20 pounds the first year, 25 pounds second year, 30 pounds third year, 35 pounds fourth year ... Wit: WA CARILES, JO CHAPPELL. (E:pg 346)

311. 18 Jul 1719. WILLIAM DONNE, CHARLES HARFORD, EDWARD LLOYD, ABRAHAM LLOYD, RICHARD COOL, CALEB LLOYD & GEORGE WHITEHEAD being the committee of joynt traders in the City

of Bristoll, the transportation of workmen & servants into America for planting, propagating, dressing & importing of flews in agreement with ROBERT VEFFEY ... this is to certify that ROBERT hath faithfully performed his part according to tenor of said articles ... Wit: JOHN PHILLIPS, WILLIAM COLLINS, JOHN HOLLIDAY, SOLOMON VEFFEY, ABSALOM CUFF. (E:pg 348)

312. 20 Jul 1719. To whomsoever it doth or may concern, ROBERT VEFFEY haveing lived in our neighborhood the whole time [above] mentioned has to the best of our knowledge ... faithfully & truly discharged his duty. In testimony whereof we have putt our hands & caused to be affixed the seal of the said county of Dover Town ... (signed) RICHARD RICHARDSON justice, TIMOTHY HANSON justice, SAMUEL BERRY justice. (E:pg 348)

313. 15 Apr 1718. Bond of Conveyance. NATHANIEL HUNN of Kent Co yeoman am bound unto JOHN BOWERS of same place yeoman for 500 pounds ... NATHANIEL HUNN shall assign unto JOHN BOWERS a tr of land n side of Murther Cr 300 a. of land and 170 a. of marsh called [?] but now called Mullbery Point in the occupation of JOHN BOWERS ... Wit: [?] EMERSON, BENJAMIN HURBER. Ackn 12 Nov 1718. (E:pg 349)

314. 12 Feb 1718. Deed. JAMES CLAYTON of Kent Co yeoman for 5 shillings sold to GEORGE HART of same place yeoman ... a tr of land called New Bristol in Dover Hund whereon GEORGE HART now dwells 100 a. ... Wit: JOSUAH GREENWOOD, GEORGE ASTER? Ackn 14 Aug 1718. (E:pg 350)

315. 16 Mar 1717/8. Deed. JOHN CURTIS of Phila marriner for 30 pounds sold to WILLIAM BRINCKLE of Kent Co esqr ... a tr of land called Pasture Point s side of Murther Cr beginning at the corner of the land of JOHN CABELLIS ... 50 a. (warrant unto JOHN CURTIS for 1200 a. 25 Feb 1681/2) ... and one other tr 400 a. granted by warrant bearing date -- Apr 1681 and surveyed 28 Jan 1681 unto JOHN COBLY and by his deed did convey same unto JOHN CURTIS and the said JOHN CURTIS in his lifetime the 22 Apr 1698 did make his will and did bequeath unto his grandchild JOHN CURTIS 200 a. adj to the land of RICHARD C[?] ... [last page missing] (E:pg 352)

316. 1 Oct 1718. Bond of Conveyance. WILLIAM MULRONY of Kent Co yeoman am bound unto WILLIAM BRINCKLE of same place esqr for 400 pounds ... WILLIAM MULRONY to convey tr of land 310 a. unto WILLIAM BRINCKLE ... Wit: [?] BRINCKLOE, JAMES BOWMAN. (E:pg 353)

317. 1 Nov 1718. Deed. WILLIAM MULRONY of Kent Co yeoman for 70 pounds sold to WILLIAM BRINCKLE of same place esqr ... a tr of land called Virgin Chance se side of Murther Cr 310 a. ... Wit: WILLIAM RODENEY, HENRY MOLESTON. Ackn 13 Nov 1718. (E:pg 354)

Deed Record F Vol. 1 Pt 1

318. 3 Feb 1717 at Phila. Appointment. JOHN BRINCKLOE, JAMES STEEL, BENJAMIN SHURMER, RICHARD RICHARDSON, TIMOTHY HANSON, ROBERT GORDON, EVAN JONES, SAMUEL BERRY, WILLIAM BRINCKLOE, THOMAS FRENCH, ADAM FISHER, MARK MANLOVE, JOSEPH BOOTH & CHARLES HILLYARD of Kent Co appointed justices for the County Court of Common Pleas ... (signed) WILLIAM KEITH Lieutenant Governor. (F:pg 2)

319. 3 Feb 1717 at Phila. To WILLIAM RODENEY of Kent Co gentleman ... whereas the [above] have been appointed justices ... I give full authority to you to administer to the said justices the several oaths or solemn affirmations by law required ... (signed) WILLIAM KEITH Lieutenant Governor. (F:pg 2)

320. 17 Feb 1717/8 at Phila. Nomination. To Majesty's Justices of Kent Co ... not having received any presentment from your bench for appointing a clerk ... I nominate BENJAMIN SHURMER a worthy member of your bench to be clerk of peace ... (signed) WILLIAM KEITH, Lieutenant Governor. (F:pg 3)

321. 12 Feb 1717 at Phila. Appointment. BENJAMIN SHURMER of Kent Co appointed clerk of the peace & prothonotary of the Court of Common Pleas for Kent Co ... (signed) WILLIAM KEITH, Lieutenant Governor. (F:pg 4)

322. 1 Feb 1717. Deed. SAMUEL BROOK of Kent Co yeoman for 120 pounds sold to HENRY SMITH of same place blacksmith ... a tr of land on Murther Cr ... to br that divides this from STEPHEN SIMONS' land ... 75 a. ... Wit: WM BRINKLE, MARK MANLOVE Senr. Ackn 13 Feb 1717. (F:pg 4)

323. 9 Feb 1710. Deed. ROBERT EDMONDS of Kent Co planter for 35 pounds sold to JOHN BROWN cordwainer ... a tr of land 600 a. called Williams Choice n side of Murder Cr binding upon the uppermost line of PETER BISSALLION's land ... Wit: WILLIAM ANNAND, THOMAS SKIDMORE. Ackn 10 Feb 1709. (F:pg 5)

324. 13 Nov 1717. Deed. DANIEL RUTTEY of Kent Co for a valuable consideration to him in hand paid sold to MICHAEL LOWBAR of same co ... 400 a. granted by virtue of a warrant bearing date 22 Feb 1681/2 w side of Island Br of Murther Cr ... called South Hampton ... Wit: THOMAS NOCK, ROBERT WEBB. 13 Nov 1717. (F:pg 6)

325. 11 Feb 1717. Deed. JACOB SMITH of Kent Co planter for [blank] pounds sold to ROBERT GORDON of town of New Castle ... a tr of land n side of Dover River a pt/o Aberdeen beginning at the corner of land belonging to ROBERT FRENCH ... to corner near JOHN STURGIS fence ... 100 a. ... Wit: THOMAS CRAWFORD, WILLIAM COCA. Ackn 13 Feb 1717. (F:pg 7)

326. 10 May 1718. Deed. SAMUEL FREEMAN of Little Cr Hund Kent Co planter and ELIZABETH his wife dau of RICHARD WHITEHART decd and JAMES SATERFIELD of same co planter and MARY his wife dau of said WHITEHART ... whereas RICHARD WHITEHART late of Kent Co decd ... in his lifetime was seized of a tr of land s side of sw br of Duck Cr being pt/o a tr called Denby Town ... 150 a. ... by his will dated 11 Oct 1701 did give his worldly goods to be equally divided amongst his children ... SAMUEL FREEMAND and ELIZABETH his wife and JAMES SATERFIELD & MARY his wife for 10 pounds sold to RICHARD WHITEHARD of Little Cr Hund Kent Co planter ... their part, right and title in afsd tr of land ... Wit: HUGH DURBOREW, MARGARET JACKSON. Ackn 15 Aug 1718. (F:pg 8)

327. 12 Aug 1718. Deed. MARY RICHARDSON widow & executrix of JOHN RICHARDSON late of Kent Co yeoman for 67 pounds sold to JOSHUA CLAYTON of Little Cr same co yeoman ... a tr of land (patent dated 7 Nov 1683 recorded 22 Nov 1687 at Phila patent book page 215 unto JOHN RICHARDSON) called Willingbrook nw side of Duck Cr ... to land where JOHN HALL now dwelleth ... to land formerly belonging to ROBERT PORTER decd ... to land where JOSHUA CLAYTON now dwelleth ... 130 a. ... Wit: TIMOHTY HANSON, SAMUELL GREENWOOD, JAMES TRAITT. Ackn 16 Aug 1718 by BENJAMIN SHURMER atty for MARY RICHARDSON. (F:pg 9)

328. 24 Jun 1718. Power of Atty. MARY RICHARDSON appoint my trusty friend BENJAMIN SHURMER clerk of the co my atty to ackn [above] deed of sale in open court ... Wit: TIMOTHY HANSON, WILLIAM COE. Proved 16 Aug 1718. (F:pg 11)

329. 7 Aug 1718. Deed. BENJAMIN SHURMER, WILLIAM BRINKLE and RICHARD RICHARDSON of Kent Co gentlemen ... (whereas by an act of assembly past at Newcastle in 1717 are impowered in behalf of the

inhabitants of Kent Co to survey lotts and make sale of a tr of land adj court house called Town of Dover formerly purch by the inhabitants of RICHARD WILLSON who bought same from JOHN WALKER all of Kent Co 500 a. being pt/o a tr of 800 a. call Brother's Portion originally taken up by said WALKER by virtue of a warrant from St. Jones Court ... beginning at Dover Cr adj DAVID MORGAN's calfe pasture) ... BENJAMIN SHURMER, WILLIAM BRINKLE and RICHARD RICHARDSON for 3 pounds 9 shillings sold to ABSALUM CUFF of Town of Salisbury same co yeoman ... a lott of land pt/o afsd tr ... to land lately granted unto JOHN MIFFLIN ... in the line of EPHRAIM EMMERSON's land ... 13 8/10 a. ... Wit: TIMOTHY HANSON, WM RODENY. Ackn 16 Aug 1718. (F:pg 11)

330. 7 Aug 1718. Deed. BENJAMIN SHURMER, WILLIAM BRINKLE & RICHARD RICHARDSON of Kent Co gentlemen for 3 pounds 9 shillings sold to SAMUEL GREENWOOD of Little Cr Hund planter ... [same as #329] ... a lott of land ... next to a lott lately granted to JOHN MIFFLIN ... to line of DAVID MORGAN's calf pasture ... 13 8/10 a. ... Wit: TIM HANSON, WM RODNEY. Ackn 16 Aug 1718. (F:pg 13)

331. 7 Aug 1718. Deed. BENJAMIN SHURMER, WILLIAM BRINKLE of Kent Co gentlemen for 4 pounds 6 shillings sold to RICHARD RICHARDSON of same co gentleman ... [same as #329] ... a lott of land beginning at the square laid out for a courthouse ... 4 3/10 a. ... Wit: TIMOTHY HANSON, WM RODENEY. Ackn 16 Aug 1718. (F:pg 14)

332. 12 Aug 1718. Deed. JOHN MORRIS of Kent Co drover for 17 pounds sold to JOHN HALL of same place brickmaker ... a tr of land n side of Mossmillion Cr nw side of Fishing Cr ... 100 a. ... Wit: JONATHAN MANLOVE, WATTMAN SIPLE, ANDREW CALDWELL. Ackn -- Aug 1718. (F:pg 16)

333. 14 Aug 1718. Deed. DAVID PUGH and ANN his wife widow of JOHN POWELL late of Kent Co decd ... whereas JOHN POWELL in his lifetime sold but did not effectually convey unto JOHN THOMPSON late of Kent Co ... 200 a. s side of sw br of Duck Cr ... e side of Wilson's Br and the land of WILLSON ... JOHN THOMPSON sold all his rights and interest to said land unto ANDREW HAMILTON of Phila gentleman and since assigned his right to said 200 a. unto PLINEAS GREENWOOD of Kent Co planter ... whereas DAVID PUGH and ANN his wife are impowered by an order of the Court of Common Pleas to sell lands of JOHN POWELL for the payment of his debts for 50 pounds sold to PHINEAS GREENWOOD afsd tr of land ... Wit: JAMES STEEL, DANIEL HUDSON. Ackn 16 Aug 1718. (F:pg 16)

334. 15 Aug 1718. Deed. MARK MANLOVE Senr of Kent Co for 30 pounds sold to MATHEW MANLOVE of same place ... a tr of land called The Exchange being a tr of land made over in open court by PETER GROUNDICK adminr to the estate of CORNELIUS VERHOOFE to JOHN HILLYARD [page torn] for an execution against the estate of CORNELIUS VERHOOFE ... a tr of land 420 a. ... (signed) MATHEW MANLOVE. Wit: RICHARD SHURLEY, JAMES STEEL. Ackn 15 Aug 1718. (F:pg 17)

335. -- Aug 1718. Deed. JOHN HILLYARD of Kent Co for 25 pounds sold to CHARLES HILLYARD of same place ... a tr of land s side of Little Duck Cr being pt/o a greater tr called The Exchange formerly taken up by JOHN HILLYARD father to the said HILLYARD's decd ... Wit: THOMAS GREEN, THOMAS ADAMS. Ackn 14 Aug 1718. (F:pg 18)

336. 26 Jul 1718. Deed. JOHN BERRY of Talbot Co MD son and heir of WILLIAM BERRY late of Kent Co decd for 60 pounds sold to THOMAS BERRY of Talbot Co planter ... a tr of land called Burburys Lott which was made over unto WILLIAM BERRY afsd father unto the said JOHN BERRY by deed of conveyance from SAMUEL BURBURY bearing date 1 Mar 1685 (original survey by RICHARD MITCHELL bearing date 23 Jan 1683) is also called Burbury's Berry or Bury ... beginning on the nw side of Bishops Br and Murderkill Cr ... to land formerly surveyed for STEPHEN? MOORE ... 600 a. ... Wit: BENJAMIN SHURMER, SAMUEL BERRY, TIMOTHY HANSON. Ackn 13 Aug 1718 by ANDREW CALDWELL atty for JOHN BERRY. (F:pg 19)

337. 11 Aug 1718 at MD. Power of Atty. JOHN BERRY of Talbott Co MD signed [above] deed of sale ... and appoint my well beloved friend ANDREW CALDWELL to ackn in open court same deed ... Wit: JOHN WILLSON, THOMAS BAYNARD. (F:pg 20)

338. 20 May 1718. Deed of Gift. JOHN HILLYARD of Kent Co for goodwill and affection give to my grandson JOHN HILLYARD the son of THOMAS and RACHELL HILLYARD ... a tr of land called Hillyard Benly being pt/o a greater tr formerly taken up by JOHN HILLYARD decd called The Exchange ... 100 a. ... Wit: PHILIP DANEY, PHINEAS GREENWOOD, EVAN JONES. Ackn 14 Aug 1718. (F:pg 20)

339. 1 Aug 1718. Deed. RANDALL DONOVAN of Kent Co yeoman for 13 pounds sold to JEREMIAH HICKERSON of same place yeoman ... a parcell of marsh land n side of Murther Cr ... 26 a. ... Wit: GEORGE LESTER, JAMES CLAYTON. Ackn 14 Aug 1718. (F:pg 20)

340. 1 Aug 1718. Deed. MATHEW MANLOVE son & heir of MARK

MANLOVE late of Kent Co yeoman decd for 30 pounds sold to WILLIAM MULRONEY of same place yeoman ... a tr of land n side of Mispillian Cr 100 a. pt/o a 300 a. tr sold by JOHN CURTIS late of Kent Co decd unto MARK MANLOVE decd bearing date 5 Jan 1693 ... on the eastern line of THOMAS JESTER's land ... binding with a tr of land called Maidens Plott ... Wit: BENJAMIN SHURMER, A HAMILTON. Ackn 13 Aug 1718. (F:pg 21)

341. 13 Aug 1718. Release. CHARLES HILLYARD of Kent Co ... whereas there was a deed of bargain and sale duly executed under the hand of THOMAS HILLYARD about 1716 for all his right to a tr of land called The Exchange except 100 a. ... know ye for in consideration in the deed mentioned by me now in hand I ackn myself repaid ... I release to said THOMAS all my rights of afsd land ... Wit: THOMAS ADAMS, THOMAS GREEN. (F:pg 22)

342. 1 Feb 1719. Deed. RICHARD LEVICK of Kent Co for 20 pounds sold to STEPHEN PARADEE of same place yeoman ... two parcells of land in Dover Hund n and s side of Pipe Elm Br ... near PATRICK HIGGINS plantation ... behind LEVICK's plantation ... containing in the whole 687 a. ... Wit: WILLIAM RODENEY, BENJAMIN SHURMER. Ackn 10 Feb 1719. (F:pg 23)

343. 25 Mar 1719. Deed. ELIZABETH HILL of Phila widow sole executrix and legatee of the will of JOHN HILL her late husband decd for 4 pounds sold to FRANCIS RICHARDSON of Phila goldsmith ... a tr of land (by warrant granted unto JOHN HILL bearing date 21 Feb 1681/2 surveyed 5 Dec 1683 800 a.) one half pt/o said 800 a. ... ELIZABETH HILL appoint TIMOTHY HANSON of Kent Co yeoman her atty to deliver these presents in open court ... Wit: ANTHONY MORRIS, TIMOTHY HANSON, SAMUEL HANSON, ELIZABETH MORRIS. Ackn 15 May 1719. (F:pg 24)

344. 15 Aug 1718. Deed. PHINEAS GREENWOOD of Duck Cr Kent Co planter for 80 pounds sold to ANDREW HAMILTON of Phila gentleman ... a tr of land n side of sw br of Duck Cr ... in the line of a tr of land called Whitewells Chance ... 226 a. being the land purch by JONAS GREENWOOD of JOHN HILLYARD and by his will devised to said PHINEAS ... Wit: JAMES STEEL, JOHN HILLYARD, EVAN JONES. Ackn 15 Aug 1718. (F:pg 24)

345. 10 Sep 1717. Deed. ELIZABETH HILL widow of JOHN HILL late of Suss Co decd and sole executrix of his will ... by virtue of a warrant granted by Kent Co Court unto JOHN HILL bearing date 21 Feb 1682 surveyed 5 Dec 1683 a tr of land 800 a. and in his lifetime did sell but not

actually convey tr unto FRANCIS RICHARDSON then of NY City but since decd ... ELIZABETH HILL in consideration of afsd sale and for 10 shillings sold to FRANCIS RICHARDSON of Phila goldsmith the son afsd tr of land ... ELIZABETH appoints TIMOTHY HANSON of Kent Co to deliver these presents in open court ... Wit: ROBERT OWEN, JOSHUA TOMKINS, JAMES STEEL, TIMOTHY HANSON, SAMUEL HANSON, RICHARD ANNITT?, ELIZABETH MORRIS. Ackn 15 May 1719. (F:pg 25)

346. 12 Jan 1720/21 at NY. Patent. Patent for a parcel of land granted unto WALTER DICKINSON ... whereas THOMAS MERRITT obtained a patent bearing date 17 Jun 1671 for a parcell of land 400 a. nw side of St. Jones Cr about a mile from Warder Cr ... bounded on the se with land of WALTER WHARTON ... having not been improved by the said THOMAS MERRITT who hath not appeared ever since and is supposed to be dead the same granted to WALTER DICKINSON and there being another parcell of land adj heretofore belonging to WALTER WARTON who having likewise a patent from Governor LOVELACE (dated 5 Sep 1676) had in part but since sold for debt ... ne side of St. Jones Cr ... bounded on the sw with land of ROBERT JONES 400 a. ... the said WALTER DICKINSON for some years been in possession by virtue of the dendue? not performed by JOHN OGLETHE ... whole compliment of 800 a. to WALTER DICKINSON ... (signed) J REYNOLDS. (F:pg 25)

347. 9 Feb 1705. Deed. ROBERT EDMONDS of Kent Co planter for 35 pounds sold to JOHN BROWN cordwainer ... a tr of land 200 a. being the upper pt/o a 600 a. tr called William's Choice n side of Murder Cr binding upon the upper most line of PETER BISALLION ... heretofore in the tenure of WILLIAM DERVALL and now in possession of JOHN BROWN ... Wit: WILLIAM ANNAND, THOMAS SKIDMORE. (F:pg 26)

348. 12 Jun 1718. Deed. SUSANNAH ROWE relict and sole executrix of the will of DAVID ROWE (ROE) late of Kent Co decd ... whereas DAVID ROWE in his lifetime was seized of a 2000 a. tr of land in Mispilan Hund called Fairfields ... by the Kings Road ... and did sell but not convey 500 a. pt/o said tr unto THOMAS FISHER of Suss Co yeoman ... THOMAS FISHER having purch from DAVID ROWE the 500 a. made his will 17 Nov 1713 with these words "I give and bequeath to my dau MARGARET FISHER the now wife of JOSEPH BOOTH Junr of Kent Co yeoman 500 a. which I purch of DAVID ROWE" and soon after dyed ... whereas DAVID ROWE since made his will bearing date 20 Aug 1717 and therein did appoint SUSANNAH ROWE his sole executrix with these words "I do hereby authorize & impower my said executrix to make over ... all lands that I have sold" and soon after dyed ... for 50 pounds paid by THOMAS FISHER in his life time unto DAVID ROWE before his decease and for

10 shillings paid by JOSEPH BOOTH and MARGARET his wife unto SUSANNAH ... SUSANNAH conveys afsd land ... Wit: JOHN STEEL, JOHN CAIN, JOHN MIFFLIN. Ackn 13 Aug 1718. (F:pg 28)

349. 12 Jun 1718. Deed. SUSANNAH ROWE relict & sole executrix of the will of DAVID ROWE late of Kent Co decd ... whereas DAVID ROWE in his lifetime was seized of a 2000 a. tr of land in Mispilan Hund called Fairfields ... did sell but not convey unto THOMAS WHARTON of Phila taylor a pt/o said tr beginning at the corner of THOMAS FISHER's land ... 200 a. ... in consideration of [above] will and 30 pounds paid to DAVID ROWE before his decease and 10 shillings paid to SUSANNAH ... SUSANNAH conveys afsd tr of land unto THOMAS WHARTON ... Wit: JAMES STEEL, JOHN MIFFLIN, JOHN PAIN. 13 Aug 1718. (F:pg 28)

350. 4 May 1720. Deed. JOHN EDMONDS (EDMUNDS) of Kent Co yeoman for 20 pounds sold to MARY ROBINSON of same place ... a tr of land n side of Murther Cr in Motherkill Hund being pt/o a parcell of land called the Dowery which was also pt/o a greater 1600 a. tr called Ousbey ... 100 a. ... Wit: GRIFF JONES, WM RODENEY. Ackn 11 May 1720. (F:pg 29)

351. 13 May 1720. Deed. SAMUEL BROOKS of Kent Co yeoman for 65 pounds sold to JOHN EDMONDS of same place yeoman ... a tr of land whereupon HENRY SMITH now dwells 75 a. (is pt/o a greater tr called Ousbey) ... to the Long Br then along the marshes of Murther Cr ... Wit: WILLIAM NOWELL, JOSEPH NICKERSON, ANDREW CALDWELL. Ackn 13 May --. (F:pg 30)

352. 1 May 1718. Deed. According to an award made by VINCENT EMERSON, THOMAS FISHER & WILLIAM ANNAND arbitrators ... in consideration of DANIEL HUDSON son & heir of ROBERT HUDSON late of Kent Co yeoman decd gives unto JOHN HUDSON of same co yeoman that land in Murtherkill Hund now in the tenure of JOHN HUDSON being pt/o that 800 a. tr called Hudson's Lott ... beginning at the corner of Division Br ... nw side of Hudson's Br ... 300 a. ... Wit: HENRY JOYCE, MOSES FREEMAN. Ackn 12 May 1718. (F:pg 31)

353. 5 Mar 1717. Deed. THOMAS EDMONDSON of Talbot Co MD gentleman & MARY his wife for 22 pounds 10 shillings sold to ISAAC MASON of Kent Co PA ... a tr of land 150 a. now called Masons Lott being pt/o a greater tr formerly laid out for ANIMADAB WRIGHT & afterwards surveyed by RICHARD MITCHELL for JOHN SHARP & sold by him to JOHN EDMONDSON ... s side of Murder Cr on Benester's Br or Mill Cr beginning at the corner of JOHN TRIPIT's land ... to line surveyed for WILLIAM TRIPPET now belonging to WM TRIPET's son

& grandson ... ANDREW CALDWELL atty signs for MARY EDMONDSON ... Wit: ROBERT HOWARD, JOHN HALL Junr, JAMES HOWARD. Ackn 10 Feb 1717. (F:pg 32)

354. 12 Feb 1718/9. Deed. GEORGE MILLS of Kent Co yeoman for 17 pounds sold to HUGH DURBOROW (DURBORROW) of same co surveyor ... a tr of land warrant dated at Phila 8 Sep 1716 unto GEORGE MILLS 200 a. in the forrest and surveyed 18 Mar 1716/7 near northern side of head of sw br of Dover River beginning at the corner by the road that goes from BLACKSAWS to REYNOLDS ... Wit: JOHN BRADSHAW Senr, WILLIAM HAWKEY. Ackn 16 May 1719. (F:pg 33)

355. 6 May 1719. Marriage. These are to certifie that EDWARD PARIS and SUSANAH MOLTON did publish their intentions of marriage ... and did solemnize their marriage ... Wit: EDWARD PARIS, MARK MANLOVE, WATERMAN SIPPLE, JOHN TALLMUM, PETER DUKE, WATERMAN SIPPLE Junr, EBENEZER MANLOVE, SUSANAH PARIS, ADAM FISHER, WILLIAM MANLOVE, RICHARD WILKINS, ABSALOM MANLOVE, MARK MANLOVE, RACHEL MANLOVE, MARY NEEDHAM. (F:pg 33)

356. 9 May 1717/8. Deed. WILLIAM BICKNELL (BIGNAL) of Kent Co shoemaker and JURY his wife for 25 pounds sold to JOHN REGISTOR (REGISTER) of same co carpenter ... a tr of land whereon BIGNAL now dwelleth s side of Dover River being pt/o a greater tr called Brinkloes Range ... 105 a. ... Wit: BEN SHURMER, JOHN EDMUNDS, EDWARD JENNINGS. Ackn 14 Aug 1718. (F:pg 34)

357. 14 Aug 1718. Deed of Release. THOMAS SHARP of Duck Cr Hund Kent Co yeoman sometime ago sold to JOHN POWELL of Duck Cr since decd a tr of land se side of Duck Cr 150 a. now in the tenure of PHINEAS GREENWOOD of Duck Cr same co planter to whom same was since transferred ... for 5 shillings ... THOMAS SHARP releases unto PHINEAS GREENWOOD afsd tr of land ... Wit: JOHN BRINKLOE, A HAMILTON. Ackn 15 Aug 1718. (F:pg 35)

358. 5 Aug 1718. Deed of Gift. JAMES JACKSON of Duck Cr Kent Co yeoman & MARGARET his wife for natural love and affection as well as 10 shillings give to their cousins JAMES SATERFIELD of Duck Cr same co planter & MARY his wife ... a tr of land beginning at Ellinsworth's Br ... 50 a. ... Wit: JOHN HILLYARD, JAMES STEEL. Ackn 15 Aug 1718. (F:pg 36)

359. 12 Aug 1718. Deed. EPHRAIN EMERSON of Kent Co yeoman & MARY his wife sole dau & heir of RICHARD WILSON late of same co

decd for 75 pounds sold to ANDREW HAMILTON of Phila gentleman ... a tr of land now in the tenure of ANDREW HAMILTON being the southern pt/o a larger tr called Whitehall n side of the southernmost br of Duck Cr ... n by the land of CHARLES HILLYARD ... w by the late JAMES GREENWOOD's to the land of Whitewell's Chance ... 414 a. ... tr was confirmed unto JOHN HILLYARD of Kent Co eldest son of JOHN HILLYARD of same co by patent bearing date 10 Oct 1687 ... was vested in RICHARD WILLSON ... Wit: JAMES STEEL, JOHN BRADSHAW, JAMES MORRICE, GRIFF JONES. Ackn 14 Aug 1718. (F:pg 37)

360. 12 Nov 1718. Deed. PHILIP MORGAN & ABRAHAM MORGAN of Talbot Co MD being the surviving legatees of the three grandsons to whom JOHN EDMONDSON late of Talbot Co decd did by his will give unto his three grandsons PHILIP MORGAN, JAMES MORGAN & ABRAHAM MORGAN 800 a. at the head of Murther Cr ... and JAMES MORGAN being decd ... for 15 pounds sold to ANDREW CALDWELL of Kent Co ... a tr of land on Hudsons Br s side of Murder Cr ... to corner of land called Burberrys Berry ... to the division line made for ISAAC MASON ... to corner of HENRY LISENBIE's land ... 400 a. ... Wit: NICHOLAS NICKSON, GEORGE ROBBINSON Junr, DAV MACK QUEEN. Ackn -- -- 1718. (F:pg 38)

361. 13 Nov 1718. Deed. WILLIAM HOWELL of Kent Co planter & JANE his wife for 19 pounds 18 shillings sold to GEORGE LESTER of same co planter ... a tr of land called Lesterfield being pt/o a greater tr called Ricom taken up by pattent by GABRIEL JONES and conveyed by him to ALEXANDER ANTER & from him to his dau the said JANE HOWELL ... n side of Dover River beginning at the corner of JAMES GORDON's land ... to line of said ANTER's land ... to line of JOHN JONES' land ... to line of DICKISON ... to JAMES FITZGERALD's fence ... 25 a. ... Wit: THOMAS PARKE, SIMON HIRONS, JAMES POTTER. Ackn 13 Nov 1718. (F:pg 39)

362. 5 Nov 1718. Deed. JAMES STEEL of Phila yeoman for 25 pounds sold to RICHARD WALKER of Duck Cr Kent Co planter ... a tr of land s side of sw br of Duck Cr bounded on the n with land of SAMUEL WHITEHART on the e with land of THOMAS ELLIT on s with other land of JAMES STEEL and on the w with land of JAMES SATERFIELD ... 120 a. ... Wit: JOHN BRINKLOE, JACOB TAYLOR. Ackn 12 Nov 1718. (F:pg 40)

363. 10 Nov 1718. Deed. SIMON HIRONS of Kent Co in consideration of a tr of land in Little Cr Hund to be made over by JOHN HIRONS ... SIMON sold to JOHN HIRONS of same place ... a tr of land in the forrest on s side of sw br of Duck Cr on the w & nw side of a tr of land

called The Exchange now in the occupation of JOHN HILLYARD adj the plantation which the said SIMON did lately dwell being 400 a. called Hirons Choice ... Wit: RICHARD SMITH, WILLIAM HIRONS. Ackn 12 Nov 1718. (F:pg 41)

364. 10 Nov 1718. Deed. JOHN HIRONS of Kent Co yeoman in consideration of [above] tr of land ... sold to SIMON HIRONS of same place ... a tr of land being one half of the plantation of SIMON HIRONS his father decd & his pt/o land thereunto given him by his fathers will with his pt/o the addition bounded according to pattent & according to ye division line run between him & his brother WILLIAM except 50 a. sold to JOHN HALL ... below the line of JAMES POTTER ... called Brobshays or Sowels Point ... Wit: RICHARD SMITH, WILLIAM HIRONS. Ackn 12 Nov 1718. (F:pg 41)

365. -- Nov 1718. Deed. PHILIP MORGAN & ABRAHAM MORGAN both of Talbot Co MD planters [see #360] for 1500 pounds of tobacco and 5 pounds currant money sold to ROBERT GRUNDY of same co merchant ... a tr of land ... n side of Murder Cr being the greater pt/o a 800 a. tr called New Line ... to the division line of WILLIAM RODENEY's land ... 400 a. ... Wit: NICHOLAS NIXON, GEORGE ROBBISON Junr, DA MACK QUEEN, ANDREW CALDWELL. Ackn 12 Nov 1718. (F:pg 42)

366. 10 Aug 1719. Deed. NICHOLAS NIXON of Murderkill Hund Kent Co smith for 30 shillings sold to JOHN WILLSON of Turrolio in Queen Anne Co MD joyner ... a tr of land warrant dated at Phila 6 Feb 1717/8 granted to said NICHOLAS NIXON 200 a. to be laid out in the forrest on the western side of Black Swamp including a plantation lately made by ALEXANDER WINDFORD ... 200 a. called Willsons Fancy ... Wit: NATHANIEL SMITH, WILLIAM BIRKETT, HUGH DURBOROW. Ackn 13 Nov 1719. (F:pg 43)

367. 10 Nov 1718. Release. WILLIAM HIRONS of Kent Co for 70 pounds release all my rights, title and interest to SIMON HIRONS of same co ... in 200 a. of land ... Wit: RICHARD SMITH, JOHN HIRONS. Ackn 12 Nov 1718. (F:pg 44)

368. 6 Nov 1718. Deed. THOMAS ALLSTON of Little Cr Hund Kent Co yeoman, eldest son of ARTHUR ALLSTON decd, and SARAH his wife for 40 pounds sold to JOHN STOTT of same place yeoman ... a tr of land (being pt/o patent dated at Phila 26 Mar 1684 granted to ARTHUR ALSTON called Chester s side of Western (or sw) Br of Duck Cr ... 800 a. ... ARTHUR ALSTON by deeds and his will sold and gave some parcells of land out of said tr, did also by his will give to his eldest son THOMAS ALLSTON all the remaining pt/o said tr) ... 100 a. ... Wit: HUGH

DURBOROW, JAMES WHITEHEART. Ackn 12 Nov 1718. (F:pg 45)

369. 23 Sep 1718. Deed. ISAAC SEELY marriner legitimate son of MARY SEELY of Great Yarmouth in Great Britain one of the dau & co-heirs of THOMAS ROUSE late of Kent Co decd and atty to HANNAH DENNIS & MARY SEELY both legitimate daus & coheirs of THOMAS ROUSE decd, ABRAHAM TODD, MARY TODD & THOMAS SEELY all of Great Yarmouth in Great Britain for 140 pounds sold to MARK MANLOVE Senr of Kent Co ... a tr of land called Heatherds Adventure n side of Murther Cr near the head ... 300 a. together with 150 a. the one halfe of a tr called Edmonds Chance ... Wit: JNO TOWNSEND, NICHOLAS NIXON. Ackn 9 Nov 1718. (F:pg 46)

370. 11 Nov 1718. Deed. RICHARD WALKER of Little Cr Hund Kent Co yeoman son of JOHN WALKER decd for 25 pounds sold to JAMES WHITEHART (WHITEHEART) of same place yeoman ... (whereas JOHN WALKER in his lifetime was seized of a tr of land s side of sw br of Duck Cr being pt/o a larger tr called Denby Town and in his will bequeathed to his two sons THOMAS WALKER & RICHARD WALKER all his said tr or 100 a. together with plantation to be equally divided between them ...) the afsd tr of land called Walker's Landing ... to corner of land now in possession of ELISHA SNOW ... 50 a. ... Wit: HUGH DURBOROW, THOMAS ALLEN. Ackn 12 -- 1718. (F:pg 48)

371. 6 Nov 1718. Deed. WILLIAM HIRONS & JOHN HIRONS both of Little Cr Hund Kent Co yeoman sons of SIMON HIRONS late of same place decd for 40 pounds sold to JAMES POTTER of same place yeoman ... (whereas SIMON HIRONS in his lifetime was seized of a tr of land called Brulshaw and by his will bequeathed to his sons WILLIAM & JOHN HIRONS all said tr of lands only excepting 50 a. he gave to his wife PERCISS who dying intestate the said 50 a. descended into the possession of the eldest son WILLIAM HIRONS) ... a tr of land beginning at a line where the land called Chip Norton (being the land where THOMAS HUDSON now dwelleth) passeth over the lands called Brulshaw ... 100 a. ... Wit: JOHN CLARK, HUGH DURBOROW. (F:pg 49)

372. 12 Nov 1718. Power of Atty. WILLIAM HIRONS of Kent Co appoint my friend & brother JOHN HIRONS of same place to be my atty to ackn deed of sale in open court for 200 a. and one for 500 a. to SIMON HIRONS ... Wit: JOHN HALL, ANNA HALL. Proved 9 Nov 1718. (F:pg 50)

373. 11 Nov 1718. Deed. JOHN RENNALLS (RENNALS) of Kent Co labourer for 23 pounds sold to WILLIAM TARRING of same co ... a tr of

land being pt/o a larger tr called Dundee s side of Isaacks Br of Dover Cr ... to corner of THOMAS WITHOLL's plantation ... 200 a. ... Wit: RICHARD LEVICK, GEORGE GREEN. Ackn 13 Nov 1718. (F:pg 51)

374. 14 Sep 1718. Deed. HENRY TRACY of Town of Salisbury Kent Co surveyor for 10 pounds sold to EDWARD LOWDER of same co lawyer ... a lott of ground on the head of Duck Cr within or near the Town of Salisbury beginning at the stake upon the edge of High Street ... 6 pence to be paid by the year and every year to the Chief Lords for ever on the 23 Dec ... HENRY TRACY appoint EDWARD CLUFF of same co to be my atty to deliver these presents in open court ... Wit: JOHN PARKER, JOHN PARSON, ABSALOM CUFF. Ackn 12 Nov 1718. (F:pg 52)

375. 10 Feb 1717/8. Deed. JAMES STEEL of Duck Cr Kent Co yeoman for 20 pounds sold to THOMAS ELLET of same place yeoman ... a tr of land s side of sw br of Duck Cr ... by Wilson's Br being also a corner of a tr of land called Denby ... by other land of JAMES STEEL ... 100 a. (granted to JAMES STEEL by warrant bearing date 24 Dec 1716 and surveyed 20 Jan) ... Wit: JOHN FOSTER, LANCELOT LEWIS, NATHANIEL LAMPLUGH. Ackn 12 Nov 1718. (F:pg 54)

376. 13 Dec 1716. JOHN FRENCH of Newcastle Co gentleman surviving executor of the will of WILLIAM MORTON late of Kent Co decd for 32 pounds sold to JOHN FOSTER of Duck Cr Kent Co yeoman ... whereas WILLIAM MORTON in his lifetime was seized of a tr of land s side of sw br of Duck Cr ... bounded on the w with land of ARNANT HENDRICKSON ... on the e with land of RICHARD KING ... 350 a. being pt/o a larger tr, patent bearing date 10 Oct 1687 unto JOHN HILLYARD of Kent Co and vested in WILLIAM MORTON ... Wit: JAMES STEEL, JOHN RUSSELL. Ackn 11 Nov 1718 by RICHARD RICHARDSON & TIMOTHY HANSON attys for JOHN FRENCH. (F:pg 55)

377. 25 Apr 1718. Power of Atty. JOHN FRENCH appoints RICHARD RICHARDSON and TIMOTHY HANSON esqr his attys or either of them to make over the [above] deed in open court ... Wit: BEN SHURMER, GRIFF JONES. (F:pg 56)

378. 1 Oct 1718. Deed. JOHN CLARK of Kent Co yeoman for 50 pounds sold to JOHN HALL late of Summerset Co MD but now of Kent Co bricklayer ... (whereas by virtue of an order of court at St. Jones bearing date 21 Sep 1683 there was surveyed 13 Jan next following unto WILLIAM CLARK of Suss Co gentleman a tr of land called Mount Pleasant n side of Mispillion Cr beginning by the Beaver Dam Br ... by Fishing Br ... 412 a. of land and 88 a. of marsh adj said land were confirmed unto WILLIAM CLARK by patent 26 Mar 1684 ... together

with another tr adj thereunto 600 a. purch of BAPTISTA HERCOMB and made over by WILLIAM CLARK unto GRIFFITH JONES of Phila merchant 13 Sep 1685 recorded by WILLIAM BERRY clerk and likewise conveyed from GRIFFITH JONES unto MARK MANLOVE of Kent Co 10 Sep 1694 from whom it descended unto MATHEW MANLOVE son and executor unto MARK MANLOVE which MATHEW MANLOVE did sell 10 Jun 1701 unto JOHN CLARK 500 a. of the same land) ... JOHN CLARK confirms unto JOHN HALL 500 a. being pt/o afsd tr of 412 a. called Mount Pleasant and also one other tr of land being the remaining pt/o 300 a. which JOHN CLARK bought of ROBERT BETTS, SAMUEL WEBSTER & their wives out of which said CLARK sold 100 a. unto afsd JOHN HALL pt/o the 200 a. ... Wit: ANDREW CALDWELL, ABSALOM CUFF. Ackn 7 Nov 1718. (F:pg 56)

379. 5 Nov 1718. Deed. THOMAS EDMONDSON of Talbot Co MD gentleman (sole surviving heir of his late father JOHN EDMONDSON) and MARY his wife for 12 pounds sold to JOSEPH WORRELL of Kent Co yeoman ... a tr of land patent confirmed unto WILLIAM WILSON late of Kent Co decd called Cambridge n side of sw br of Duck Cr and WILLIAM WILSON by deed bearing date 5 May 1689 sold unto JOHN DUNSTON of Kent Co pt/o tr of land ... 100 a. ... JOHN DUNSTON by his deed bearing date 10 Jun 1690 did convey unto JOHN EDMONDSON late father of the afsd THOMAS 100 a. ... Wit: THOMAS BERRY, ANDREW CALDWELL, JAMES PEMBERTON. 13 Jan 1718 THOMAS EDMONDSON received full consideration of JOSEPH WORRELL. Ackn 12 Feb 1718 by BENJAMIN SHURMER atty for THOMAS EDMONDSON & MARY EDMONDSON. (F:pg 60)

380. 2 Jan 1718. Power of Atty. THOMAS EDMONDSON & MARY EDMONDSON his wife of Talbot Co MD appoint our trusty friend BENJAMIN SHURMER our atty to deliver [above] deed of sale in open court ... Wit: THOMAS BERRY, ANDREW CALDWELL. (F:pg 62)

381. 9 Feb 1718. Mortgage. THOMAS EDMONDSON of Talbott Co MD gentleman and MARY his wife for 273 pounds and for certain other sums of money and tobacco still remaining out, sold to PHILEMON LLOYD of Queen Anne Co MD gentleman ... a tr of land called Flower Field 1200 a., one other tr called Pellton? 1200 a., one other tr called Little Janeway 400 a., one other tr called Great Geneva 600 a. and all other lands whatsoever lying in Kent, New Castle or Suss Cos ... THOMAS EDMONDSON and MARY his wife to pay PHILEMON LLOYD 273 pounds upon 10 Jun 1719 at the dwelling house of PHILEMON LLOYD in Wye River in Queen Ann Co ... if paid this sale will be utterly void ... THOMAS EDMONSON & MARY his wife appoint WILLIAM RODENEY and ANDREW CALDWELL both of Kent Co gentlemen to be their attys to ackn this

deed in open court ... Wit: JOHN BERRY, JOHN HACKER. THOMAS EDMONDSON received 273 pounds being pt/o consideration mentioned. Ackn 13 Feb. 1718. (F:pg 62)

382. 10 Feb 1718. Deed of Gift. JOSEPH WORRELL of Duck Cr Kent Co for love goodwill and affection give to my dear and well beloved son JOHN WORRELL ... 700 a. (n side of sw br of Duck Cr 500 a. being half pt/o a tr called Berry Field formerly granted unto one FRANCIS WHITWELL and by several persons transferred untill I came to be legally possessed, also 200 a. w of Berry Field) ... JOHN WORRELL is to pay all the arrears rent due upon the 700 a. ... Wit: MATHEW MORGAN, JOHN BRADSHAW Senr, PHINEAS GREENWOOD. Ackn 12 Feb 1718. (F:pg 64)

383. 10 Feb 1718. Deed of Gift. JOSEPH WORRELL of Duck Cr Kent Co for love good will and affection give to my well beloved son JAMES WORRELL ... 400 a. being one halfe pt/o the 800 a. tr of land I now dwell upon n side of sw br of Duck Cr ... JAMES WORRELL to pay all the arrears rent due and payable upon the land ... Wit: MATHEW MORGAN, PHINEAS GREENWOOD, JNO BRADSHAW Senr. Ackn 12 Feb 1718. (F:pg 65)

384. 10 Feb 1718. Deed. JOHN CLIFFORD (CLIFORD) of Kent Co yeoman (son and heir of THOMAS CLIFFORD late of same co decd) and ANN his wife for 26 pounds sold to BENJAMIN BARRET of Little Cr same co taylor ... a tr of land called Simsons Choice n side of Little Cr (404 a. patent bearing date 25 Mar 1676 granted by Sir EDMOND ANDROSS then Governor of NY under his Royall Higness JAMES DUKE of York unto WILLIAM SIMSON) ... pt/o which tr of land 50 a. was conveyed late in the tenure of THOMAS CLIFFORD decd unto JOHN CLIFFORD ... bounded by the land of ANDREW HAMILTON to the w and the land where BENJAMIN BARRET dwelleth to the e ... afsd 50 a. ... Wit: JOHN BRADSHAW Senr, GRIFFITH JONES. Ackn 12 Feb 1718. (F:pg 66)

385. 9 Dec 1718. Deed. THOMAS EDMONDSON of Talbot Co MD gentleman & MARY his wife ... whereas by an act of assembly made at Annapolis MD 11 Nov 1709 THOMAS EDMONDSON was impowered to sell the lands left in the will of his deceased father JOHN EDMONDSON for payment of his debts ... for 200 pounds sold to ROBERT GRUNDY of same place merchant ... all the lands, plantations, tenements within the bounds of the cos of New Castle, Kent and Suss ... belonging to THOMAS EDMONDSON as surviving executor of his late decd father JOHN EDMONDSON ... Wit: JOHN BUTTEN, THOMAS BERRY, DAV MACKQUEEN. Ackn 11 Feb 1718 by RICHARD RICHARDSON & TIMOTHY

HANSON attys for THOMAS EDMONDSON & MARY EDMONDSON. (F:pg 68)

386. 13 Jan 1718. Power of Atty. THOMAS EDMONDSON & MARY his wife of Talbot Co MD appoint our trusty friends RICHARD RICHARDSON & TIMOTHY HANSON esqr our attys to ackn & deliver [above] deed in open court ... Wit: THOMAS BERRY, DAVE MACK QUEEN. (F:pg 70)

387. 10 Dec 1718. Deed. ROBERT GRUNDY of Talbot Co MD merchant ... whereas THOMAS EDMONDSON of same place gentleman & MARY his wife by deed of sale 9 Dec 1718 did convey unto ROBERT GRUNDEY the lands belonging unto THOMAS EDMONDSON as he is surviving executor of his late decd father JOHN EDMONDSON anywhere bounded within the limits of the cos of Kent, New Castle & Suss ... for 100 pounds sold to THOMAS EDMONSON half pt/o all afsd lands ... Wit: JOHN BUTTEN, THOMAS BERRY, DAV MACK-QUEEN. (F:pg 70)

388. 12 Jan 1718. Power of Atty. ROBERT GRUNDY of Talbot Co MD merchant appoint my trusty friends THOMAS FRENCH esqr and EDWARD JENNINGS of Kent Co to be my attys to ackn and deliver [above] deed in open court ... Wit: THOMAS BERRY, DAV MAC-QUEEN. Ackn 12 Jan 1718 by THOMAS FRENCH & EDWARD JENNINGS attys for ROBERT GRUNDY. (F:pg 72)

389. 6 Feb 1718. Deed. JOHN HILLYARD of Kent Co for 24 pounds sold to EVAN JONES of same co esqr ... a tr of land [page torn] e side of Hillyard's Br ... br between [?] and SIMON HIRONS ... 75 a. being pt/o a greater tr called The Exchange being the sw pt/o that tr ... Wit: WILLIAM FORBES, JOHN PAIN, GEORGE MARTIN. Ackn 10 Aug 1718 by CHARLES HILLYARD atty for JOHN HILLYARD. (F:pg 73)

390. 6 Feb 1718. Power of Atty. JOHN HILLYARD of Kent Co appoint my well beloved friend & brother CHARLES HILLYARD of same co to be my atty to ackn and make over the [above] deed in open court ... Wit: JOHN PAIN, GEORGE MARTIN. (F:pg 75)

391. 1 May 1719. Deed. JEREMIAH NICKOLDSON of Kent Co yeoman sold for 8 pounds to JOHN NEWIL of same place yeoman ... a tr of marsh land n side of Murther Cr ... 13 a. being half pt/o a 26 a. tr of marsh granted by the commissioners of property unto RANDALL DONOVAN and he did sell unto JEREMIAH NICKOLDSON ... Wit: WILLIAM RODENEY, ARTHUR BROOKE. Ackn 13 Nov 1719. (F:pg 75)

392. 15 May 1719. Deed. BENJAMIN SHURMER of Kent Co esqr for 3

pounds sold to HUGH DURBOROW surveyor of same co ... a tr of land ... n side of Dover River called Canterbury ... 50 a. ... Wit: WM RODENEY, THOMAS CRAWFORD. Ackn 16 May 1719. (F:pg 77)

393. 12 May 1719. Deed. ZACHARIAH GOFORTH of Kent Co yeoman for 80 pounds sold to MATHEW MANLOVE of same place ... a tr of land being pt/o a tr called Kickmans Worth se side of Murther Cr ... to corner of GEORGE ROBINSON's land ... 96 a. purch from ABRAHAM SKIDMORE ... Wit: THOMAS FRENCH, THOMAS CRAWFORD. Ackn 13 May 1719. (F:pg 77)

394. 10 May 1719. Deed. HENRY SMITH of Kent Co blacksmith & SARAH his wife for 120 pounds sold to SAMUEL BROOK of same place ... a tr of land 75 a. (which SAMUEL BROOK sold unto HENRY SMITH 1 Feb 1717) ... Wit: WILLIAM NEVIL, JOSEPH NICKERSON, ANDREW CALDWELL. Ackn 13 May 1719. (F:pg 79)

395. 13 May 1719. Deed. ANDREW CALDWELL of Kent Co for 8 pounds sold to CHRISTOPHER NUGAN planter ... a tr of land (warrant dated at Phila 10 Oct 1714 granted unto ANDREW CALDWELL 500 a. surveyed 24 Jun 1716 ... bounded by WILLIAM WILLSON's land ... to line of PHILIP CARNY's land) ... 100 a. ... Wit: WM BRINCKLE, MARK MANLOVE. Ackn 13 May 1719. (F:pg 80)

396. 20 May 1719. Deed. SAMUEL GREENWOOD of Little Cr Hund Kent Co planter for 3 pounds 9 shillings sold to BENJAMIN SHURMER clerk of same co ... a parcell of land lying within the Town of Dover beginning at the ne corner of a street near a parcel of land lately granted to JOHN MIFFLIN but now in the tenure of BENJAMIN SHURMER ... in the line of land called Lissen or DAVID MORGAN's calf pasture ... 15 8/10 a. was granted unto SAMUEL GREENWOOD 7 Aug 1718 under the hands of BENJAMIN SHURMER, WILLIAM BRINCKLE & RICHARD RICHARDSON gentlemen authorized & appointed by act of assembly to lay out and grant the same ... Wit: ABSALOM CUFF, GRIFF JONES. Ackn 22 May 1721. (F:pg 81)

397. 20 May 1719. Deed. ABSALOM CUFF of Duck Cr Kent Co planter for 3 pounds 9 shillings sold to BENJAMIN SHURMER clerk of same co ... a lott of land being within the Town of Dover beginning at the se corner of the street near a parcell granted unto JOHN MIFFLIN but now in the tenure of BENJAMIN SHURMER ... by the line of EPHRAIM EMERSON's land ... 13 8/10 a. same as granted to ABSALOM CUFF by deed 7 Aug 1718 by BENJAMIN SHURMER, WILLIAM BRINKLE & RICHARD RICHARDSON gentlemen authorized by act of assembly to lay out and grant the same ... Wit: GRIFF JONES, SAMUEL GREENWOOD.

Ackn 22 May 1719. (F:pg 82)

398. 13 May 1718. Deed. BENJAMIN SHURMER and RICHARD RICHARDSON of Kent Co gentlemen for 16 pounds sold to JOHN MIFFLIN late of Phila but now of Kent Co ... (by an act of assembly 1717 impowered on behalf of the inhabitants to survey and layout lotts and make sale of a tr of land adj the courthouse called the town of Dover formerly purch by the inhabitants of RICHARD WILLSON who bought the same of WILLIAM SOUTHBY to whome it came conveyed by deed of sale from JOHN WALKER all of same co 500 a. being pt/o a tr of 800 a. called Brother's Portion originally taken up by said WALKER by virtue of a warrant from the court of St. Jones granted to FRANCIS WHITWELL in his behalfe) ... beginning at the nw corner of EPHRAIM EMMERSON's land ... to corner of DAVID MORGAN's calf pasture late in the possession of WILLIAM ANNAN decd ... 69 a. ... Wit: TIMOTHY HANSON, WATERMAN SIPPLE, SIMON HIRONS. Ackn 14 May 1718. (F:pg 84)

399. 1 Aug 1718. Deed. MOSES BROOKS late of Kent Co PA carpenter but now of Queen Anns Co MD & ELIONER his wife for 55 pounds sold to THOMAS MACKELANY of Kent Co planter ... a tr of land called Hudsons Lott nw side of Hudsons Br of Murtherkill ... 100 a. ... Wit: VINCENT EMERSON, JONATHAN STURGIS. Ackn 13 Aug 1619. (F:pg 86)

400. 8 May 1719. Power of Atty. MOSES BROOKS and ELIONER my wife both of Queen Anns Co MD appoint my well beloved and trusty friend GRIFFEN JONES of Kent Co my atty to convey [above] deed of sale in open court ... Wit: JAMES GOULD, JONATHAN STURGIS. (F:pg 87)

401. 12 Aug 1719. Deed. JOHN KILLINGSWORTH eldest son and heir of EDWARD KILLINGSWORTH decd of Kent Co yeoman for 35 pounds sold to LUKE MANLOVE yeoman of same place ... 100 a. being pt/o a tr of land formerly laid out for JOHN WALKER and pt/o a tr of land formerly laid out for RICHARD WILLIAMS s side of Murtherkill Cr formerly sould unto afsd EDWARD KILLINGSWORTH 10 Feb 1687 ... Wit: SAMUEL BROOKE, MARK MANLOVE Senr. Ackn 13 Aug 1719. (F:pg 87)

402. 12 Nov 1719. Deed. WILLIAM WINSMORE of Kent Co yeoman for 33 pounds sold to JAMES GORDON of same place yeoman ... pt/o a tr of land called Great Pipe Elm s side of Little Cr ... bounded by land formerly laid out for HENRY AMOS ... 100 a. ... Wit: BEN SHURMER, RICHARD RICHARDSON. Ackn 17 Nov 1719. (F:pg 89)

403. 16 Nov 1719. Deed. WILLIAM WINSMORE of St. Jones Hund Kent Co yeoman son of WILLIAM WINSMORE of same co decd & grandson of WILLIAM WINSMORE the elder also of same co decd for 33 pounds sold to HENRY AMOS of same place planter ... whereas WILLIAM WINSMORE ye grandfather in his life time by virtue of a pattent dated - - -- 1680 became seized of a tr of land called Great Pipe Elm in St. Jones Hund bounded to the n by Little Cr and by his will bequeathed the greater pt/o said land to his son WILLIAM WINSMORE for and during his natural life & after his decease it descended to WILLIAM WINSMORE the grandson ... 50 a. ... Wit: HUGH DURBOROW, JAMES GORDON. Ackn 17 Nov 1721. (F:pg 90)

404. 14 Nov 1719. Deed. WILLIAM WINSMORE of Jones Hund Kent Co son of WILLIAM WINSMORE late of same co decd and grandson of WILLIAM WINSMORE ye elder also of same co decd for 33 pounds sold to ENEAS MAHAN of same place planter ... whereas [same as above] ... 100 a. Wit: HUGH DURBOROW, JOSEPH ASTON. Ackn 17 Nov 1719. (F:pg 92)

405. 9 Feb 1719. Deed. JOHN MIFFLIN of Kent Co yeoman & SARAH his wife for 16 pounds sold to BENJAMIN SHURMER prothonotary of same co ... a lott of land [same as #396] ... 69 a. ... Wit: GRIFF JONES, RICHARD RICHARDSON, THOMAS WARD. Ackn 10 Feb 1721. (F:pg 94)

406. 1 Feb 1719. Deed. WILLIAM WILLIAMS of Kent Co yeoman for 60 pounds sold to REYNOR WILLIAMS of same place yeoman ... a tr of land in Mispillion Hund pt/o a tr called Bridge Town 650 a. nw side of Mispillion Cr between Swan Cr and Gooseberry Br ... now in possession of WILLIAM LEDGAR ... Wit: THOMAS SKIDMORE, WM RODENEY. Ackn 11 Feb 1721. (F:pg 95)

407. 1 Feb 1719. Deed. WILLIAM RODENEY of Kent Co yeoman for 125 pounds sold to WILLIAM WALTON of Suss Co yeoman ... a tr of land being pt/o a greater tr called Hudsons Lott w side of Division Br ... 300 a. ... Wit: REYNEAR WILLIAMS, THOMAS SKIDMORE. Ackn 11 Feb 1721. (F:pg 97)

408. 10 Feb 1719/20. Deed. MICHAEL LOWBAR of Kent Co for a valuable consideration in hand paid sold to ANDREW CALDWELL ... a tr of land 400 a. being first due unto DANIEL RUTTEY of same co by virtue of a warrant granted unto him bearing date 22 Feb 1681/2 executed on 29 Feb ... w side of Island Br of Murther Cr ... DANIEL RUTTEY sold unto MICHAEL LOWBAR by deed of sale bearing date 15 Nov 1717 ... one halfe of afsd tr of land ... Wit: TIMOTHY HANSON,

EDWARD RUTLEDGE, DAVID MACKQUEEN. Ackn 13 Feb 1719. (F:pg 98)

409. 11 May 1720. Deed. ISAAC MASON of Kent Co for 23 pounds sold to WILLIAM TRIPPET of same place ... a tr of land which was made over to ISAAC MASON by THOMAS EDMONDSON & MARY his wife 5 Nov 1717 s side of Murther Cr beginning at the corner of JOHN TRIPIT's land ... to line of tr formerly surveyed for WILLIAM TRIPPET Senr but now decd ... 150 a. being pt/o a 500 a. tr called Rights Lott ... Wit: SAMUEL BROOKE, JOHN MIFFLIN, ANDREW CALDWELL. 13 May 1720. (F:pg 99)

410. 30 Nov 1718. Deed. JOSEPH BOOTH of Murderkill Hund Kent Co yeoman & ELINOR his wife for 11 shillings sold to RICHARD UNDERWOOD of Mispillion Hund same co ... a tr of land patent bearing date 26 Feb 1716/7 granted unto JOSEPH BOOTH 200 a. surveyed 10 Apr 1718 n side of Pemberton's Br ... se side of the present dwelling of RICHARD UNDERWOOD ... Wit: HUGH DURBOROW, DANIEL RODENEY. Ackn 11 May 1720. (F:pg 100)

411. 10 Nov 1719. Deed. ELISHA SNOW of Duck Cr Hund Kent Co yeoman for 25 pounds sold to ARTHUR ALSTON of Little Cr Hund yeoman ... a tr of land n side of sw br of Duck Cr beginning at the corner of land called Walker's Landing also the corner of land now in the possession of JAMES WHITEHART ... 53 a. being pt/o land formerly granted by patent to THOMAS WILSON decd and has descended into the possession of ELISHA SNOW by an indenture by THOMAS WALTER 6 Feb 1716 ... Wit: THOMAS BERRY, HUGH DURBOROW. Ackn 11 May 1720. (F:pg 101)

412. 6 May 1720. Lease. JAMES STEEL of Phila gentleman & MARTHA his wife for 10 shillings lease to JOHN CURTIS of same city mariner for one full year ... a tr of land, patent under the hands of RICHARD HILL, ISAAC MORRIS and JAMES LOGAN commissioners bearing date of 25 Mar 1717 granted unto JAMES STEEL ... n side of Murther Cr which divides this from the land of JOHN EDMONDS ... 440 a. ... Wit: ANDREW HAMILTON, JOHN BETTLE. Ackn 13 May 1721. (F:pg 102)

413. 7 May 1720. Deed. JAMES STEEL of Phila gentleman & MARTHA his wife for 160 pounds sold to JOHN CURTIS of same city mariner ... a tr of land [same as above] ... Wit: ANDREW HAMILTON, JOHN BEETLE. Ackn 13 May 1721. (F:pg 103)

414. 5 Nov 1719. Deed. JAMES STEEL of Phila gentleman & MARTHA his wife for 110 pounds sold to WILLIAM HAWKEY of Duck Cr Kent Co

yeoman ... several parcells of land, one patent bearing date 8 May 1714 granted unto JAMES STEEL n side of sw br of Duck Cr 135 a. ... and by virtue of a warrant 14 Apr 1718 there was surveyed and laid out for JAMES STEEL a parcel of land by Dawson's Br 45 a. and by indenture 15 Feb 1715/6 WILLIAM HAWKEY did convey unto JAMES STEEL a parcel of land 11 a. ... to corner of other land of JAMES STEEL & THOMAS SHARP ... to line of a tr called Coventry ... by Dawson's Br 150 a. ... Wit: ANDREW HAMILTON, JOHN BOOTH. Ackn 11 May 1720. (F:pg 105)

415. 9 May 1720. Lease. JAMES STEEL of Phila gentleman for 5 shillings lease to SAMUEL HANSON of Kent Co carpenter ... a tr of land s side of sw br of Duck Cr beginning at the line of JOHN FOSTER's land ... to line of the land late of JOHN KELLY ... to Wilson's Br ... 325 a. ... for one year ... Wit: GEORGE FITZWATER, HUGH DURBOROW Junr. Ackn 11 May 1721. (F:pg 107)

416. 10 May 1720. Deed. JAMES STEEL of Phila gentleman for 105 pounds sold to SAMUEL HANSON of Kent Co carpenter 325 a. [same as above] ... a tr of land patent bearing date 4 May 1715 granted unto JAMES JACKSON of Kent Co yeoman & MARGARET his wife s side of sw br of Duck Cr 750 a. ... by indenture bearing date 5 Feb 1717 JAMES JACKSON & MARGARET his wife sold unto JAMES STEEL afsd 750 a. ... some parcels thereof granted to other persons ... by a deed of SAMUEL MANLOVE & ELIZABETH his wife [date blank] did grant unto JAMES STEEL 140 a. pt/o the afsd 750 a. being one of the parcells sold ... Wit: GEORGE FITZWATER, HUGH DURBOROW Junr. Ackn 11 May 1720. (F:pg 108)

417. 10 Aug 1720. Deed. ALEXANDER WINDFORD late of Kent Co yeoman for 20 pounds sold to JOHN SHEPHERD of White Marsh in Dosset Co MD yeoman ... a tr of land adj the Black Swamp called Windford's Design ... to the line of MOSES WHITATEE's land ... 500 a. surveyed 4 Nov 1718 ... ALEXANDER WINDFORD appoints his trusty friend ANDREW CALDWELL to be his atty to ackn afsd deed in open court ... Wit: HUGH DURBOROW Junr, SARAH DURBOROW. Ackn 12 Aug 1720. (F:pg 110)

418. 8 Aug 1720. Deed of Gift. JOHN HILLYARD Senr of Duck Cr Kent Co for love, goodwill and affections I have for my well beloved dau ELIZABETH the now wife of ARTHUR COOK ... give to ARTHUR COOK and ELIZABETH his wife ... a tr of land being pt/o a greater tr called The Exchange s side of sw br of Duck Cr beginning at Hillyard's Br ... it intersect with the land which I gave to my grandson JOHN HILLYARD ... it intersects with land of EVAN JONES ... 220 a. ... Wit:

JOHN BRADSHAW Senr, GEORGE MARTIN. Ackn 10 Aug 1721. (F:pg 111)

419. 10 Aug 1720. Deed. MOSES FREEMAN (adminr of the goods, chattels, rights & credits which were belonging to MARGARET BISHOP late of Kent Co decd) for 38 pounds sold to OWEN GARVEY of same place yeoman ... a tr of land s side of one of the forks of Murther Cr called Mill Cr ... to line of BENJAMIN RENNALS land ... 100 a. ... Wit: MATHEW MANLOVE, JAMES HOWARD. Ackn 11 Aug 1721. (F:pg 112)

420. 5 Aug 1720. Deed. RICHARD LEVICK of Kent Co yeoman for 105 pounds sold to CHARLES MARAM of same place carpenter ... a parcell of land called Cardiff n side of Little Cr adj to the lands now belonging to SIMON HIRONS, ABRAHAM FIELDS, JOHN MORGAN & JOHN PLEASANTINE severally being pt/o a greater tr called York formerly in the tenure of WILLIAM STEVENS then of JOHN RICHARDSON and lately of said RICHARD LEVICK but now in the occupation of EVAN JONES plasterer ... 200 a. ... Wit: BEN SHURMER, WM RODENEY. Ackn 12 Aug 1721. (F:pg 113)

421. 10 Aug 1720. Deed. CHARLES MARAM (MARIM) of Kent Co carpenter for 110 pounds sold to EVAN JONES of same place carpenter ... [above] tr of land ... Wit: BEN SHURMER, WM RODENEY. Ackn 12 Aug 1721. (F:pg 114)

422. 28 Jan 1719. Deed. JAMES PORTER of Phila carpenter for 65 pounds sold to EVAN JONES of Kent Co plasterer ... a tr of land near the western br of Duck Cr ... to Freeman's Br ... bounding upon lands of WILLIAM REYNOLDS ... 200 a. pt/o 400 a. patent granted 26 Mar 1684 unto JOHN COLLIER who by indenture of sale 15 Jul 1684 conveyed unto JOHN RENNALS who dying lawfully seized in the said land, his son & heir WILLIAM REYNOLDS by deed 11 Oct 1704 unto EDWARD WILLIAMS, and JAMES PORTER by deed 20 Apr 1705 purch from EDWARD WILLIAMS ... Wit: JNO CADWALDER, MARY SHEPARD, SAMUEL SHEPARD. Ackn 10 Aug 1721 by EVAN JONES atty for JAMES PORTER. (F:pg 115)

423. 28 Jan 1719. Power of Atty. JAMES PORTER appoints EVAN JONES of Kent Co gentleman my atty to ackn [above] deed ... Wit: MARY SHEPARD, SAMUEL SHEPARD, JNO CADWALDER, EVAN JONES, THOMAS SHARP. (F:pg 117)

424. 9 Aug 1720. Deed. Whereas WILLIAM MANLOVE by virtue of certain goods conveyance to him made and executed in open Court of Common Pleas 15 Aug 1716 by EPHRAIM EMERSON of Kent Co &

MARY his wife became lawfully seized in a tr of land in Little Cr Hund adj to the n side of Muddy Br 300 a. ... corner of land late in the possession of JOHN HALL called Content ... said WILLIAM MANLOVE of Little Cr Hund same co yeoman & SUSANNAH his wife for 29 pounds sold 100 a. of land to ALEXANDER HUMPHRYS of same place yeoman ... Wit: HUGH DURBOROW Junr, MARY FREEMAN. Ackn 12 Aug 1720. (F:pg 118)

425. 10 Aug 1720. Deed. JOHN STEVENS of Kent Co yeoman & ELIZABETH his wife for 83 pounds sold to JOHN RENALDS & JOHN MARAM of same place gentlemen ... a tr of land in Dover Hund nw side of Pipe Elm Br ... all the land that lyes between JOHN MARAM's line and DAVID FRENCH's ... Wit: ISAAC SNOW, ABRAHAM BROOK. Ackn 10 Nov 1720. (F:pg 119)

426. -- Aug 1720. Deed. BENJAMIN RENNALLS of Kent Co planter for 25 pounds sold to JOHN NEWILL of same place yeoman ... a tr of land n side of Service Br of Murther Cr ... 50 a. being pt/o a tr formerly taken up by NICHOLAS BARRET called Barretts Lott ... Wit: BENJAMIN SHURMER, MARK BARDON. Ackn 9 Nov 1720. (F:pg 120)

427. 15 May 1719. Deed. SAMUEL MANLOVE of Dover Hund Kent Co yeoman for 1 pound 3 shillings sold to JAMES PHILIPS same place labourer ... a tr of land warrant dated 10 Sep 1718 granted unto SAMUEL MANLOVE, 150 a. in the forest surveyed 30 Mar 1719 in the fork of the head of Dover River between the plantation of said SAMUEL MANLOVE and FLETCHER PAIN ... Wit: THOMAS BERRY, HUGH DURBOROW Junr. Ackn 11 Nov 1720. (F:pg 121)

428. 8 Aug 1720. Deed. GEORGE GREEN of Little Cr Hund Kent Co yeoman for 6 pounds sold to THOMAS BERRY of Murderkill Hund yeoman ... a tr of land warrant dated -- May 1718 granted unto GEORGE GREEN, 200 a. surveyed 5 May 1718 in the forrest n side of the main marsh ... below the present dwelling plantation of CHARLES MARAM ... Wit: HUGH DUBOROW Junr, JOSEPH BOOTH Junr. Ackn 12 Nov 1720. (F:pg 122)

429. 10 May 1720. Deed. JAMES PHILIPS of Dover Hund Kent Co labourer for 10 pounds sold to FLETCHER PAIN of same place weaver ... a tr of land [same as #425] ... Wit: HUGH DURBOROW Junr, JOHN REYNALLS. Ackn 12 Nov 1720. (F:pg 123)

430. 11 Nov 1720. Deed. ROBERT GORDON of town & co of New Castle gentleman for 30 pounds sold to JONATHAN STURGIS of Kent Co yeoman ... a tr of land being pt/o a larger tr called Aberdeen beginning

near a piece of land lately belonging to ROBERT FRENCH decd ... near JONATHAN STURGIS fence ... 105 a. ... Wit: PHIL KEARNY, BEN SHURMER. Ackn 11 Nov 1720. (F:pg 124)

431. 11 Aug 1719. Deed. Whereas RICHARD WHITEHART in his lifetime became seized of a parcell of land s side of sw br of Duck Cr by a deed of sale to him 10 Jun 1701 and sometime before his death did give and bequeath said land to be equally divided amongst his children as by his will dated 11 Oct 1701 ... whereas some of his children did sell their share unto their brother RICHARD WHITEHART ... RICHARD WHITEHART, SAMUEL WHITEHART & JAMES WHITEHART all of Little Cr Hund Kent Co yeomen, sons of RICHARD WHITEHART decd for 10 pounds sold to ARTHUR ALSTON yeoman ... afsd tr of land beginning at the corner of JOHN WALKER decd ... to land where said RICHARD WHITEHART now dwelleth ... 40 a. ... Wit: ISAAC SNOW, HUGH DURBOROW Junr. Ackn 11 Nov 1720. (F:pg 125)

432. 31 May 1720. Receipt. MARY CROSLEY received of JOHN REGISTER a cow and calf being full satisfaction for all debts, dues & demands ... Wit: ANDREW CALDWELL, THOMAS FOLKS. (F:pg 126)

433. 30 May 1720. Deed. FRANCIS HIRONS, SIMON HIRONS & ROBERT HIRONS of Kent Co yeomen for 8 pounds sold to DAVID MORGAN of same place yeoman ... a tr of land adj to the w side of land and plantation of said DAVID MORGAN being pt/o a tr called Mount Pleasant beginning at the corner of said DAVID's land which he late bought of JOSHUA CLAYTON ... to JAMES POTTER's land ... to land called Bradshaw ... 30 a. ... Wit: THOMAS BERRY, BEN BARRATT. Ackn 12 Nov 1720. (F:pg 127)

434. 5 May 1720. Deed. FRANCIS HIRONS, SIMON HIRONS & ROBERT HIRONS of Kent Co yeoman for 50 pounds sold to RALPH NEEDHAM of same place planter ... a tr of land in Little Cr Hund pt/o a tr called Mount Pleasant ... bounded by land called Highams Trace in the possession of JOSHUA CLAYTON ... corner of DAVID MORGAN's land ... to tr of land called Bradshaw ... w to land called Chippanorton ... [page torn] ... Wit: THOMAS BERRY, BEN BARRETT. Ackn 12 Nov 1720. (F:pg 128)

435. 10 May 1720. Deed. FRANCIS HIRONS, SIMON HIRONS & ROBERT HIRONS of Little Cr Hund Kent Co yeomen for 22 pounds sold to JOSHUA CLAYTON of same place gentleman ... a tr of land patent dated at Phila 25 Feb 1691/2 unto FRANCIS HIRONS, SIMON HIRONS & ROBERT HIRONS (& ELIZABETH HIRONS was without issue decd) called Mount Pleasant in Little Cr Hund between land called Highams &

Chippanorton ... w side of RALPH NEEDHAM's land ... 130 a. ... Wit:
THOMAS BERRY, BEN BARRATT. Ackn 12 Nov 1720. (F:pg 129)

436. 12 Nov 1720. Power of Atty. ROBERT HIRONS of Little Cr Hund
Kent Co yeoman appoint my trusty friend HUGH DURBOROW of same
co my atty to ackn [above] three deeds of sale in open court ... Wit:
THOMAS BERRY, BENJAMIN BARRET. Proved 12 Nov 1720. (F:pg
130)

437. 8 Aug 1720. Deed. JOHN HALL of Little Cr Hund Kent Co and
ANNAH his wife for 80 pounds sold to THOMAS LEATHERBURY of
same place bricklayer ... a tr of land (patent dated 26 Feb 1684 granted
unto EVAN DAVIS 410 a.) called Content s side of sw br of Duck Cr 210
a. ... whereas WILLIAM DAVIS by a deed did convey land to WILLIAM
JACOCK and WILLIAM JACOCK did convey to ZODIACK HALL brother
to JOHN HALL ... ZODIACK HALL dying intestate the land descended
into possession of said JOHN HALL & ANNAH his wife ... (JOHN HALL
sold pt/o afsd land unto SAMUEL LEWIS decd) ... Wit: THOMAS
BERRY, HUGH DURBORROW Junr. Ackn 11 Nov 1720. (F:pg 130)

438. 1 Mar 1714. Articles of Agreement. WILLIAM DONNE, TRON
MONGER, CHARLES HARFORD, EDWARD LLOYD, ABRAHAM
LLOYD, RICHYATE COOLE, merchants, CALEB LLOYD, grocer, and
GEORGE WHITEHEAD, tobacconist, all of the City of Bristol ... whereas
the parties afsd together with several other persons have agreed and are
copartners, adventurers and joynt traders in the transportation of
workmen and servants into America for ye planting, propagating, dressing
and importing of hemp and other things ... SOLOMON DESSEY
[WESSEY?] of the parish of Belton in the Isle of Acoline in the co of
Lincoln yeoman hath agreed he will serve the said committee (as their
agent) in American for the tenure of four whole years ... committee to
provide for him necessary meat, drink, washing and lodging and pay to
him the yearly sum of 20 pounds the first year, 25 pounds second year,
30 pounds third year, 35 pounds fourth year, to be paid quarterly ... Wit:
NA CARELES, JO CHAPPELL. (F:pg 133)

439. 25 Mar 1720. Appointments. JASPER YEATS, JOSEPH WOOD,
JOHN BRINKLOE, JAMES STEEL, JONATHAN BAYLY & RICHARD
HINMAN esqr appointed justices of our Supream Court in cos of New
Castle, Kent and Suss ... (signed) WILLIAM KEITH. (F:pg 134)

440. 5 Mar 1720. ROWLAND FITZGARALD of New Castle, GRIFITH
JONES of Kent Co & PRESERVED COGESHALL of Suss Co or any of
them ... to administer unto [above] justices the several oaths & other
qualifications required ... (signed) WILLIAM KEITH. (F:pg 134)

441. 11 Mar 1717. Bond. DANIEL RODENEY and WILLIAM RODENEY of Kent Co yeomen are bound and indebted unto GEORGE NOWELL of same place gentleman in the sum of 660 pounds ... due unto GEORGE RODENEY, CALEB RODENEY and SARAH RODENEY legatees of WILLIAM RODENEY late of Kent Co decd gentlemen 330 pounds being their full dividends which have come to the possession of GEORGE NOWELL and SARAH his wife executors of the will of WILLIAM RODENEY decd ... DANIEL RODENEY have indemnify the said GEORGE NOWELL ... Wit: JAMES TUE?, HENRY JOYCE. (F:pg 135)

Deed Record F Vol 2 Pt 2

442. 11 Sep 1699. Deed. WILLIAM RODENEY of Kent Co PA and WILLIAM MORTON of same co joyntly bought of JOHN and WILLIAM STEVENS of Dorchester Co MD planters sons of JOHN STEVENS of Dorchester Co MD decd a tr of land called London n side of Little Cr ... to corner of land called Sympsons Choyce ... to the line of land lately belonging to WM STEVENS of Talbot Co MD ... to corner of land of JOHN RICHARDSON ... to corner of the land late of WILLIAM FREEMAN decd 1300 a. for 300 pounds ... WILLIAM RODENEY and WILLIAM MORTON agree to divide afsd land ... WILLIAM MORTON to have land adj SAMUELL BERRY's land 600 a. more or less now called St. Andrews ... WILLIAM RODENEY to have land adj WM FREELAND decd and STEPHEN PARADDEE ... 600 a. more or less now called Tiverton ... Wit: THOMAS BEDWELL, EVAN JONES. (F:pg 1)

443. 9 Feb 1698/9. Power of Atty. ELIZABETH CLEMISON of Phila widow and sole adminr of the estate of MATHEW CLEMISON my last husband decd ... appoint my loving friend THOMAS BEDWELL of Kent Co my atty to demand and receive of all persons whatsoever all summs of money due me ... Wit: WILLIAM ALLEWAY, JNO PRSONSS, ELSTON WALLIS. Proved by JAMES FOX justice. (F:pg 3)

444. 10 Feb 1699. Deed. THOMAS EVERETT of Kent Co PA for 50 pounds sold to JOHN EVANS of same co ... a tr of land pt/o a tr called Northampton in a fork of the Little Cr ... to corner of JOHN NICKELSON's land ... to corner of JOHN EVENS his land ... 50 a. ... called Thomas His Lott ... Wit: JOHN CLAYTON, JACOB SMITH, JAMES POTTER. Ackn 12 Mar 1699. (F:pg 4)

445. 10 Feb 1699. Deed. WILLIAM MORTON of Kent Co for 100 pounds sold to JOHN NICKOLSON of same co ... a tr of land pt/o a tr called Northampton in a fork of the Little Cr ... to corner of GEORGE MORGAN's land ... 100 a. ... Wit: JOHN EVENS, JAMES POTTER. Ackn

12 Mar 1699. (F:pg 4)

446. 12 Mar 1699. Deed. JOHN NICKOLSON planter of Kent Co PA for 51 pounds sold to THOMAS EVERETT of same co planter ... a tr of land called Highmans Ferry n side of Little Cr adj a tr called Wellingbrook upon which JOHN RICHARDSON now liveth ... 138 a. surveyed 10 Dec 1683 ... Wit: JOHN EVENS, JOHN CLAYTON, JACOB SMITH, JAMES POTTER. Ackn 12 Mar 1699. (F:pg 5)

447. 1 May 1700. Deed. WILLIAM RODENEY of Kent Co PA for 110 pounds sold to JOHN CLAYTON of same co black smith ... a tr of land called Middle Wicks n side of Little Cr ... intersects with land of WILLIAM MORTON called London ... to corner of the land of WILLIAM FREELAND decd ... 180 a. which lately belonged to JOHN and WILLIAM STEVENS both of Dorchester Co MD ... Wit: JOHN EVANS, JAMES GORDON. Ackn 9 Jul 1700. (F:pg 6)

448. 24 Apr 1700. Deed. DANIELL RUTTY of Kent Co PA planter and ELLENER (ELLINOR) his wife for 10 pounds sold to DAVID GOGIN of same co planter ... a tr of land s side of St. Jones Cr alias Dover River being pt/o land of THOMAS BEDWELL called Holy Neck ... 50 a. ... Wit: STEPHEN SIMONS, EDMOND NEEDHAM. Ackn 10 Sep 1700. (F:pg 7)

449. 10 Sep 1700. Quit Claim. THOMAS PRICE of Suss Co PA planter the only brother of JOHN PRICE late of Kent Co decd ... whereas THOMAS HEATHARD and ANNE his wife late of Kent Co decd by their deed bearing date 20 Feb 1687 in consideration of a marriage then had and solemnized between JOHN PRICE decd and ANNE the dau of THOMAS HEATHARD and ANNE his wife decd did give unto their then son in law JOHN PRICE decd a tr of land called Cumberland being taken out of a tr THOMAS HEATHERD decd which he then lived upon called Ousbey beginning at the corner of JOHN ROBESON's land ... 200 a. ... whereas ANNE widdow and relict of JOHN PRICE decd is since intermarryed with EDMOND NEEDHAM of Kent Co and none of the issue neither male or female of JOHN PRICE decd being at this day left alive but all of them are also since decd ... because JOHN PRICE decd became possessed thereof only in right of his wife ANNA ... therefore THOMAS PRICE for love good will and affection quitt claim afsd tr of land unto EDMUND NEEDHAM and ANNA his wife ... Wit: STEPHEN SIMONS, NATHANIEL HUNN. Ackn 10 Sep 1700. (F:pg 8)

450. 10 Sep 1700. Deed. GEORG HART of Kent Co PA planter for 30 pounds sold to THOMAS WELLS of same co planter ... a tr of land called Shepards Lott being pt/o a tr called Leesen sw side of Dover River ... bounded by WILLIAM RODENEY's land that formerly belonged to

DANIELL JONES decd ... 100 a. ... Wit: NATHANIELL HUNN, TIMOTHY THOROLD. Ackn 10 Sep 1700. (F:pg 9)

451. 10 Sep 1700. Deed. THOMAS WELLS of Kent Co planter for 30 pounds sold to GEORG HART of same co planter ... a tr of land called Wells Purchase being pt/o a tr taken up by THOMAS BEDWELL, HENRY BEDWELL, ROBERT BEDWELL and ADAM FISHER ... 100 a. ... Wit: NATHANIEL HUNN, TIMOTHY THOROLD. Ackn 10 Sep 1700. (F:pg 10)

452. 10 Sep 1700. Deed. ADAM FISHER and SUSANNAH his wife of Kent Co PA for 26 pounds sold to THOMAS SKIDMORE of same co ... a parcell of land called Fishers Delight being pt/o a tr of land called Dover Farmes sw side of Dover River ... 92 a. ... Wit: EDMUND NEEDHAM, MATTHEW MANLOVE. Ackn 10 Sep 1700. (F:pg 10)

453. 10 Sep 1700. Deed. FRANCIS EASTGATE of Kent Co PA planter for 25 pounds sold to JAMES FITZGARRALD of same co planter ... a tr of land heretofore purch by TIMOTHY THOROLD of HENRY STEVENSON decd 50 a. being one halfe pt/o 100 a. ... n side of Dover River ... bindeth upon line of RICHARD LEVITT ...bounded by tree standing between the land of JOHN SMITH and the land formerly of said HENRY STEVENSON decd ... Wit: MATTHEW WILLSON, GRIFF JONES. Ackn 10 Sep 1700. (F:pg 12)

454. 19 Aug 1684. Deed. ALLEXANDER CHANSLEY (CHANCE) sold unto GEORG MARTIN of Kent Co all my right, title and interest in one warrant of 500 a. of land granted unto me by Kent Co Court ... Wit: HENRICH JANSEN, NICKLAS BARTLET. (F:pg 12)

455. 20 Apr 1700. Deed. ELIZABETH BASNETT of the town of Burlington in New West Jersey widdow for 250 pounds sold to STEPHEN NEWELL of Kent Co PA yeoman ... a plantation or tr of land in Jones Cr called Kingstowne Upon Hull ... bounded by land of ROBERT JONES ... by the land belonging to the Town Poynt ... 450 a. ... ELIZABETH BASNETT defends against estate rights by, from or under WILLIAM FRAMPTON decd and RICHARD BASNETT decd ... Wit: WILLIAM CLARK, JASPER YATES, RICHARD HATTWELL. Ackn 11 Mar 1700 by ARTHUR MESTON atty for ELIZABETH BASNETT. (F:pg 13)

456. 2 Nov 1700. Deed. EDMOND NEEDHAM and ANNA his wife both of Kent Co PA for 63 pounds sold to JOHN ROBESON of same co ... a tr of land called Cumberland upperside of Murder Cr being taken out of a tr of land formerly belonging to THOMAS HEATHERD called Ousbey beginning at corner of JOHN ROBESON's land ... 200 a. ... Wit:

STEPHEN SIMONS, THOMAS BEDWELL. Ackn 14 Jan 1700. (F:pg 14)

457. 10 Mar 1700. Deed. SAMUELL BURBERY of Kent Co PA planter for 225 pounds sold to ROBERT FRENCH of town and co of New Castle PA merchant ... a tr of land 170 a. pt/o a 400 a. tr belonging to WILLIAM BERRY now decd beginning at the corner of a plantation formerly belonging to JOHN BRIGGS long since decd and now in the tenure of STEPHEN NOWELL ... Wit: ALLEXANDER CHANCY, GRIFF JONES. Ackn 11 Mar 1700. (F:pg 15)

458. 11 Mar 1700. Deed. WILLIAM FREEMAN of Kent Co PA for 160 pounds sold to JOHN BRINCKLOE Junr of same co ... a tr of land called Freemans Rest n side of Mispillion ... to the corner of WILLIAM MANLOVE's land ... 450 a. ... Wit: JOHN FOSTER, WILLIAM BRINCKLOE. Ackn 11 Mar 1700. (F:pg 16)

459. 10 Feb 1700. Deed. MARY TOMSON widdow and executrix of the will of URBANUS TOMSON late of Kent Co PA decd for 46 pounds sold to JOHN FOSTER of same co ... a tr of land pt/o a tr whereon PATRICK WORD lately decd lived s side of sw br of Duck Cr called Kingsaile ... 70 a. and also one other tr of land adj unto afsd tr and is pt/o a tr called The Partners ... 100 a. ... Wit: WILLIAM RODENEY, THOMAS BEDWELL. Ackn 11 Mar 1700. (F:pg 17)

460. 11 Jun 1700. Deed. JOHN ROBESON (ROBBISON) and ELINOR his wife of Kent Co PA for a valuable consideration to them paid sold to SAMUELL BROOK of same co ... a tr of land pt/o a tr which was THOMAS HEWTHAT's called Ousbe ... by the land of STEPHEN SIMONS ... 75 a. ... Wit: WM WILLIAMS, JONAS GREENWOOD. Ackn 14 Jan 1700. (F:pg 18)

461. 13 Mar 1700. Deed. TUNIS TOBIAS of Kent Co PA planter for 17 pounds 10 shillings sold to JOHN FOSTER planter of same co ... 89 a. being pt/o a tr formerly belonging to MATHEW MASON and then to URBANUS TOMSON and now in the hands of TUNIS TOBIAS called Allams Cabines se side of sw br of Duck Cr ... binding on URBANUS TOMSON's land ... intercepts with the head line of Allams Cabins ... intercepts with SAMUELL TOMSON's land ... Wit: THOMAS SHARP, THOMAS FRENCH. Ackn 10 Jun 1701. (F:pg 19)

462. 11 Jun 1701. Deed. MATHEW MANLOVE of Kent Co PA planter for 15 pounds sold to LUKE MANLOVE of same co ... a tr of land nw side of Mispillion Cr ... at the corner of the land formerly laid out for JOHN CURTICE called Strallow ... 100 a. called Fishing Point ... Wit: JOHN CLAYTON, MATHEW WILLSON, MARK MANLOVE. Ackn 10 Jun 1701.

(F:pg 20)

463. 22 Apr 1701. Deed. JOSEPH OSBORN of Kent Co PA for 45 pounds sold to GEORGE HART of same co ... a tr of land called Reding being pt/o a tr called Burtons Delight adj to the land of JAMES CLAITON decd ... 50 a. ... Wit: WILLIAM RODENEY, JAMES FITZGERALD. Ackn 10 Jun 1701. (F:pg 21)

464. 10 Dec 1700. Deed. THOMAS WILLSON Junr of Kent Co PA for 55 pounds sold to RICHARD WHITEHART of same co ... 150 a. being pt/o a 1200 a. tr s side of sw br of Duck Cr called Darby Town formerly laid out for THOMAS WILLSON Senr and by him given to his son THOMAS WILLSON Junr by deed of gift bearing date 18 Feb 1686 ... to corner of land of HENRY ASKINS ... to corner of JOHNSTON's land ... Wit: THOMAS SHARP, JOHN BRADSHAW. Ackn 10 Jun 1701. (F:pg 22)

465. 19 Jul 1701. Deed. STEPHEN NEWELL (NOWELL) of Kent Co PA planter for a competent sume of money sold to ROBERT FRENCH of same co merchant ... a tr of land being pt/o a tr heretofore belonging unto JOHN BRIGGS of same co decd called Kingston Upon Hull on Jones Cr otherways called Dover River ... 50 a. all which were heretofore in the tenure of WILLIAM FRAMPTON or RICHARD BASSNETT or one of their tennants and late in the tenure of STEPHEN NEWELL ... Wit: JOHN BRINCKLOE, ARTHUR MESTON. Ackn 9 Sep 1701. (F:pg 23)

466. 21 Jul 1701. Deed. ANDREW MILLS of Kent Co PA planter and JANE his wife for 73 pounds 8 shillings 6 pence sold to ROBERT FRENCH of same co merchant ... a tr of land ... at the corner of JOHN ANDREWS land decd ... 50 a. ... together with the meat and cattle ... Wit: JOHN BRINCKLOE, GRIFF JONES. Ackn 9 Sep 1701. (F:pg 24)

467. 22 Jul 1701. Deed. JOHN BURTON of Kent Co PA carpenter and ELIZABETH his wife for 138 pounds sold to ROBERT FRENCH of same co merchant ... a tr of land being the remainder pt/o a tr called Burton's Delight ... adj se with land of CAPTAIN JOHN BRINCKLOE and on the ne with the land formerly sold by said JOHN BURTON to DANIELL JONES decd and on the nw with the land of JOSEPH OSBORN, on the sw with the land of WALTER DICKINSON ... 180 a. ... Wit: GRIFF JONES, WILLIAM ANNAND. Ackn 19 Sep 1701. (F:pg 25)

468. 9 Sep 1701. Deed. GEORGE MORGAN of Kent Co PA planter for 10 pounds sold to ROBERT FRENCH of same co merchant ... a tr of land being halfe pt/o a tr called Potters Lodge n side of Jones Cr ... bounded on the upper side of PORTER's land ... 100 a. heretofore in the possession of MAURICE SMITH Senr decd ... Wit: GRIFF JONES,

WILLIAM ANNAND. Ackn 9 Nov 1701. (F:pg 26)

469. 11 Oct 1701 at Phila. Deed. MARY NAYLOR of the city and co of Phila widdow executrix of the will of JOHN KING of Menienson in same co marriner decd ... JOHN KING by his will hath given full and absolute power to said MARY with the advice of SAMUELL HARRISON, JOHN CRAP and JOSEPH PIDGEON or any of them to dispose of all his real estate ... for 20 pounds sold to ROBERT FRENCH of afsd city & co merchant ... a tr of land ne side of Dover River ... in the line of MORRIS SMITH's land ... 300 a. called Troy ... MARY NAYLOR appoints WILLIAM ANNAND of Kent Co to be her atty to ackn in open court this deed ... Wit: REBECKA BULLOCK, JOHN BRINKLOE. Ackn 11 Nov 1701 by WILLIAM ANNAND atty for MARY NAYLOR. (F:pg 27)

470. 10 Dec 1701. Deed of Gift. WILLIAM FREEMAN of Kent Co PA for love, goodwill and affection give to my son in law ADAM FISHER of same co and in consideration of a marriage had and solemnized between him the said ADAM FISHER and my dau SUSANNA ... a tr of land called Fishers Delight being pt/o a tr of land said WILLIAM FREEMAN now lives on called Seven Haven ... n side of Service Br ... to land of JOHN COURTNEY ... 100 a. ... Wit: JOHN CLARK, JOHN ROBESSON. Ackn 9 Sep 1701. (F:pg 28)

471. 21 Oct 1701. Quit Claim. JOHN WELLS and THOMAS WELLS both of Kent Co PA planters and KATHARINE (CATHARINE) WELLS of same place spinster, sons and dau to JAMES WELLS late of same co decd ... whereas JAMES in his life time was seized of a plantation and tr of land called Bettyes Fortune on Duck Cr ... bounded by land of WILLIAM STEPHENS ... binding part upon the line of WILLIAM SIMPSON ... 500 a. and another tr of land called Shrewsbury n side of Little Cr adj to the land of JOHN RICHARDSON now called Symsons Choyce ... 175 a. both purch by JAMES WELLS of EVAN DAVIS of Cape May by deed dated 26 Aug 1684 and whereas JAMES WELLS dyed intestate MARY WELLS relict and adminr of said JAMES and by deed of sale bearing date 15 Feb 1685 she did sell afsd two parcells of land unto GRIFFITH JONES of Phila merchant ... JOHN WELLS, THOMAS WELLS and KATHARINE WELLS for the corroborating MARY WELLS her sale afsd quitt claime the two parcells of land unto GRIFFITH JONES ... Wit: SAMUEL BERRY, JAMES POTTER, ELIZABETH DYER. Ackn 11 Nov 1701 by SAMUEL BERRY atty for THOMAS, JOHN and KATHARINE WELLS unto WILLIAM RODENEY atty for GRIFFETH JONES. (F:pg 29)

472. 10 Feb 1701. Deed. BENJAMIN WHITE of Kent Co PA planter for four score pounds sold to CAPT JOHN BRINKLOE of same co ... a tr of land being that pt/o a tr called Lisbon n side of Dover River ... bounded

by land of WILLIAM BRINKLOE ... 400 a. ... Wit: THOMAS FRENCH, JOHN EVANS. Ackn 10 Feb 1701. (F:pg 30)

473. 10 Feb 1701. Deed. JOHN COURTNEY of Kent Co PA planter for 20 pounds sold to STEPHEN SIMONS of same co planter ... a tr of land heretofore belonging to THOMAS WILLIAMS late of same co called Leaverpoole w side of Murther Cr and n side of Service Br ... to land formerly belonging to THOMAS HEATERD ... 101 a. ... Wit: THOMAS FRENCH, JOHN BRINKLOE. Ackn 10 Feb 1701. (F:pg 31)

474. 10 Feb 1701. Deed. WILLIAM HAWKER of Kent Co PA planter and URSULA his wife relict and adminr of GEORGE MARTIN late of same co decd ... whereas the said GEORGE MARTIN at the time of his decease left behind him several young children to the nature and education of URSULA ... WILLIAM HAWKER and URSULA his wife petitioned court and at a court held 20 Dec 1699 court ordered lands of GEORGE MARTIN decd to be sold for bringing up the said children being young and chargable ... WILLIAM HAWKER and URSULA his wife for 20 pounds sold to ROBERT FRENCH of Newcastle PA merchant a tr of land called Elkes Horn lying near Duck Cr bounded with a tr called Gloucester heretofore belonging to GEORGE MARTIN decd and the land called Coventy belonging to ROBERT FRENCH on the one side and on the ne with the land of ALBURT MUNTFORD ... 85 a. ... Wit: PHILLIP JAMES, GRIFFETH JONES. Ackn 10 Feb 1701. (F:pg 32)

475. 10 Feb 1701. Deed. WILLIAM WILLSON of Kent Co PA planter for 16 pounds sold to THOMAS WILLSON of same co planter ... a tr of land being pt/o a 1200 a. tr s side of Duck Cr called Denby Town formerly laid out for THOMAS WILLSON Senr late of same co ... 100 a. lately in the tenure of one WILLIAM JONSON since decd and lately in the possession of WILLIAM WILLSON ... Wit: WM ELMANA, JAMES GORDEN. Ackn 10 Feb 1701. (F:pg 33)

476. 8 Dec 1701. Deed. WILLIAM SHERER otherwayes called WILLIAM SHERWOOD and MARY his wife of Kent Co PA for 170 pounds sold to BENJAMIN GUMBLY of Newcastle Co PA ... a tr of land 700 a. called Sherwoods Fortune alias Green Hoop s side of Duck Cr (patent granted for 900 a. at Phila 21 May 1689 unto WILLIAM SHERER by the name of WILLIAM SHERWOOD) ... he has since disposed of 200 a., 100 a. which is in the possession of RICHARD TURNER and 100 a. is possessed by FRANCIS WETTSWOOD of this co ... Wit: JOHN BRADSHAW, HENRY PERMAINE, WILLIAM GREEN. Ackn 10 Feb 1701 (F:pg 34)

477. 9 Feb 1701. Deed. RICHARD TURNER of Kent Co PA for 18 pounds sold to BENJAMIN GUMBLY of Blackbird Cr Newcastle Co ... a parcell

of land called Green Oak it being pt/o a tr called Sherers Fortune alias Green Hope n side of Permaines Br of Duck Cr ... 103 a. ... Wit: THOMAS SHARP, EVAN JONES. Ackn 10 Feb 1701. (F:pg 35)

478. 10 Feb 1701. Mortgage. JOHN DUBROIS of Kent Co PA merchant for 119 pounds 17 shillings 3 pence sold to MICHAJAH PERRY, JOHN KNIGHT, THOMAS COOPER, HENRY GOULDNEY and JOHN FREAME all of London, England merchants ... a tr of land n side of Murder Cr ... to line of WILLIAM NICKOLS land ... to corner of ROBERT NICHOLS land ... 580 a. called Kingston which plantation was invested with several more assignments on RALP ELSTION Junr and by him sold to JOHN DUBROIS by deed bearing date 1 Oct 1696 ... if JOHN DUBROIS pays to MICHAJAH PERRY, JOHN KNIGHT, THOMAS COOPER, HENRY GOULDNEY and JOHN FREAME at the dwelling house of JOHN MOORE of Phila 119 pounds 17 shillings 3 pence at or upon 10 Oct insuing the date of these presence one entire payment ... this bargain & sale to be utterly void ... Wit: JOHN BRINKLOE, WM RODENEY. Ackn 10 -- --. (F:pg 36)

479. 28 Apr 1717. Deed. SAMUEL TAYLOR of Duck Cr New Castle Co bolter for 1 pound sold to JOSEPH WELLDON of the forrest in same co yeoman ... a lott of ground being within ye line laid out for a town called Saulsbury on the head of Duck Cr ... corner of JOHN WILLIAMSON's land ... JOSEPH WELLDON to pay to SAMUEL TAYLOR 1 shilling on 23 of Dec yearly and every year forever hereafter ... Wit: JOHN PARSON, ABSALOM CUFF. Ackn 15 May 1717. SAMUEL TAYLOR received 1 pound of JOSEPH WELLDON it being the consideration money within mentioned. (F:pg 38)

480. 15 May 1717. Receipt. SAMUEL TAYLOR received 10 shillings of JOSEPH WELLDON which I do hereby ackn to be in full satisfaction and fully discharge JOSEPH WELLDON from the [above] said annual rent forever ... Wit: FRANCES JONES, BENJAMINE HIXSON. (F:pg 38)

481. 9 May 1717. Deed of Release. Whereas there was a certain sum of money in hand paid by ROBERT BEDWELL in his life time to WILLIAM RODENEY decd for a tr of land ... WILLIAM RODENEY son and heir of WILLIAM RODENEY late of Kent Co decd releases to ROBERT and JAMES BEDWELL sons and coheirs of ROBERT BEDWELL late of same co decd all his rights to tr of land called Wedmore ... 354 a. ... Wit: DANIELL RODENEY, JOHN HALL. Ackn 15 May 1717. (F:pg 39)

482. 9 Feb 1716. Deed. SAMUEL TAYLOR of Duck Cr Kent Co bolter for 1 pound sold to GEORGE GRAHAM of same place hatter ... a lott of ground being on a place layed out for a town Salsbury on the head of

Duck Cr ... corner of another lott formerly granted to said GEORGE GRAHAM ... 1/4 a. ... GEORGE GRAHAM to pay 6 pence to SAMUEL TAYLOR on 23 Dec yearly and for ever hereafter ... Wit: ABSALOM CUFF, HENRY JONES. Ackn 15 May 1717. SAMUEL TAYLOR received 1 pound 1 shilling it being the consideration money within mentioned. (F:pg 40)

483. 15 May 1717. Quit Claim. JOHN SWIFT of Phila quitt claim unto GEORGE GRAHAM [above] lott of land ... Wit: HENRY JONES, EDWARD CLUFF, ABSALOM CUFF. (F:pg 40)

484. 19 Feb 1716. Deed. SAMUEL TAYLOR of Duck Cr Newcastle Co bolter for 1 pound sold to BENJAMINE SHURMER of the Manor of Frith Kent Co gentleman ... a piece of ground being in a place laid out for a town called Salsbury on the head of Duck Cr beginning at the corner of ABSALOM CUFF's lott ... to lott of HENRY JONES ... BENJAMINE SHURMER to pay SAMUEL TAYLOR 6 pence on 23 Dec yearly and every year hereafter ... Wit: JAMES STEEL, ABSALUM CUFF. Ackn 15 -- 1717. SAMUEL TAYLOR received of BENJAMINE SHURMER 1 pound it being the consideration money within mentioned. (F:pg 41)

485. SAMUEL TAYLOR received 5 shillings of BENJAMINE SHURMER and discharges him from the annual rents ... Wit: FRANCES JONES, BENJAMINE HIXON. (F:pg 41)

486. 15 May 1717. Deed. THOMAS WELLS of Kent Co eldest son of JAMES WELLS of same co decd for 50 pounds sold to MARK MANLOV Senr of same co ... a tr of land called Farms Elsworth n side of Murther Cr ... 900 a. surveyed 20 Aug 1684 ... Wit: SAMUELL BERRY, HUGH DURBOROW. Ackn 15 May 1717. (F:pg 42)

487. 12 Nov 1706. Deed. CHRISTOPHER STANLEY of Newcastle Co PA cordwiner sold to GEORGE GREEN of Kent Co yeoman ... a tr of land patent dated 26 Mar 1684 granted unto JOHN BETTS of Kent Co called John Betts Endeavor s side of sw br of Duck Cr ... 400 a. and whereas JOHN BETTS and RICHARD WILLIAMS by their deed of sale bearing date 20 Aug 1685 did sell unto CHRISTOPHER STANLEY of Kent Co afsd tr of land and said CHRISTOPHER STANLEY died intestate the tr of land descended to the oldest son CHRISTOPHER STANLEY who also dieing left his wife MARY sole executrix of his will giving her land except a part thereof which was before sold out to pay his debts and bringing up of his children, land remaining unsold until eldest son of CHRISTOPHER STANLEY last named who is also named CHRISTOPHER STANLEY became the age of 21, the executrix became married to CHARLES RUMSEY and together with CHRISTOPHER STANLEY sold afsd land

to GEORGE GREEN but because CHRISTOPHER STANLEY was not 21 sale was not then good ... therefore CHRISTOPHER STANLEY now sells afsd tr of land to GEORGE GREEN ... Wit: THOMAS ADAMS, HUGH DURBOROW. Ackn 15 May 1717. (F:pg 42)

488. 10 Sep 1717. Deed. JOHN FRENCH of town and co of Newcastle gentleman for 135 pounds sold to JOHN BRINKLOE of Dover Hund Kent Co gentleman ... a tr of land patent under the hands of RICHARD HILL, ISAAC MORRIS and SAMUEL LOGAN commissioners bearing date 20 Sep 1715 unto JOHN FRENCH ... 588 a. recorded at Phila Patent Book A Vol 5 pg 173 13 Aug 1716 ... Wit: JOHN COOK, GEORGE MARTIN. Ackn 14 May 1718. (F:pg 44)

489. 13 Nov 1717. Deed. ROBERT GRUNDY of Talbot Co MD gentleman for his bond drawn payable to THOMAS EDMONDSON for 500 pounds and for one full third pt/o all the estate real and personall that is due to THOMAS EDMONDSON return and make back unto THOMAS EDMONDSON of same co ... one half of all lands specified in a grand deed made by THOMAS EDMONDSON unto ROBERT GRUNDEY bearing date 10 May 1710 ... ANDREW CALDWELL doth sign for ROBERT GRUNDY. Wit: MICHAEL LOWBER, PHILLIP MORGAN, JOHN BERRY, BEN SHURMER. (F:pg 45)

490. 20 Mar 1717. By this publick instrument of procuration be it known and made manifest that on Thursday 20 Mar 1717 before us THOMAS LEGRIER esqr major and justice of the peace for the Burgh of Great Yarmouth in the co of Norfolk in Great Britain and THOMAS ROYALL gentleman notary ... personally appeared HANNAH DENNIS and MARY SEELY both of Great Yarmouth widows the two daus and coheirs of THOMAS ROUSE late of Kent Co PA joyner decd and ABRAHAM TODD of Great Yarmouth taylor and MARY his wife aged 28 and upwards and THOMAS SEELY of Great Yarmouth marriner aged 30 and upwards which said MARY TODD and THOMAS SEELY are two of the children of MARY SEELY, HANNAH DENNIS has no children living ... appointed ISAAC SEELY of Great Yarmouth marriner aged 21 and upwards of small statue, swarthy complexion and wears his own black hair, the other of the children of MARY SEELY their atty to demand, recover and take possession of all lands, estate both real and personall of THOMAS ROUSE of which he dyed possessed ... in PA as well as in the Island of Barbados and to sell same ... Wit: THOMAS ROYALL. Proved 20 Mar 1717. (F:pg 46)

491. Deed. of Gift. GEORGE ROBISSON (ROBINSON) of Kent Co for love, good will and affection give to my well beloved children namely LAWRENCE ROBISSON, DANIEL ROBISSON and CHARITY

ROBISSON ... a tr of land sw side of Dover River called Whitewells Delight and is the same whereon the said GEORGE ROBISSON now dwells, divided equally, ... 774 a. (reserving unto myself and my wife SARAH our natural lives 100 a. to be laid off next adj unto Smiths Br) ... Wit: JOHN CLARK. Ackn 13 Nov 1717. (F:pg 47)

492. 21 Mar 1684 at Phila. Confirmation of Patent. Whereas there is a tr of land called Benefield s side of sw br of Duck Cr ... bounded by FRANCES WHITEWELL's land ... 1000 a. granted by a court of Suss surveyed 13 May 1680 to FRANCIS WHITWELL ... WILLIAM PENN Governor of PA confirms patent unto FRANCIS WHITEWELL ... Vol A fol. 10 ... (signed) PATRICK ROBINSON deputy. (F:pg 47)

493. 10 Jun 1686. Assignment. WILLIAM BERRY of Kent Co PA adminr of the estate of FRANCIS WHITWELL decd for 30 pounds due by said WHITEWELL to SARA JONES assign over unto GRIFFETH JONES one half of lands in [above] patent ... (signed) WM BERRY, WM SOUTHBY. Wit: JAMES THOMAS, SAMUELL BULKLEE, BARNABAS WILLCOE, WM BOYDON. (F:pg 48)

494. 23 Mar 1685. Deed. CHARLES PICKERING of New Castle PA have a just right and title to 500 a. of land on sw br of Duck Cr being half of 1000 a. that was FRANCIS WHITWELL's adj to the land that now is JOSEPH GROWDEN's which he purch of said WHITWELL and also 200 a. which was WILLIAM FREEMAN's adj the same which said lands ... together with 4 breeding cows and her increase since 1683. I do ackn to have sold unto RALPH FRETWELL of Barbadoes esqr for 100 pounds afsd 700 a. ... Wit: JOHN EDMONDSON, THOMAS [?]. Recorded 1 Mar 1718 by order of JOSEPH WORRELL. Attest: BEN SHURMER clerk. (F:pg 48)

495. -- -- 17--. Deed. BENJAMIN SHURMER of Duck Cr Kent Co and SARAH his wife for 40 pounds sold to WILLIAM FARSON of Newcastle Co husbandman ... a tr of land on Western Br or Gravelly Run of Duck Cr warrant dated at Phila 26 Feb 1714 by special commission given to him for that purpose from JACOB TAYLOR surveyor 8 Mar 1716 ... to corner near the intersection of eastern line of the Mannor of Freith with an e se line of a tr called Brewford formerly taken up by one RIDGEWAY ... 200 a. ... Wit: THOMAS HACKETT, ROBERT DOSSY, JOHN MESSING. Ackn 13 Feb 1718/19. (F:pg 49)

496. 6 Nov 1718. Deed. JOHN PHILLIPS of Duck Cr Newcastle Co merchant and HANNAH his wife for 30 pounds sold to JOHN STOOPS of Salsbury Kent Co ... a piece of ground lying in the town of Salisbury on the head of Duck Cr ... to corner of lott already belonging to said JOHN

STOOPS ... to Greens Br ... 1 a. ... 1 shilling to be paid yearly and every year hereafter on 23 Dec to the chief lord ... Wit: JOHN HACKETT, ABSALOM CUFF. (F:pg 50)

497. 5 Feb 1717. Deed. JAMES JACKSON of Duck Cr Kent Co yeoman and MARGARET (MARGARETT) his wife for 200 pounds sold to JAMES STEEL of same place yeoman ... a tr of land patent bearing date 4 May 1715 granted and confirmed unto JAMES JACKSON and MARGARET his wife s side of sw br of Duck Cr ... to corner of JOHN FOSTER's land called Alloms Cabbins ... to n of THOMAS WILLSON's br ... to JOHN HALL's land called Galaway ... 750 a. ... excepting a 70 a. parcell formerly sold from the e side to JOHN FOSTER and also 140 a. sold from the s to SAMUEL MANLOVE and also a small parcell on Willson's Br granted to WILLIAM KELLY ... Wit: JOHN FOSTER, ANN FOSTER. Ackn 12 Feb 1717. (F:pg 51)

498. 1735. [note on side of page] [?] BENJAMIN SHURMER former recorder althrough the leaves folding it was left blank and in his alphabet includes for [?] which neglect appearing to MARK MANLOE and his associates then justices was ordered by them to record it. (signed) JAMES HOUSMAN receiver. (F:pg 52)

499. 5 Feb 1717/18. Deed. JAMES STEEL of Duck Cr Kent Co yeoman for 50 pounds sold to JAMES JACKSON of same place yeoman and MARGARET his wife ... a parcell of land s side of sw br of Duck Cr beginning at the mouth of Ellensworths Br ... 200 a. being pt/o a tr called Ferry Bridges ... Wit: JOHN FOSTER, GEORGE MORTON, ANN FOSTER. Ackn 12 Feb 1717. (F:pg 52)

500. 13 May 1717. Deed. GEORGE MARTIN of Duck Cr Kent Co for 50 pounds sold to SAMUEL POUNDS of Newcastle Co ... a tr of land n side of sw br of Duck Cr ... by the Black Princes Br ... 100 a. ... Wit: JAMES STEEL, RICHARD EMERSON. Ackn 14 Aug 1717. (F:pg 53)

501. 20 May 1712. Deed. CHARLES RUMSEY of Cecil Co MD and MARY his wife executrix of the will of CHRISTOPHER STANLEY late of Newcastle decd and CHRISTOPHER STANLEY eldest son of CHRISTOPHER STANLEY decd sold to GEORGE GREEN of Phila yeoman [see #485] ... a tr of land called John Betts Endeavour s side of sw br of Duck Cr ... 400 a. ... Wit: JOHN WATERS, JAMES STEEL. Ackn 13 Aug 1712. (F:pg 54)

502. 6 Nov 1713. Quit Claim. FRANCIS RICHARDSON of Phila silver smith quit claim unto GEORGE MARTIN of Duck Cr Kent Co yeoman ... all actions, suits, bills, bonds, debts, sums of money whatever which I said

FRANCIS RICHARDSON ever had against GEORGE MARTIN ... Wit: JOHN HARPER, TO LAWRENCE. (F:pg 56)

503. 1 Mar 1717. Power of Atty. MARY EDMONDSON wife of THOMAS EDMONDSON of Talbert Co MD appoint ANDREW CALDWELL my atty to deliver and ackn in open court conveyance of any tr of land that my husband THOMAS EDMONDSON doth make unto any person ... Wit: JOHN BERRY, MARMA DUKE PENWELL. Proved 13 Feb 1717. (F:pg 56)

504. 20 Apr 1708. Deed. ROBERT PARVISS surviving son and heir of ROBERT PARVISS late of Kent Co gentleman decd for 25 pounds sold to JOHN WILSON of Talbert Co MD ... a tr of land called Gilford n side of Murther Cr ... corner of Bishops Br ... 600 a. warrant bearing date -- Oct 1682 unto ROBERT PARVISS decd ... Wit: WILLIAM ANNAND, WILLIAM ELLOIT. Ackn 11 May 1708 by VINCENT EMERSON atty to ROBERT PARVISS. (F:pg 57)

505. 30 Apr 1708. Power of Atty. ROBERT PARVISS appoint VINCE EMERSON of Kent Co to be my atty to ackn and deliver the [above] deed of sale in open court ... Wit: WILLIAM ANNAND, WILLIAM ELLOIT. (F:pg 57)

506. 8 Jan 1717/18. Deed. Whereas JOSHUA CLAYTON of Kent Co yeoman by deed dated 15 Feb 1715/16 did sell unto DAVID MORGAN a tr of land whereon said MORGAN now dwelith ... beginning at the path which goes from Little Cr to the plantation formerly belonging to RICHARD WILLSON decd ... by the line of JOHN RICHARDSON's land ... 50 a. being pt/o a tr called Higham Ferry ... DAVID MORGAN of Little Cr Hund Kent Co planter and SARAH his wife for 20 pounds conveys land back to JOSHUA CLAYTON ... Wit: HENRY JOYCE, HUGH DURBOROW. Ackn 13 Feb 1717. (F:pg 57)

507. 10 Feb 1718. Deed. JOSHUA CLAYTON of Little Cr Hund Kent Co yeoman and SARAH his wife for 20 pounds sold to DAVID MORGAN of same place planter ... a tr of land where DAVID MORGAN now dwelleth in Little Cr Hund ... to line of JAMES POTTER's land ... near the corner of tr called William Brook formerly laid out for JOHN RICHARDSON decd ... to corner of land which formerly did belong to ROBERT PORTER decd ... to tr of land called Higham Ferry ... to line of JAMES PORTER's land ... 50 a. (being pt/o two trs of land one called Highams Ferry and the other William Brook both formerly taken up by JOHN RICHARDSON decd) ... Wit: HENRY JOYCE, HUGH DURBOROW. Ackn 13 Feb 1717. Attest: WILLIAM RODENEY. (F:pg 58)

508. 1 May 1718. Deed. JOHN LUCUS and REBECCA his wife adminr of JAMES BROOKS late of Kent Co yeoman decd to satisfy judgment recovered by NICHOLAS NIXON in the Court of Common Pleas held at Dover 14 Aug ... sold to NICHOLAS NIXON of same place black smith ... a tr of land in Murtherkill Hund 400 a. being pt/o a 800 a. tr of land called The Plains ... Wit: THOMAS CRAWFORD, WM RODENEY. Ackn 13 May 1718. (F:pg 59)

509. 13 May 1718. Deed. NATHANIEL ROCH of Little Cr Hund Kent Co planter and DEBORAH his wife, dau of JOHN WILLSON decd ... whereas a tr of land (patent dated at Phila 1 Oct 1685 granted unto THOMAS WILLSON 1200 a. called Denby Town) s side of sw br of Duck Cr and is the lower pt/o that neck now called Whiteharts Neck ... w side of Racoon Br ... to the line of SAMUEL WHITEHART's land ... whereas THOMAS WILLSON by deed of gift bearing date 18 Feb 1686 did give unto his son JOHN WILSON 350 a. being pt/o afsd tr and said JOHN WILSON dying without disposing of land and also all his children dying in their minority without issue except one dau named DEBORAH, the 300 a. descended to DEBORAH WILSON now the wife of NATHANIEL ROCH ... NATHANIEL ROCH and DEBORAH his wife for 28 pounds sold 95 a. to THOMAS ALSON of same place planter ... Wit: RICHARD WHITEHART, HUGH DURBOROW. Ackn 14 May 1718. (F:pg 60)

510. 14 May 1718. Deed. RICHARD WHITEHART of Little Cr Hund Kent Co yeoman for 10 pounds sold to SAMUEL FREEMAN of same place yeoman ... a tr of land in Little Cr Hund being pt/o that piece of land whereon said RICHARD WHITEHART now dwelleth ... to corner of land of JOHN WALKER decd ... to land of SAMUEL FREEMAN ... 20 a. ... Wit: HUGH DURBOROW, NATHANIEL ROCK. Ackn 16 May 1718. (F:pg 61)

511. 19 May 1713. WILLIAM STARKEY went upon a tr of land s side of Dover River between the land the court house is built upon and the land sold by WILLIAM SOUTHBE to EDWARD STARKEY 500 a. ... plots made by JONAS GREENWOOD surveyor ... and did deliver possession to EPHRAIM EMERSON in behalf of EPHRAIM and MARY his wife and THOMAS EMERSON and ELIZABETH his wife according to judgment had at the Court of Common Pleas held 12 May 1713 against said WILLIAM ... Wit: JONATHAN STURGIS, ISAAC FREELAND, HENRY SHAW. (F:pg 62)

512. 15 Apr 1718. Bond of Conveyance. NATHANIEL HUNN of Kent Co yeoman am bound unto JOHN BOWERS of same place yeoman for 500 pounds ... NATHANIEL HUNN to sell unto JOHN BOWERS a tr of land ... n side of Murther Cr 300 a. of land and 170 a. of marsh called

Whitewells Delight but now by the name of Mulbery Point now in the tenure of JOHN BOWERS ... Wit: JOHN EMERSON, BENJAMIN FURBER. Proved 12 Nov 1718. Attest: BENJAMINE SHURMER clerk. (F:pg 62)

513. 1 May 1718. Deed. JAMES CLAYTON of Kent Co yeoman for [?] shillings sold to GEORGE HART of same place yeoman ... a tr of land called New Bristol in Dover Hund being the same whereon said GEORGE HART now dwelleth 100 a. ... Wit: GEORGE LESTER, J GREENWOOD. Ackn 13 Aug 1718. (F:pg 63)

514. 19 Mar 1718/19. Deed. JOHN CURTIS of Phila mariner for 30 pounds sold to WILLIAM BRINKLOE of Kent Co esqr ... a tr of land called Pasture Point s side of Murder Cr ... to corner of land of JOHN CALBELLES ... 50 a. (granted unto JOHN CURTIS by virtue of a warrant for 1200 a. dated 21 Feb 1681/2 surveyed 18 Oct 1687) and one other tr s side of Murther Cr ... 200 a. lower half part (400 a. granted by virtue of a warrant bearing date 20 Apr 1681 surveyed 28 Jan 1681 unto JOHN CABLEY and JOHN CABLEY sold to JOHN CURTIS) ... JOHN CURTIS in his life time 22 Apr 1698 did make his will ... I give to my grandchild JOHN CURTIS 270 a. of land s side of Murther Cr adj land of RICHARD CURTIS and on the other side that which is called Ceder Landing Neck ... JOHN CURTIS appoint my friend WILLIAM RODENEY of Kent Co to be my atty to ackn these presents in open court ... Wit: JAMES MAXWELL, WILLIAM MANLOVE. Ackn and Proved 13 May 1719. (F:pg 63)

515. 1 Nov 1718. Deed. WILLIAM MULRONY of Kent Co yeoman for 70 pounds sold to WILLIAM BRINKLOE of same place esqr ... a tr of land called Virgin Chance se side of Murther Cr ... 310 a. ... Wit: WILLIAM RODENEY, HENRY MOLESTON. Ackn 13 Nov 1718. (F:pg 64)

516. 1 Oct 1718. Bond of Conveyance. WILLIAM MULRONY of Kent Co am bound unto WILLIAM BRINKLOE of same place for 500 pounds ... WILLIAM MULRONY to convey [above] tr of land ... Wit: JOHN BRINKLOE, JAMES BOWMAN. (F:pg 65)

517. 13 May 1714. Deed. Whereas WILLIAM DARVALL of PA merchant by indenture bearing date 7 Nov 1689 ... purch of RICHARD DRASGATE several parcells of land, one 800 a. tr se side of Jones Cr called Canoan Mannor formerly laid out for JOSHUA BARKSTEAD ... to line of ROBERT BEDWELL ... and also a 1200 a. tr of land s side of Jones Cr to the lands of ROBERT BEDWELL to the nw and to lands of EDMOND GIBBONS to the se and also a 600 a. tr of land called Williams Chance n side of Murther Cr ... surveyed 20 Jan 1680 to THOMAS WILLIAMS and

also a 400 a. tr of land called The Downs between Dover River and Murther Cr ... granted by a warrant 22 Feb 1680 surveyed 23 Jan 1683 unto BRYAN ONEAL and also a 1200 a. tr of land n side of Murther Cr ... granted by a warrant 21 Mar 1682 surveyed 23 Nov 1683 unto WILLIAM CLARK and WILLIAM DARVELL and also a 700 a. tr of land in Suss Co called Poplar Hill n side of Cedar Cr ... granted 16 Nov 1681 surveyed 21 Jan following unto ROBERT HART and also a 600 a. tr of land called The Graves End n side of Maid Stone Br ... along the line of land called Maidstone ... granted by a warrant 20 Jun 1682 resurveyed 14 Feb 1683 unto CHARLES MARSH ... payment of WILLIAM DARVALL due RICHARD DRASGATE of 179 pounds 10 shillings and the interest thereof on the 8 Nov 1691 was not paid on said date ... this indenture RICHARD DRASGATE citizen and girdler of London sold to THOMAS BISHOPP citizen and haberdasher of London and THOMAS HUDSON citizen and draper of London afsd parcells of land ... Wit: SPRINGATE HAMILTON, RICHARD PARKER. (F:pg 66)

Deed Record G Vol 1

518. 22 Feb 1723. By virtue of a former survey of RICHARD MITCHELL's bearing date 23 Jan 1683 by warrant bearing date 21 Jun 1682 granted unto JOHN COURTNEY and by him assigned to SAMUELL BURBERRY the 23 Jun 1683 & directed by WILLIAM CLARKE chief surveyor of Suss & Kent resurveyed for SAMUELL BURBERRY the tr of land called Burberrys Berry n side of Bishops Br beginning at the corner of land called Sheusworth ... 600 a. resurveyed 11 Jul 1686 by JOSHUA BARKSTEED deputy surveyor ... ANDREW CALDWELL aged about 47 years on his solemn affirmation ... the above written copy was by him taken from an original signed by JOSHUA BARKSTEED deputy surveyor ... Attest: BENJAMIN SHURMER. (G:pg 3)

519. 24 Feb 1723. Personally came before the subscriber one of the Kings chief justices of the Supream Court ... THOMAS BERRY gentleman aged about 45 years by his solemn affirmation (allowed by law to the people called Quakers of which he is one) that he had in his keeping about 2 years ago the original paper above mentioned signed with the name of JOSHUA BARKSTEED deputy surveyor and that the same to the best of his remembrance contained the land portion laid as are expressed in the above ... (signed) THOMAS BERRY. Attest BENJAMIN SHURMER. (G:pg 3)

520. 9 Feb 1720. Deed. JOHN CLIFFORTH (CLIFFWORTH) of Kent Co yeoman, only surviving son & heir of THOMAS CLIFFORTH late of same

place decd, and ANN his wife for 17 pounds sold to BENJAMIN SHURMER of same co gentleman ... a tr of land (by virtue of a warrant granted unto THOMAS CLIFFORTH for 300 a. bearing date 21 Sep 1682) ... being on the nw side of Jones Cr ... to corner of tr of land laid out for ROBERT BEDWELL ... to corner of land called London formerly laid out for DANIEL JONES ... 300 a. called Skiptop surveyed 17 Jan 1683 ... JOHN CLIFFORTH and ANN his wife appoint TIMOTHY HANSON esqr & EDWARD JENNINGS their atty to deliver these presents in open court ... Wit: WILLIAM BIRKETT, JOHN PLESENTON, BEN BARRATT. Ackn & Proved 15 Feb 1720. (G:pg 6)

521. 4 Feb 1720. Deed. GEORGE BROWN of Motherkill Hund yeoman for 15 pounds sold to RICHARD HUDSON & his wife ELIONER (ELIOUNR) HUDSON & ELIZABETH PENNENTON the said ELENOR HUDSON & ELIZABETH PENENTON being full sisters ... a tr of land (called Williams Choice 600 a. which JOHN CURTIS has 400, GEORGE BROWN 100 a. and the other 100 a. layd for RICHARD HUDSON, ELINOR HUDSON & ELIZABETH PENNINGTON) ... by Motherkill Br ... adj to EDMONDS land ... 100 a. which JOHN BROWN father to GEORGE BROWN sold in his lifetime to said HENRY PENNENTON but was not made over, father to ELENOUR (LENOUR) HUDSON now wife to RICHARD HUDSON & ELIZABETH PENENTON ... Wit: WM WINSMORE, JOHN CURTIS. Ackn 15 Feb 1721. (G:pg 8)

522. 30 Oct 1719. Deed of Conveyance. WILLIAM JACKSON of Kent Co yeoman am bound unto ARTHUR STEELE of same co yeoman for 100 pounds ... ARTHUR STEEL hath by certain writing obligatory ackn himself to be bound unto WILLIAM JACKSON for 40 pounds ... WILLIAM JACKSON to assign (as soon as full payment of the above mentioned obligatory be made) unto ARTHUR STEEL 100 a. of land in Murtherkill Hund being pt/o a tr of land which WILLIAM JACKSON took up by virtue of a warrant ... said 100 a. shall be laid off the co pt/o the afsd tr owed to EDWARD RUTHLEDGE and that the same shall be free and clear from all incumberances ... Wit: WM RODENEY, STEPHEN HARGROVE Junr, RUTH RODENY. (G:pg 9)

523. 17 Feb 1721. Deed. FERDINANDO ODOCHARTIE (ODOWGHERTY) of Kent Co planter for 18 pounds sold to ROBERT GORDON of same place merchant ... a tr of land called Dundee ... to br proceeding out of ISAAC WEBB's ... 50 a. ... Wit: BENJAMIN SHURMER, GRIFF JONES. Ackn: 17 Feb 1721. (G:pg 9)

524. 8 Aug 1720. Deed. JOHN HIRONS of Kent Co yeoman for [blank] pounds sold to SIMON HIRONS of same place husbandman ... a plantation and two parcells of land in the forrest s side of sw br of Duck

Cr 400 a. (200 a. in each tr) being the same plantation and two tr that was lately conveyed to me from the said SIMON HIRONS ... excepted JOHN MIFFLIN has the use of the said plantation and housing by lease for two years ... Wit: ROBERT HIRONS, MARY NIXON. Ackn 16 Feb 1721 by JOHN HALL atty for JOHN HIRONS. (G:pg 10)

525. 2 Feb 1720. Power of Atty. JOHN HIRONS of Kent Co labourer constitute my trusty friend JOHN HALL esqr to be my atty to make over unto SIMON HIRONS a tr of land [see above] adj on land called The Exchange on Hilyards Br ... Wit: ROBERT HIRONS, MARY NIXON. Proved 16 Feb 1721. (G:pg 10)

526. -- Feb 1720/21. Deed. EVAN JONES of Kent Co esqr for 17 pounds sold to ROBERT KARR (CARR) of town of Salisburry Kent Co merchant adminr of CHARLES HARPER late of town of Salisburry taylor decd who died intestate ... a lott lying within the limits of the town of Salisbury on the head of Duck Cr ... beginning at stake belonging to the lott of ROBERT READ ... 1/2 a. ... JNO PAIN, JNO COOK. Ackn 17 Feb 1721 by GEORGE MARTIN atty for EVAN JONES. (G:pg 10)

527. 16 Feb 1720. Power of Atty. EVAN JONES esqr of Kent Co constitute my loving friend GEORGE MARTIN of Kent Co my atty to make over [above] deed of sale for a dwelling house and lott belonging to CHARLES HARPER decd unto ROBERT KARR ... Wit: CHARLES HILLYARD, JOHN COOK. Proved 17 Feb 1721. (G:pg 11)

528. 30 Jan 1721. Deed. FRANCES MAROM of Kent Co widow for 45 pounds sold to JOHN MAROM of same place ... a parcell of land called Rooding being pt/o a tr called Edington formerly laid out for RICHARD LEVITTE ... 50 a. ... Wit: TIMOTHY HARBOT, JOHN MORISSON, WM BIRKETT. Ackn 16 Feb 1721. (G:pg 11)

529. 14 Feb 1720. Deed. BENJAMIN RENNALS eldest son & heir of FRANCIS RENNALS late of Kent Co decd for 10 pounds sold to JOHN TOUNZIN Junr of same place ... a tr of land s side of nw br of Murtherkill Cr ... to corner of a pt/o land sold by said BENJAMIN RENNALS to SAMUEL WATKINS ... 50 a. pt/o a tr called Indian Field ... BENJAMIN RENNALS appoint my trusty & well beloved friend ROBARD CUMING to ackn afsd deed in open court ... Wit: JOHN SIPPLE, MARK MANLOVE, WILLIAM MANLOVE Junr. Ackn 15 Feb 1721. (G:pg 12)

530. 10 Feb 1720/21. Deed. CHRISTOPHER SIPPLE (SIPLE) of Murtherkill Hund Kent Co for 2 pounds sold to JOHN MORRISS (MORRIS) of Mispillion Hund same co ... a tr of land warrant dated at

Phila 30 Oct 1717 granted to said CHRISTOPHER SIPPLE 200 a. to be laid out in the forrest in Mispillion Hund surveyed 10 Dec 1720 ... the plantation where JOHN MORRISS now dwelleth ... by Browns Br of Murther Cr ... to line of LEWIS DAVIS land ... Wit: HUGH DURBORROW Junr, RICHARD UNDERWOOD. Ackn 10 May 1721. (G:pg 13)

531. 10 Jun 1721. Deed. JOHN HALL of Kent Co gentleman and ANNA his wife & ELIZABETH PARNELL (PARNEL) wife of EDWARD PARNELL late of same co yeoman for 60 pounds sold to RICHARD WILSON (WILLSON) of same place gentleman ... a tr of land s side of Dover River called Elizabeth's Chance beginning at the white oak of MARY CLAYTON & HENRY BEDWELL's land at the head of Muddy Br ... to JOHN COR's land ... 150 a. ... Wit: WM RODENEY, SIMON HIRONS. Ackn 21 Jun 1721. (G:pg 15)

532. 6 May 1721. Deed. STEPHEN PARRADEE of Kent Co yeoman and MARGARET my wife for 12 pounds sold to TIMOTHY HIRONS (IRONS) of same co yeoman ... a tr of land in Dover Hund being pt/o a tr of land called Edingtons Tract ... adj land called Burtons Tr ... 26 a. ... Wit: JNO HART, STEPHEN PARADEE, WILLIAM BIRKETT. Ackn 10 May 1721 (G:pg 16)

533. 11 May 1721. Deed. Whereas THOMAS BANISTER formerly of Kent Co decd, uncle to RICHARD JAMES of New Castle Co yeoman, had due unto him 700 a. called Norring n side of Banister's Br or Hudson's Br of Murther Cr ... now said RICHARD JAMES heir at law to his uncle THOMAS BANISTER for 100 pounds sold to ANDREW CALDWELL of Kent Co yeoman afsd tr of land ... and further RICHARD JAMES is grandson unto PETER BAROM formerly of Kent Co decd and now heir at law to his said grandfather, sold to ANDREW CALDWELL 880 a. call Arondeck n side of Bannister's Br or Hudson's Br adj below the afsd tr of land called Norring ... Wit: RICHARD UNDERWOOD, ROBERT WILLSON. Ackn 11 May 1721. (G:pg 17)

534. 10 Apr 1721. Deed. WILLIAM RODENEY (RODNEY) of Kent Co for 27 pounds paid by THOMAS DOWNHAM in his lifetime sold to AGNES DOWNHAM executrix of the will of THOMAS DOWNHAM late of same co decd ... a tr of land s side of Dover River on n side of Mill Cr pt/o a greater tr of land called Dover Farms ... to corner of THOMAS SKIDMORE's land ... 55 a. ... Wit: JAMES MACKY, BENJAMIN SHURMER. Ackn 10 May 1721. (G:pg 18)

535. 10 May 1721. Deed. WILLIAM TRIPPET (TRIPET) Junr of Kent Co yeoman for 10 pounds 10 shillings sold to SAMUEL WILSON of same co

yeoman ... (WILLIAM TRIPPET Junr is lawfully possessed with 75 a. of land being due unto him by his father WILLIAM TRIPPET Senr of Kent Co yeoman late decd in his will dated 3 Aug 1716) ... a tr of land called Tripington ... near the fence of said WILLIAM TRIPPET ... 75 a. ... Wit: ANDREW CALDWELL, ROBERT BLACKSHER. Ackn 10 May 1721. (G:pg 19)

536. 1 Feb 1720. Deed. GEORGE ROBISSON Senr of Kent Co yeoman for 14 pounds sold to JOHN BOWERS of same co cooper ... a tr of land s side of Dover River pt/o a tr called Whitwells Delight ... near the present dwelling house of JOHN BOWERS ... by the line of a tr of land now in the possession of JOHN BOWERS ... 28 1/4 a. ... Wit: CALEB OFFLEY, JAMES STEEL. Ackn 10 May 1721. (G:pg 20)

537. 1 May 1721. Deed. WILLIAM WINSMORE son and heir of WILLIAM WINSMORE late of Kent Co esqr decd for 160 pounds sold to GEORGE ROBISSON Junr of same place gentleman ... a tr of land s side of Little Cr called Great Pipe Elme ... at the head of Dragons Cross Br ... to line of RICHARD LUKE ... bounded by DANIEL JONES ... 728 a. ... (100 a. given by WILLIAM WINSMORE grandfather of WILLIAM WINSMORE the younger, party to these presents by his will, to ABEL WILSON decd only excepted) ... Wit: THOMAS SKIDMORE, WM RODENEY. Ackn 12 May 1721. (G:pg 21)

538. 11 May 1721. Deed. THOMAS GONSEALA of Kent Co planter for 40 pounds sold to ROBERT GORDON of town & co of New Castle merchant ... a tr of land n side of Little Cr ... at the corner of JOHN FOSTER's land ... to the land called Simsons Choice ... 120 a. being pt/o 175 a. sold to GRIFFITH JONES by MARY WELLS adminr of JAMES WELLS bearing date 17 Feb 1685 who on 6 Oct 1698 granted 120 a. unto THOMAS GONSEALA ... Wit: EDWARD JENINGS, CHARLES HILLYARD. Ackn 13 May 1721. (G:pg 22)

539. 13 May 1721. Deed. JOHN HALL of Little Cr Hund gentleman for 25 pounds sold to LANCELOT LEWIS of same place yeoman ... a tr of land in Little Cr Hund adj n side of Mudy Br called Content ... (whereas JOHN HALL did convey unto THOMAS LEATHERBURY 200 a. forest tr of land, only excepting 100 a.) ... this indenture 100 a. being pt/o afsd tr which was excepted ... northerly corner of JOHN LEWIS ... to corner of THOMAS LEATHERBURY's land ... Wit: HUGH DURBOROW Junr, JAMES WORRALL. Ackn 13 May 1721. (G:pg 24)

540. 3 May 1721. Deed. JOHN REGISTER of Kent Co carpenter & SARAH his wife for 32 pounds 10 shillings sold to EDWARD JENNINGS of same place ... a tr of land being pt/o a larger tr called Berrys Range

formerly in the tenure of JAMES MAXWELL in Dover Hund near the head of Dover River ... 81 a. ... Wit: WM RODENEY, JOSEPH ASHTON. Ackn 11 May 1721. (G:pg 25)

541. 4 May 1721. Deed. JAMES SATERFIELD of Kent Co for 20 pounds sold to WILLIAM HILLYARD of same place planter ... a tr of land being pt/o a larger tr called Ferry Brigg s side of sw br of Duck Cr 50 a. bounded by the land late of JAMES JACKSON decd to the n and the land of JAMES STEEL to the e & se and Ellingsworth Br to the nw ... was lately in the tenure of JAMES STEEL and from him conveyed to JAMES JACKSON and from him to JAMES SATERFIELD ... Wit: JNO CLAYTON, MOSES FREEMAN, DANIEL HAMMOND. Ackn 13 May 1721. (G:pg 26)

542. 10 May 1721. Deed. JOHN HALL of Little Cr Hund Kent Co gentleman for 25 pounds sold to JOHN LEWIS of same co son of LANCELOT LEWIS blacksmith decd ... a tr of land in Little Cr Hund n side of Muddy Br called Content ... (whereas JOHN HALL did sell unto THOMAS LEATHERBURY of same place 200 a.) ... 100 a. being the upper pt/o 200 a. called Content ... to the corner of land now in the possession of LANCELOT LEWIS son of LANCELOT LEWIS decd ... HUGH DURBOROW Junr, JAMES WORRELL. Ackn 13 May 1721. (G:pg 27)

543. 10 May 1721. Deed. ARTHUR ALSTON of Kent Co yeoman son of ARTHUR ALSTON of same place decd for 25 pounds sold to JASPER HARWOOD of same place yeoman ... whereas ARTHUR ALSTON decd by his will did bequeath unto his son ARTHUR ALSTON 100 a. to be laid off at the upper end of a parcel he was then possessed ... to corner of that parcel of land whereon JASPER HARWOOD how dwelleth ... to land late in the possession of ISAAC ELLET decd ... to land now in the possession of RICHARD WALKER ... to land now in the possession of JOHN SCOT ... in Little Cr Hund and is pt/o a greater tr granted by patent to ARTHUR ALSTON ye father ... Wit: HUGH DURBOROW Junr, JAMES POTTER. Ackn 12 May 1721. (G:pg 28)

544. 8 Aug 1721. Deed. WILLIAM MAXWELL eldest son of JAMES MAXWELL late of Kent Co decd & ROBERT MAXWELL younger son of the said JAMES MAXWELL decd & MELISTON his wife all of Little Cr Hund ... whereas JAMES MAXWELL in his lifetime became seized of a tr of land adj e side of Dover River called Berrys Range whereon he did then dwell ... dying intestate the land descended unto his sons WILLIAM, JAMES and ROBERT MAXWELL ... JAMES MAXWELL by a deed of sale dated 10 May 1712 did sell to JOHN REGISTER a parcel of land of the lower end of the tr as his share ... WILLIAM MAXWELL by one

other indenture did sell to JOHN MAHAN a parcel of afsd tr including pt/o the plantation whereon THOMAS PARBO now dwelleth (Book D folio 15) ... this indenture WILLIAM MAXWELL and ROBERT MAXWELL and MELISTON his wife for 30 pounds sold to EDWARD JENNINGS (JENINGS) of Dover same co one parcel of land between the two afsd parcels ... 130 a. ... Wit: HUGH DURBOROW Junr, JOHN LAUDE. Ackn 12 Aug 1721. (G:pg 30)

545. 9 Aug 1721. Deed. RICHARD WALKER of Little Cr Hund Kent Co yeoman & MARY his wife for 40 pounds sold to THOMAS ELLITT (ELLETT) of same place yeoman ... a tr of land patent at Phila granted unto ARTHUR ALSTON late of Little Cr Hund same co decd, bounded on the n by sw br of Duck Cr 800 a. ... ARTHUR ALSTON did convey 400 a. unto THOMAS BOLSTOCK then of same co ... THOMAS BOLSTOCK dying intestate the 400 a. descended into the possession of MARY FITZGARRALL (FITZJARRELL) grandau & only surviving heir to the said THOMAS BOLSTOCK ... MARY FITZGARRALL dau to EDWARD FITZGARRALL & ANN his wife (which said ANN was dau of the said THOMAS BOLSTOCK) is now become lawfully married to RICHARD WALKER afsd ... 230 a. that pt/o the afsd 400 a. tr whereon said THOMAS BOLSTOCK did in his lifetime dwell ... Wit: HUGH DURBOROW Junr, JAMES POTTER. Ackn 9 Aug 1721. (G:pg 31)

546. 11 Aug 1721. Deed. JOHN TOWNSEND (TOWNZIN) Junr of Murderkill Hund Kent Co yeoman for 20 shillings sold to ROBERT HOWARD of same place yeoman ... a tr of land (200 a. patent dated at Phila 6 Feb 1717/18 granted unto JOHN TOWNSEND Junr in the forrest) ... a small distance nw from the Black Swamp ... 100 a. ... to land called Long Tract ... Wit: HUGH DURBOROW Junr, ROBERT MAXWELL. Ackn 12 Aug 1721. (G:pg 33)

547. 10 Aug 1721. Deed. SAMUEL WILLOBE (WILBEE) of the forest of Murderkill Hund Kent Co yeoman for 20 pounds sold to RICHARD MORLEY late of Talbot Co MD yeoman ... a tr of land whereon said SAMUEL WILLIBE now dwelleth ... 100 a. ... Wit: HUGH DURBOROW Junr, FRANCIS ALLEXANDER, WM NEWELLE. Ackn 10 Aug 1721. (G:pg 33)

548. 4 Sep 1707. Bond of Conveyance. HENRY BECKWITH of Dorchester Co MD planter am bound unto JOHN MOLLESTON of Kent Co PA gentleman for 88 pounds ... HENRY BECKWITH shall convey unto JOHN MOLLESTON before the second Tuesday in Aug next ensueing a perfect and absolute estate of inheritance unto a tr of land called Gainsbrough 445 a. ... Wit: BENJAMIN DABBS, THEODORUS BONNER. (G:pg 34)

549. 10 Nov 1702. Deed. WILLIAM WINSMORE of Kent Co PA for 30 pounds sold to THOMAS WILLSON of same co planter ... a tr of land called Denby Town being pt/o a tr on the s side of Little Cr called Great Pipe Elme ... by Levicks Br ... to corner of MATHEW WILLSON's land ... 50 a. ... Wit: WILLIAM ANNAND, SAMUEL BURBARY. Ackn 10 Feb 1702. (G:pg 35)

550. 1 May 1719. Deed. WILLIAM STARKEY son & heir of ANN (PORTER alias) EDMONDS late of Kent Co decd for 12 pounds sold to NICHOLAS NIXON of same co blacksmith ... a tr of land n side of Murther Cr called Egmonds Chance ... bounded by THOMAS HEATHARD's land ... 300 a. granted by patent unto ROBERT EDMONDS late of Kent Co decd bearing date 26 Mar 1684 ... ROBERT EDMONDS in his lifetime the 26 Nov 1706 did make his will ... bequeathed remaining pt/o my estate both real & personal unto my beloved wife ANN EDMONDS ... Wit: ANDREW CALDWELL, JOHN THOMSON. Ackn 15 May 1719. (G:pg 37)

551. 15 Nov 1721. Deed. NICHOLAS NIXON of Kent Co blacksmith for one merchantable cow and calfe to him in hand paid sold to MARK MANLOVE of same place yeoman ... one half pt/o [above] tr of land whereon SAMUEL MOTT formerly dwelleth ... Wit: THOMAS BERRY, THOMAS ROCK. 17 Nov 1721. (G:pg 38)

552. 1 Nov 1721. Deed. WILLIAM RODENEY of Kent Co yeoman & RUTH his wife ... whereas a tr of land called Dover Farms s side of Dover River ... by the line of WILLIAM DARVAL's land ... by Mill Cr ... 840 a. being made up of several parcels of land: 400 a. granted by patent from Sir EDMOND ANDREWS to HUBERT FRANCIS, 210 a. granted by Court of St. Jones and laid out 21 Mar 1684 to JOHN BURTON and whereas EDMOND GIBBONS decd did in his lifetime purch of HUBERT FRANCIS the 400 a. and of the JOHN BURTON the 200 a. & devised the same by his will to his brother FRANCIS GIBBONS and resurveyed and found to contain 695 a. and afterwards conveyed by said FRANCIS GIBBONS to WILLIAM RODENEY decd father of the afsd WILLIAM RODENEY and 50 a. more purch by WILLIAM RODENEY of JAMES MAXWELL and 100 a. granted by a warrant and being resurveyed together was found to contain 840 a. as afsd and by confirmation by pattent bearing date 17 Oct 1701 by WILLIAM PENN esqr Governor of PA confirmed unto WILLIAM RODENEY, and said WILLIAM RODENEY did afterwards in his life time by deed 25 Mar 1699 sell unto ADAM FISHER of same co 92 a. pt/o afsd 840 a. and also 1 May 1708 did make his will ... I bequeath unto my two eldest sons WILLIAM & THOMAS RODENEY all that tr of land called Dover Farms containing at this time 748 a. to be divided between them ... when my son WILLIAM shall attain

the age of 21 ... THOMAS RODENEY dyeing without issue and before WILLIAM RODENEY the brother came of age the same WILLIAM RODENEY is heir to the whole 748 a. ... WILLIAM RODENEY (after his attaining the age of 21) did sell to ISAIAH WHITEHEAD 50 a. & to AGNES DOWNHAM executrix of the will of THOMAS DOWNHAM decd 57 a. ... this indenture WILLIAM RODENEY for 350 pounds sold to WAITMAN SIPPLE of same place yeoman remaining pt/o 748 a. ... Wit: CHARLES HARRISON, ISABEL JUCH Ackn 18 Nov 1721. (G:pg 39)

553. 18 Nov 1721. Power of Atty. RUTH RODENEY appoint my friend JOHN CURTIS & MOSES FREEMAN of either of them to be my atty to ackn [above] deed in open court ... Wit: CHARLES HARRISON, ISABEL JUCH. Proved 18 Nov 1721 by CHARLES HARRIS. (G:pg 42)

554. 17 Nov 1721. Deed. JAMES WORRALL of Kent Co gentleman ... whereas a tr of land pattent granted unto WILLIAM WILLSON late of Kent Co decd called Cambridge n side of sw br of Duck Cr and by deed bearing date 5 May 1689 did sell unto JOHN DUNSTONBY and JOHN DUNSTONBY by deed bearing date 10 Jun 1690 did sell unto JOHN EDMONDSON of Talbot Co MD afsd tr of land ... 100 a. was by THOMAS EDMONDSON son and heir at law of afsd JOHN EDMONDSON by his deed bearing date 5 Nov 1718 sold to JOSEPH WORRALL father of said JAMES WORRALL ... this indenture JAMES WORRALL (surviving son & heir at law of his late father JOSEPH WORRALL decd) for 31 pounds 5 shillings sold afsd tr of land to JOHN POUND of Kent Co yeoman ... Wit: NICHOLAS LOOCKERMAN, THOMAS ADAMS, BENJAMIN SHURMER. Ackn 18 Nov 1721. (G:pg 42)

555. 17 Oct 1721. Deed of Release. FRANCIS HIRONS of Kent Co yeoman son & heir of SIMON HIRONS late of same place decd ... by virtue of a warrant bearing date 20 Jun 1682 there was surveyed the 12 Nov 1686 unto SIMON HIRONS a tr of land called The Range 1000 a. n side of Dover River and by patent granted bearing date 30 Mar 1688 ... SIMON HIRONS in his life time did sell afsd tr of land unto WILLIAM BERRY and JOSEPH PHIPS joyntly and by indenture bearing date 1 Feb 1689 they did sell the same unto JOHN RICHARDSON Senr late of same co decd and by his will dyed possessed of the 1000 a. to be divided between MARY RICHARDSON his executrix, JOHN RICHARDSON, his grandson JOHN LEVICK and the children of GEORGE and JUDITH ROW ... 300 a. of afsd tr do now belong unto JOHN HALL & BENJAMIN SHURMER of Kent Co gentlemen and because the first mentioned conveyance from SIMON HIRONS has been misplaced ... FRANCIS HIRONS for 10 shillings release unto JOHN HALL & BENJAMIN SHURMER 300 a. pt/o the 1000 a. to be laid out by virtue of the will afsd

... Wit: THOMAS WARD, EDWARD JENINGS, ROBERT BYGRAVE. Ackn 17 Nov 1721. 18 Oct 1721 Memorandum that peaceable possession of the lands was delivered by FRANCIS HIRONS unto JOHN HALL & BENJAMIN SHURMER. Wit: THOMAS WARD, GEORGE METCALFE, ROBERT BYGRAVE. (G:pg 44)

556. 12 Jan 1721. Gift. MARY RICHARDSON of Kent Co widow for natural love and affection which I have for my grandchildren MARY LEVICK, WILLIAM LEVICK and JOHN LEVICK sons & dau of RICHARD LEVICK and MARY his wife ... I give unto my grandchild MARY LEVICK my negro girl called HANNAH aged 4 years, I give unto my grandchild WILLIAM LEVICK my negro girl called PHILLIS aged two years, and I give unto my grandchild JOHN LEVICK my negro called DIRK aged 17 years, after my decease ... Wit: BENJAMIN SHURMER, SARAH SHURMER, ROBERT BYGRAVE. (G:pg 46)

557. 19 Dec 1721. Articles of Agreement between BENJAMIN SHURMER of Kent Co esqr and JOHN HALL of same co esqr ... whereas the afsd BENJAMIN SHURMER & JOHN HALL joyntly with ANDREW CALDWELL & HUGH DURBOROW both of same co yeoman lately purch of JOHN ROW of Queen Anns Co MD yeoman tr of land formerly belonging to old JOHN RICHARDSON of Kent Co yeoman decd by deed of sale from JOHN ROE to PHILIP KEARNY of Kent Co esqr executed in trust to the only use of afsd BENJAMIN SHURMER, JOHN HALL, ANDREW CALDWELL & HUGH DURBOROW ... division of all tr hath lately been made between the four purch in two equal parts ... one to remain to BENJAMIN and JOHN and the other to ANDREW and HUGH ... it is agreed between BENJAMIN SHURMER and JOHN HALL to the division of all lands purch joyntly ... BENJAMIN to have 300 a. of land call The Range at the head of Dover River above the plantation late of JOHN MACHAN which FRANCIS HIRONS hath lately conveyed to them [see #553] ... JOHN HALL by his deed of sale and 85 pounds due from RICHARD LEVICK by bond being pt/o the 120 pounds purch money which he is to pay for 200 a. of land sold to him before any agreement of division ... and JOHN HALL shall have for his part tr of land called Chipping Norton ... Wit: TIMOTHY HANSON, JAMES WORRALL. Ackn 19 Dec 1721. (G:pg 47)

558. 3 Aug 1704. Deed. JOHN TOAS (TOAES) of Kent Co MD gentleman for 5 pounds sold to JOHN RAYNOLDS of Kent Co son of THOMAS RAYNOLDS decd ... a tr of land called Dundee w side of Dover River s side of Isaacs Br ... to THOMAS MICHOLDS plantation ... 200 a. ... Wit: WILLIAM WILLSON, JOHN CLARKE, ROBERT REGISTER. Ackn 8 Aug 1704. (G:pg 48)

559. 4 Aug 1704. Power of Atty. JOHN TOAES of Kent Co MD gentleman appoint my well beloved friend WILLIAM MORTON of Kent Co PA to be my atty to ackn one parcel of land called Dundee, 200 a. to WILLIAM REGISTER & 500 a. to JOHN RAYNOLDS son of THOMAS RAYNOLDS decd in open court ... Wit: JOHN CLARKE, WILLIAM WILLSON, ROBERT REGESTER. Proved 8 Jul 1704 by JOHN BRINCKLE. (G:pg 49)

560. 1 Oct 1718. Receipt. JOHN FRENCH received from SIMON HIRONS full satisfaction for a bond of 18 pounds ... Attest: BEN SHURMER. (G:pg 50)

561. 15 Nov 1718. Receipt. WM HIRONS received of SIMON HIRONS 10 pounds being in full of all amounts, bills, bonds, debts, deus and demands whatsoever ... Attest: ELIZABETH HIRONS, RICHARD SMITH. (G:pg 50)

562. 14 Feb 1721. Deed. JOHN MILLS of Kent Co planter son & heir of JOHN MILLS late of same co decd ... whereas a 500 a. tr of land patent bearing date 5 Jul 1684 granted unto EDWARD PINER then of same co ... s side of Murtherkill Cr ... and EDWARD PINER by his deed bearing date 14 Jun 1692 conveyed to JOHN MILLS the father who being possessed of said tr of land soon after dyed whereby tr descended unto JOHN MILLS the son ... this indenture JOHN MILLS the son for 23 pounds 10 shillings sold to WILLIAM MANLOVE of same place carpentor afsd tr of land ... at Virgins Br ... to Mills Br ... 150 a. ... Wit: ANDREW CALDWELL, MATTHEW MANLOVE. Ackn 14 Feb 1721. (G:pg 50)

563. 15 Feb 1720. Deed. SIMON HIRONS of Kent Co yeoman for 100 pounds sold to BENJAMIN SHURMER & JOHN HALL both of same place gentlemen ... a tr of land (patent granted unto JOHN RICHARDSON late of Kent Co gentleman) called Wellingbrook 1000 a. on Little Cr Hund late in possession of RICHARD LEVICK and now of EVAN JONES and other lands of GEORGE RODENEY's called York to the se and by the lands of RODENEY formerly in possession of STEPHEN PARADEE to the s & sw ... to lands of JOSEPH CLAYTON & RALPH NEEDHAM to the w & of DAVID MORGAN to the nw ... whereas there is also another tr called Bristol being of the afsd larger tr called York beginning at the corner of land late of RICHARD LEVICK ... 200 a. ... Wit: TIMOTHY HANSON, GRIFF JONES. Ackn 15 Feb 1720. (G:pg 51)

564. 15 Feb 1720. Deed. THOMAS NIXON of Kent Co yeoman and MARY his wife, adminr of BENJAMIN BRADY the father and also of BENJAMIN BRADY the son late of same place decd ... whereas a tr of

land (patent bearing date 9 June 1683 granted unto JOHN RICHARDSON late of same co gentleman) called Chipping Norton in Little Cr Hund ... bounded formerly by JOHN BETTS ... to line formerly of RICHARD WILLSON ... in line formerly of JOHN STEVENS ... 800 a. ... JOHN RICHARDSON by deed of gift bearing date 16 Oct 1689 did give unto JOHN BRADY Senr, JOHN BRADY Junr, DANIEL BRADY & BENJAMIN BRADY afsd tr of land ... all are dead and gone and no heirs of their body remain and said MARY adminr becoming seized of afsd tr of land ... this indenture THOMAS NIXON and MARY his wife for 120 pounds sold afsd tr of land to JOHN HALL and BENJAMIN SHURMER both of same co gentlemen ... Wit: TIMOTHY HANSON, MARK MANLOVE. Ackn 15 Feb 1720. (G:pg 52)

565. 29 Dec 1721. Lease. JAMES STEEL of Phila gentleman and MARTHA his wife lease to NICHOLAS GREENAWAY of Duck Cr Kent Co merchant ... a tr of land s side of sw br of Duck Cr ... corner of JOHN FOSTER's land ... to land of SAMUEL HANSON ... to Wilsons Br ... 300 a. ... for one whole year ... Wit: A HAMILTON, CLEM PLUMSTED. Akcn 14 Feb 1721. (G:pg 54)

566. 30 Dec 1720. Deed. JAMES STEEL of Phila gentleman and MARTHA his wife for 130 pounds sold to NICHOLAS GREENAWAY of Duck Cr Kent Co merchant ... [above] 300 a. tr of land (patent bearing date 4 May 1715 granted unto JAMES JACKSON late of Duck Cr & MARGARET his wife for 750 a. recorded at Phila Book A Dot 5 pg 109) and they by deed 5 Feb 1717/8 sold to JAMES STEEL excepting 70 a. sold to JOHN FOSTER and 140 a. sold to SAMUEL MANLOVE and a small parcel granted to WILLIAM KELLY ... Wit: A HAMILTON, CLEM PLUMSTED. Ackn 15 Feb 1721. (G:pg 55)

567. 1 Mar 1720. Deed. JOHN ROE of Queen Anns Co MD planter, son of GEORGE ROE late of Kent Co decd, and JUDETH his wife and nephew to JOHN RICHARDSON Senr late of same co gentleman ... whereas JOHN RICHARDSON decd in his life time became seized of sundry trs of land and JOHN RICHARDSON by deed of gift bearing date 16 Oct 1689 did grant unto his son in law JOHN BRADY Senr and his grandchildren JOHN BRADY Junr, DANIEL BRADY and BENJAMIN BRADY a tr of land called Chippenorton 800 a. and the said BRADY's all deceasing, the said land descended into the possession of BENJAMIN BRADY son of said BENJAMIN BRADY decd and only surviving heir of all the BRADY's decd ... and JOHN RICHARDSON by deed of gift bearing date 14 Jun 1698 gave his grandson JOHN RICHARDSON 200 a. called Bristol being pt/o a tr called York ... and JOHN RICHARDSON by his will bequeathed to his grandson JOHN RICHARDSON 500 a. being one halfe of a tr called Willingbrook and said JOHN RICHARDSON the

grandson decd before he became the age of 21 and without lawfull issue the two parcels of land became into the possession of BENJAMIN BRADY son of BENJAMIN and greatgrandson of JOHN RICHARDSON the grandfather and only surviving heir to the BRADY's afsd which BENJAMIN BRADY is now also decd without lawfull issue and under age ... this indenture JOHN ROE heir at law of BENJAMIN BRADY for 80 pounds sold to PHILLIP KERNEY of same place gentleman all afsd parcells of land ... Wit: THO WARD, JOHN THOMSON, JOHN LEVICK. Proved 13 May 1721. (G:pg 56)

568. 15 Feb --. Deed. JAMES HOWELL of Kent Co planter for 10 pounds sold to JOHN BARNS of same place yeoman ... a tr of land n side Fishing Br in Mispillion Hund ... by Cullings Br ... 100 a. being pt/o a tr called Cullings Purchase formerly in the tenure of GEORGE CULLEN and by him sold to JAMES HOWELL father to the said JAMES HOWELL by indenture bearing date 10 Aug 1697 Book C Fol 194 and the will of afsd JAMES HOWELL decd bequeathed unto JAMES HOWELL his son ... Wit: MATTHEW MANLOVE, ROBERT BYGRAVE, THOMAS TESTER. Ackn 15 Feb 1721. (G:pg 58)

569. 20 Feb 1721. Deed of Gift. MICHEAL LOWBAR (LOWBER) of Kent Co yeoman for love and fatherly respect give to my dau SUSANAH and her husband BENJAMIN FURBY ... 100 a. where BENJAMIN FURBY now dwelleth it being pt/o a 400 a. tr of land I bought of DANIEL RUTTY called Southhemton which 100 a. is now called Furbys Lott ... to land I before sold to ANDREW CALDWELL ... Wit: ANDREW CALDWELL, SAMUELL WILSON, MOSES WHITAKER. Ackn 15 Feb 1721. (G:pg 60)

570. 17 Feb 1721. Deed. GEORGE HART & JOHN HART both of Kent Co yeomen & HENRY HART of same place yeomen & MARY his wife for [blank] pounds sold to THOMAS WELLS of same place yeoman ... a tr of land n side of Isaacs Br called Wellses Purchase being pt/o a greater tr of land formerly taken up by THOMAS BEDWELL, HENRY BEDWELL, ROBERT BEDWELL and ADAM FISHER then called Long Reach ... 100 a. which came to belong to GEORGE HART father to the afsd GEORGE HART, JOHN HART & HENRY HART who by his will bearing date 25 Nov 1702 did give to his sons to be equally divided between them ... Wit: ISRAEL RIKY, JOHN JONES, ROBERT BYGRAVE. Ackn 17 Feb 1721. (G:pg 60)

571. -- -- 1721. Deed. Whereas JOHN CLIFFWORTH and ANN his wife did by indenture bearing date 9 Feb 1720 convey unto BENJAMIN SHURMER of Kent Co gentleman a 300 a. tr of land called Skiptop n side of Jones Cr ... at corner of land formerly laid out for ROBERT BEDWELL ... to corner of land called London formerly laid out for DANIEL JONES

... this indenture BENJAMIN SHURMER in consideration of afsd and 10 shillings sold to JOHN CLIFFWORTH 100 a. being pt/o afsd tr called Skiptop adj land now in the possession of JOHN CLAYTON, MARK BARDON, GEORGE HAYPOLE and afsd BENJAMIN SHURMER ... to Walker's Br ... Wit: TIMOTHY HANSON, CHARLES HILLYARD. Ackn 17 Feb 1721. (G:pg 62)

572. 9 May 1721. Deed of Release. Whereas JOHN ELLIS decd in his life time became seized of a tr of land in Little Cr Hund s side of sw br of Duck Cr near a place called Chestnut Landing being the uppermost corner of a tr called Denby Town ... 100 a. being pt/o a tr called Denby Town ... JOHN ELLIS by his will dated 1 Feb 1719/20 ... bequeath all his estate to his son WILLIAM ELLIS as by the will recorded in the Registers Office for Kent Co MD ... JOHN ELLIS the father did in his life time receive of SAMUEL WHITEHART of Kent Co yeoman 23 pounds payment for afsd 100 a. ... WILLIAM ELLIS of Kent Co MD son of JOHN ELLIS decd release unto SAMUEL WHITEHART afsd tr of land being his present dwelling ... Wit: THOMAS LEATHERBURY, HUGH DURBOROW Junr. Ackn 15 Feb 1721. (G:pg 63)

573. 12 Apr 1722. Assignment. WILLIAM KEITH Baronet by our Royal Approbation & Appointment Governour assigns COLONEL JOHN FRENCH & SAMUEL LOWMAN of New Castle Co, JAMES STEEL & BENJAMIN SHURMER of Kent Co and JONATHAN BAILLIE & BERKLEY TODD of Suss Co esqrs justices of our Supream Court ... to inquire by affirmations of honest and lawfull men of the respective cos ... the truth of the matter may be better known of all treasons, murders and such other crimes ... be made capital or felonies of death ... (G:pg 65)

574. 29 Mar 1722. Appointments. SIR WILLIAM KEITH Baronet by our Royal Approbation and Appointment Governour appoints COLONEL JOHN FRENCH, SAMUEL LOWMAN, JAMES STEEL, BENJAMIN SHURMER, JONATHAN BAILLIE and BERKLEY TODD esqrs ... Supream Court Justices of Kent Co. (G:pg 66)

575. 17 May 1722. Appointment. SAMUEL LOWMAN collector by virtue of commission and instruction given unto me appoint BENJAMIN SHURMER esqr of Kent Co to be deputy collector ... (G:pg 66)

576. 15 Feb 1721/2. Gift. THOMAS KNOX (NOCK) of Motherkill Hund Kent Co farmer for love, goodwill and affection give to CHERITY BROOKS of same place ... one cow & one calve ... Wit: JOHN NEWELL, JOHN ALLEE. (G:pg 66)

577. 9 May 1722. JOHN NEWELL & JOHN ALLEE made oath ... that

they saw the [above] instrument of writing or deed of gift as his act unto
REBECKA BROOKS ... (signed) THOMAS FRENCH. (G:pg 67)

578. 1 Mar 1720. Deed. PHILIP KEARNY of Kent Co gentleman ...
whereas JOHN ROE of Queen Anns Co MD planter, son of GEORGE
ROE late of Kent Co decd, and JUDITH his wife, and nephew of JOHN
RICHARDSON Senr late of Kent Co gentleman by his deed of sale sold
unto PHILIP KEARNY of Kent Co gentleman ... parcels of land in Little
Cr Hund [see #565] ... sold to BENJAMIN SHURMER, JOHN HALL,
HUGH DURBOROW and ANDREW CALDWELL all of Kent Co yeomen,
afsd parcels of land ... Wit: THOMAS WARD, JOHN TOMSON, JOHN
LEVICK. (G:pg 67)

579. 4 May 1722. Deed. Whereas EVAN JONES esqr late of same co decd
for 205 pounds paid by ISAAC SNOW & ELISHA SNOW by indenture
bearing date 14 Jan 1712 for a tr of land on which said ELISHA SNOW
now dwells n side of sw br of Duck Cr 199 1/2 a. (recorded in Book E
3,4,5 & 6) ... ISAAC SNOW of Kent Co yeoman for 100 pounds sold unto
ELISHA SNOW afsd tr of land ... Wit: RICHARD WALKER, JOHN
TILTON. Ackn 9 May 1721. (G:pg 68)

580. 3 May 1722. Deed. EVAN JONES of Kent Co plasterer for 200
pounds sold to ISAAC SNOW of same co yeoman ... a tr of land n side of
sw br of Duck Cr being the plantation where ISAAC SNOW now dwelleth
having been in 1684 granted by patent (wherein called Intollahay) unto
JOHN GALE ... to land of FRANCIS WHITWELL ... to line of MICHAEL
SIMKINS ... 400 a. ... Wit: JOHN TILTON, JAMES WORRALL. Ackn 10
May 1721. (G:pg 69)

581. 28 Apr 1722. Deed. THOMAS ELLET of Duck Cr Kent Co yeoman
for 21 pounds sold to JOHN JONES of the town of Salisbury Kent Co
miller ... a tr of land s side of sw br of Duck Cr ... by Willsons Br and a
corner of a tr of land called Denby ... to land of JAMES STEEL ... 100 a.
was granted by warrant bearing date 24 Dec 1716 & surveyed 20 Jan to
JAMES STEEL afterwards sold to THOMAS ELLET 10 Feb 1717/8
(recorded Book F folio 54) ... Wit: ISAAC SNOW, JOHN ALLEE
ROBERT BYGRAVE. Ackn 9 May 1722. (G:pg 71)

582. 12 May 1722. Deed. JOHN CURTIS late of Kent Co gentleman and
SARAH his wife for a valuable consideration in hand paid sold to JOHN
MATHON of same place yeoman ... a tr of land called The Reserve sw
side of Dover River 400 a. ... Wit: THOMAS CRAWFORD, JOHN
BLAND, GEORGE MARTIN. Ackn 12 May 1722. (G:pg 72)

583. 7 Apr 1722. Power of Atty. JOHN CURTIS of Kent Co yeoman (son

& heir of CALEB CURTIS late decd of same co gentleman) and SARAH his wife appoint our trusty friend ANDREW CALDWELL of same co gentleman to be our atty to deliver & convey [above] deed of sale in open court ... Wit: NATHANIEL BOWMAN, THOMAS JESTER, JAMES MAXWELL. Proved 12 May 1722. Attest: BENJAMIN SHURMER clerk. (G:pg 73)

584. 15 May 1711 at NY. Confirmation of Patent. FRANCIS LOVELACE esqr confirms patent unto THOMAS YOUNG for a tr of land 400 a. ne side of St. Jones Cr being about a mile above Murder Cr ... se with the land of THOMAS MERRITT ... patent dated 17 Jun 1671. (signed) H WILEMAN secretary. (G:pg 73)

585. 27 Apr 1722. Deed. JOHN BRADSHAW & FRANCIS his wife of Kent Co yeoman for 38 pounds sold to OWEN DAVID of same place husbandman ... a tr of land called Bradshaws Chance n side of sw br of Duck Cr being pt/o a 300 a. tr formerly in the tenure of JOHN BRADSHAW of same co decd ... since in 1722 by decease of said JOHN BRADSHAW, JOHN BRADSHAW Junr became seized of pt/o land ... to corner of JOHN HIGHAM ... 140 a. ... Wit: NICOLAS GREENAWAY, JOHN ALLEE. Ackn 11 May 1722. (G:pg 73)

586. Memorandum. EPHRAIM EMERSON and THOMAS PARKE did hear NICH GREENAWAY and JOHN ALLEY say that they saw FRANCIS BRADSHAW sign and deliver the [above] deed ... (G:pg 74)

587. 12 May 1722. Deed. ENEAS MAHAN of Dover Hund Kent Co yeoman and ORPHA his wife for 200 pounds sold to RANDALL DONNAVAN of Murtherkill Hund same co yeoman ... a tr of land lately belonging to WILLIAM WINSMORE & by him granted unto the said ENEAS MAHAN by deed bearing date 14 Nov 1719 ... by Cattail Pond ... 100 a. ... Wit: THOMAS ADAMS Senr, JOHN BLAND, EDMOND BOWMAN. Ackn 11 May 1721. (G:pg 75)

588. 26 Aug --. Deed. WILLIAM WINSMORE of Kent Co yeoman for 20 pounds sold to JOHN WILLSON of same co yeoman ... a tr of land in Dover Hund called MATHEW WILLSON's plantation and was in the tenure of ISAAC FREELAND 100 a. ... Wit: MARY HART, JOHN GLOVER, JOHN HARTT. Ackn 10 May 1722. (G:pg 76)

589. 4 May 1722. Deed. ISAAC MASON and SUSANNA his wife of Kent Co for 16 pounds sold to JOHN TOMBLIN labourour of same co ... a tr of land s side of Murder Cr in Mispillion Hund being pt/o a 2000 a. tr called Fair Field ... to line of ROBERT CUMMINGS land ... 120 a. ... Wit: GEORGE ROBBISSON Junr, NATHANIEL WHITEHEAD. Ackn 11 May

1722. (G:pg 77)

590. 8 May 1722. Deed. SAMUEL WATKINS and ANN his wife of Kent Co for 11 pounds sold to JOHN TOWNZIN Senr of same place ... a tr of land called Watkins Dear Purchase being pt/o a tr called Indian Fields s side of nw br of Murtherkill ... by Pine Br ... 50 a. ... Wit: RICHARD LEVICK, JOHN CLAYTON, JOHN EVAMS. Ackn 10 May 1722. (G:pg 78)

591. 21 Nov 1721. Deed. ANNE GORLEN (GARLEN) (alias ROE) wife of WILLIAM GURLEN of Sumerset Co planter (who hath authorized his said wife ANNE by power of atty bearing date 1 Nov 1721) to sell and convey a tr of land ... ANNE for 10 pounds sold unto ANDREW CALDWELL of Kent Co yeoman ... a tr of land being 100 a. bequeathed unto her by her unckle JOHN RICHARDSON late decd of Kent Co in his will ... Wit: THOMAS BERRY, JAMES WILLSON Junr, ROBERT HODGSON. Ackn 11 May 1722. (G:pg 79)

592. 1 Nov 1721. Power of Atty. ANN GORLEN alias ROE appoint my trusty friend THOMAS BERRY to ackn and deliver [above] deed of sale in open court ... (G:pg 80)

593. 9 May 1722. Deed. RANDOL DONOVAN and ELIZABETH his wife of Kent Co for 200 pounds sold to AENES MAHON of same place ... a parcel of land called Simons Folly formerly belonging to STEPHEN SIMONS of same co decd and bequeathed by his will ... to my dau ELIZABETH and RANDOL DONOVAN that plantation called Simons Folly to be delivered to them at the day of marriage ... n side of Murtherkill Cr ... by Servis Br ... bounded by JEREMIAH NICKERSON's land ... 100 a. ... Wit: JON MCDOWELL, MICHAELL RICHMOND. Ackn 10 May 1722. (G:pg 80)

594. 9 May --. Deed. EPHRAIM EMERSON of Kent Co yeoman & MARY his wife for 80 pounds sold to JOHN HALL of same place gentleman ... a tr of land s side of sw br of Duck Cr ... in the line of land formerly laid out for SIMON HIRONS called Chippanorton ... in the line of land laid out for JOHN RICHARDSON ... to side of Muddy Br ... 400 a. warrant dated 21 Sep 1680 and laid out 11 Dec 1686 unto RICHARD WILLSON late of Kent Co yeoman decd and by him by his will bequeathed unto his dau MARY WILLSON now wife of afsd EPHRAIM EMERSON ... Wit: NICHOLAS LOOCKERMAN, ROBERT BYGRAVE. Ackn 10 May 1722. (G:pg 81)

595. 11 May 1722. Deed. HENRY HALL of Mispelion Hund Kent Co yeoman for 30 pounds sold to MATHEW MANLOVE of same place

yeoman ... a tr of land called Mount Pleasant n side of Mispillion Cr ... by Beaver Dam Br ... by Fishing Br ... 412 a. of land and 88 a. of marsh adj ... granted by order of St. Jones court 21 Sep 1680 surveyed 13 Jan following to WILLIAM CLARK and confirmed by patent 26 Mar 1684 and conveyed unto GRIFFITH JONES late of Phila merchant decd ... 10 Sep 1694 GRIFFITH JONES by deed sold to MARK MANLOVE late of same co decd father of MARK MANLOVE ... which MARK MANLOVE in his lifetime 24 Nov 1694 did make his will ... bequeath unto my son MARK the afsd plantation ... MARK MANLOVE the younger by deed sold unto ROBERT BETTS of Kent Co 200 a. and 1 Jan 1716 sold unto HENRY HALL of same co yeoman the residue of afsd tr of land ... Wit: JOHN CURTIS, NICOLAS GREENAWAY, ROBERT BYGRAVE. Ackn 11 May 1722. (G:pg 83)

596. 17 Apr 1721/2. Writ of Execution. CHARLES HILLYARD esqr sheriffe of Kent Co ... whereas ROBERT GORDON and MARY his wife at a Court of Common Pleas held 11 May ... one DANIEL SMITH late of Kent Co marriner ... owing a debt of 111 pounds 16 shillings 5 pence with 7 pounds costs which ROBERT & MARY were adjudged for their damages which they had sustained by occasion of the detention of that debt ... writt 10 Nov directed GRIFFITH JONES then sheriff to sell goods and chattels of DANIEL SMITH to pay debt ... 16 Nov 1716 seized in execution two parcells of land containing in the whole 195 a., one begins at the corner of land of JOHN COURTNEY decd ... called Coventry the other begins at a corner of SAMUEL BURBERRY's land ... by WILLIAM MORTON's land ... down the br by BARTLETT's ... jurors appraised to afsd vallue of debt ... GRIFFITH JONES afterwards dyed ... another writ bearing date 17 Feb directed to CHARLES HILLYARD sheriff ... for 80 pounds sold to THOMAS CRAWFORD of Kent Co yeoman 195 a. taken in execution as afsd ... Wit: EDWARD JENINGS, BENJAMIN SHURMER. Ackn 8 May 1722. (G:pg 85)

597. Petition. ROBERT GORDON esqr requesting justices to impower the present sheriff to convey lands of DANIEL SMITH as it was not done before the death of GRIFFITH JONES sheriff ... [see above] (G:pg 87)

598. 15 Feb 1721/2. Affidavit. JOHN HILLYARD aged about 60 years doth declare that he became acquainted with one PETER BACOME (BOACOMB) about 1682 and he became acquainted with a young woman named RUTH and the above PETER BACOME said she was his only dau, about 2 or 3 years after PETER BACOME died and he did hear PETER BACOME did make a will which he often see amongst some papers belonging to GEORGE MARTIN who did adminr with RUTH BACOME and by that will PETER BACOME did leave all his lands to RUTH. RUTH his dau married and your deponent was present with one

RICHARD JAMES ye father of RUTH JAMES who lived in Newcastle Co who was eldest son to above RICHARD & RUTH his wife ... Proved 15 Feb 1721/2 by THOMAS BERRY. (G:pg 87)

599. 7 Feb 1721. Affidavit. JOHN BRADSHAW Senr aged about 63 years doth declare that he became acquainted with one PETER BACOME in 1683 and said BOUCOM had their a young woman who he ackn to be his dau named RUTH and all his lifetime did ackn the said RUTH to be his dau and said BOUCOM died in or about Oct 1685 & GEORGE MARTIN adminr of the estate & ISAAC WEBB & THOMAS STRATON were appraisers and your deponent sayeth there was a tr of land on Mother Cr near ROBERT HODGSON's containing 880 a. ... sometime in Aug 1686 one RICHARD JAMES married the said RUTH BOUCOM as I was told and that the RICHARD JAMES and RUTH lived together as man and wife and had several children ... in the year 1696 came one GEORGE ROBINSON & one CONSTANCE his wife brought a suit against the above said land of 880 a. and claimed as dau of PETER BOARCOM decd and one ROBERT FRENCH defended the cause & imployed ye deponent as atty to plead the suite against the plantiffe and GRIFFITH JONES atty for the plantiff went and discontinued ye suite ... and deponent further declareth that he heard old JOHN CURTIS say in open court that PETER BOACOM did make a will and did give all his land to his dau RUTH ... Proved 7 Feb 1721 by EVAN JONES. (G:pg 88)

600. 11 Mar 1717. Bond. DANIEL RODENEY & WILLIAM RODENEY of Kent Co yeoman am bound unto GEORGE NOWELL of same place gentleman in the amount of 660 pounds ... DANIEL RODENEY hath taken possession the several portions of money belonging unto GEORGE RODENEY, CESAR RODENEY & SARAH RODENEY legatees of WILLIAM RODENEY late of Kent Co decd gentleman amounting to 330 pounds being their full dividends ... DANIEL RODENEY shall save harmless GEORGE NOWELL & SARAH his wife executrix of the will of WILLIAM RODENEY decd from all suites, troubles, judgments & incumberances which may happen to said GEORGE NOWELL by the Orphans Court by reason of DANIEL RODENEY's taking into his possession as afsd ... Wit: JAMES TYRE, HENRY JOYCE. (G:pg 88)

601. 16 Aug 1722. Deed. MARK MANLOVE of Kent Co for 20 pounds sold to WILLIAM CRIPPEN of same place ... a tr of land being pt/o a tr formerly laid out for DANIEL BROWN of same co decd (surveyed 26 Aug 1684) called Elsworth and sold to JAMES WELLS of same co by deed bearing date 24 Jan 1684 and sold to MARK MANLOVE by THOMAS WELLS eldest son & heir to afsd JAMES WELLS decd by deed bearing date 14 May 1717 ... n side of Murtherkill Cr ... by Spring Br ... 150 a. ... Wit: WILLIAM MANLOVE, JOHN MORRICE. Ackn 16 Aug 1722. (G:pg

88)

602. 23 Dec 1721. Deed. THOMAS WELLS of Kent Co yeoman & ANN his wife ... whereas there is a tr of land called Worcester w side of Bishops Br of Murther Cr ... 350 a. was sold by THOMAS HODGKINS unto JAMES WELLS father of afsd THOMAS WELLS by indenture bearing date 16 Sep -- (Book B folio 147) ... THOMAS WELLS and ANN his wife for 20 pounds sold ANDREW CALDWELL of Kent Co yeoman afsd tr of land ... Wit: BENJAMIN SHURMER, EDWARD JENINGS. Ackn 15 Aug 1722. (G:pg 90)

603. 8 May 1722. Deed. NATHANIEL LUFF of Kent Co yeoman for 40 pounds sold to NATHANIEL BOWMAN of same co yeoman ... 200 a. granted by pattent to HUGH LUFF father of said NATHANIEL LUFF ... except the right of dower belonging to SARAH his mother the present wife of NATHANIEL BOWMAN afsd ... Wit: THOMAS WARD, WM RODENEY. NATHANIEL LUFF received of NATHANIEL BOWMAN the full consideration money. Wit: GEORGE ROBBISSON Junr, ROBERT HOWARD. Ackn 15 Aug 1722. (G:pg 91)

604. 8 May 1722. Deed. JOHN ROADS Junr of Suss Co gentleman son & heir of JOHN ROADS Senr late of Suss Co decd ... whereas a tr of land surveyed by virtue of a warrant from Whorkill Court 23 Nov 1679 under the hand of CORNELIUS VERHOOF surveyor on Tidberry Br of Jones Cr ... 2000 a. called Roads Forrest ... JOHN ROADS Junr for 200 pounds sold to ANDREW CALDWELL of Kent Co yeoman afsd tr of land ... Wit: ROBERT HODGSON, ROBERT WILLSON, JOSEPH CALDWELL, JOHN HUDSON. Ackn 15 Aug 1722. (G:pg 91)

605. 16 Aug 1722. Deed. Whereas ANDREW CALDWELL of Kent Co yeoman is now possessed of a tr of land n side of Deep Br of Murther Cr ... at upper corner of land called The Exchange now in the possession of MARK MANLOVE ... 600 a. now called Roads Choice by virtue of warrant granted by HUGH DURBOROW surveyor 20 Jan 1719 and another tr [same as #598] ... ANDREW CALDWELL for 100 pounds sold afsd parcells of land to JOHN ROADS of Suss Co gentleman ... Wit: JOHN WILLSON, JOHN RUDOLPH, ? BUNDELYN. Ackn 15 Aug 1722. (G:pg 92)

606. 12 Jun 1722. Deed. DANIEL RUTTEY of Kent Co yeoman for 20 pounds sold to WILLIAM RODENEY of same place yeoman ... a tr of land called Ruttington 400 a. s side of sw br of Murther Cr ... corner of land called Gendington ... along the line of Hunting Quarter ... Wit: LYDIA SIPPLE, RICHARD WILLSON. Ackn 16 Aug 1722. (G:pg 93)

607. 15 Aug 1722. Deed. ANDREW CALDWELL of Kent Co yeoman for 25 pounds sold to THOMAS MCCLANEY of same co yeoman ... whereas THOMAS BANISTER had unto him 700 a. called Norring (surveyed by EPHRAIM HARMAN surveyor 2 Apr 1681) ... and THOMAS BANISTER late of same co decd and RICHARD JAMES of New Castle Co yeoman being cousin and the nearest apparent heir unto said land hath by his deed of sale bearing date 11 May 1721 sold afsd land to ANDREW CALDWELL ... 200 a. pt/o afsd tr ... by Banisters Br ... to line of HARPER's land ... on WILLIAM PICKERIL's line ... 200 a. ... Wit: JOHN GORDON, SAMUELL WILLSON. Ackn 16 Aug 1722. (G:pg 94)

608. 10 Aug 1722. Deed. ANDREW CALDWELL of Kent Co Yeoman for 16 pounds sold to GEORGE ROBBISSON of same co gentleman ... 150 a. pt/o a tr of land [see #600] ... Wit: JOHN GORDON, ROBERT HODGSIN. Ackn 15 Aug 1722. (G:pg 95)

609. 20 Jun 1722. Deed. SAMUEL WILLSON of Kent Co yeoman and JOANNAH his wife for 20 pounds sold to JOHN GORDON of same co yeoman ... a tr of land called The Golden Thubett purch of DANIEL RUTTEY 15 Aug 1718 ... to Hudsons Br ... 200 a. ... Wit: ANDREW CALDWELL, THOMAS MACKELANEY. Ackn 15 Aug 1722. (G:pg 96)

610. 7 Apr 1722. Deed. JOHN CURTIS son & heir of CALEB CURTIS to whom JOHN CURTIS Senr late of Kent Co gentleman decd, father of said CALEB CURTIS, devised the hereafter mentioned land by his will bearing date 22 Apr 1698 ... & JOHN CURTIS Junr now of same co yeoman, son & heir of said CALEB, & SARAH his wife for 60 pounds sold to JAMES MAXWELL of same co yeoman ... 400 a. which JOHN CURTIS Senr was lawfully possessed (pattent granted from York 29 Sep 1678) unto JOHN BRIGGS who sold same by an assignment on the pattent bearing date 5 May 1679 ... JOHN CURTIS and SARAH his wife appoint their trusty friend ANDREW CALDWELL of same co gentleman to be their atty to ackn & deliver deed in open court ... Wit: NATHANIEL BOWMAN, THOMAS JESTER. Ackn 15 Aug 1722. (G:pg 97)

611. 9 Aug 1722. Deed. JOHN TURNER of Kent Co yeoman for 52 pounds 13 shillings 6 pence sold to ELIZABETH BRINKLE widow & JOHN CURTIS esqr of same place ... a tr of land nw side of Swan Cr and nw side of Mispillion Cr ... 300 a. ... Wit: WM RODENEY, JAMES WHITE, AN MAGILL. Ackn 15 Aug 1722. (G:pg 99)

612. 9 Aug 1722. Power of Atty. JOHN TURNER appoint my friend JOHN BRINKLE of Kent Co gentleman my atty to ackn and deliver [above] deed of sale in open court ... Wit: WM RODENEY, JAMES WHITE, AN MAGILL. Proved 15 Aug 1722. (G:pg 99)

6013. 8 Aug 1722. Deed of Release. JOHN FLOWERS of Kent Co son and heir of JOHN FLOWERS late of same co yeoman decd ... whereas JOHN FLOWERS the father in his lifetime for a valluable consideration to him in hand paid by JOHN DAWSON then of same co did sell to JOHN DAWSON a tr of land s side of Isaacks Br of Dover River being pt/o a larger tr called Dundee .. by HARDIN ANDREWS br ... 150 a. ... by sundry mean conveyances the 150 a. are rightfully in the possession of ALEXANDER PENDOR (PENDER) of same co yeoman ... this indenture JOHN FLOWERS the son for the afsd consideration and 6 pounds release unto ALEXANDER PENDOR afsd tr of land ... Wit: ELIZABETH PEPPER, HUGH DURBOROW Junr. Ackn 15 Aug 1722. (G:pg 100)

614. 1 Aug 1722. Deed. EDWARD LOWDER of Newcastle Co weaver and MARY his wife for 12 pounds sold to ROBERT CARR of Salisbury Town on Duck Cr Kent Co ... a tr of land within the towne of Salisbury ... to Greens Br ... 1 a. ... Wit: JOHN COWGILL, THOMAS DAKEYNE, D MACBRIDE. Ackn 16 Aug 1722. (G:pg 101)

615. 1 Aug 1722. Deed. ROBERT CARR of Salisbury Town on Duck Cr Kent Co merchant for 6 pounds sold to ROBERT ELLIOTT of same place taylor ... the [above] tr of land ... Wit: THOMAS DAKEYNE, EDWARD LOWDER, D MACBRIDE. Ackn 16 Aug 1722. (G:pg 102)

616. 17 Aug 1722. Deed. WILLIAM ELLIS of Kent Co MD yeoman executor of the will of BENJAMIN ELLIS late of same place decd ... whereas BENJAMIN ELLIS in his lifetime and at the time of his death was seized of a tr of land being pt/o a larger tr called Denby Town formerly granted unto THOMAS WILLSON in Little Cr Hund nw side of Willsons Br ... by land of THOMAS WILLSON ... by land of WILLIAM WILLSON ... by former estimation 327 a. but actually 240 a. ... BENJAMIN ELLIS in his lifetime for 100 pounds (receiving 50 pounds in part payment) sold unto SAMUEL FREEMAN afsd land deemed at 300 a. ... but both parties happening to dye before the afsd bargain could be forfeited the said BENJAMIN ELLIS did in his will bearing date 26 Oct 1721 impower executor to confirm the contract ... this indenture WILLIAM ELLIS in consideration of the 50 pounds paid and other 50 pounds to him paid sold afsd tr of land to SAMUEL WHITMAN of Kent Co yeoman assignee of JOHN FOSTER and ELIZABETH FREEMAN executors of the will of SAMUEL FREEMAN late of Kent Co decd ... (G:pg 103)

617. 29 Jun 1722. Deed. NICHOLAS NIXON of Kent Co blacksmith & ELIZABETH his wife ... whereas NICHOLAS NIXON in 1717 in a Court of Common Pleas obtain judgment against REBECCA BROOKS adminr

of JAMES BROOKS decd for 30 pounds ... she was ordered to dispose of so much of the lands appertaining to the estate as sufficient to satisfie the judgment ... she with JOHN LUCOS with whome she had intermarried by deed bearing date 1 May 1718 sold unto NICHOLAS NIXON 2/3 pt/o a 400 a. tr of land late in the tenure of afsd JAMES BROOKS at Murderkill Hund being pt/o a larger tr called The Plains ... this indenture NICHOLAS NIXON and ELIZABETH his wife for 40 pounds sold afsd tr of land to WILLIAM MARONEE of same place yeoman ... Wit: BENJAMIN SHURMER, ROBERT BYGRAVE. Ackn 17 Aug 1722. (G:pg 104)

618. 29 Jun 1722. Power of Atty. NICHOLAS NIXON of Kent Co blacksmith & ELIZABETH his wife appoint our trusty & good friends BENJAMIN SHURMER & THOMAS BERRY of Kent Co gentlemen and EDWARD JENNINGS inholder of same place or any one of them our atty to ackn and deliver [above] deed in open court ... Wit: BENJAMIN SHURMER, ROBERT BYGRAVE. Proved 17 Aug 1722. (G:pg 106)

619. 5 Aug 1721. Deed. WILLIAM FORBUSH late of Kent Co labbourer for 6 pounds sold to JOHN BRIAN of Murderkill Hund yeoman ... a 200 a. tr of land JOHN BRIAN and WILLIAM FORBUSH joyntly purch in the forest of Murderkill Hund ... Wit: JOHN THOMSON, DANIEL GOODIN, LAWRENCE BEDSHOLD. Ackn 18 Aug 1722. (G:pg 106)

620. 13 Aug 1719. Deed. JOHN BRADSHAW of Kent Co adminr of JAMES WALLIS, RICHARD CROSLEY, CHARLES JONES Junr and THOMAS TAYLOR of Kent Co ... whereas a tr of land called Whitwells Chance n side Duck Cr ... 1000 a. which tr of land JOSEPH CROWDEN of Bensalem Burks Co PA gentleman formerly mortgaged unto ANDREW ROBESON late of Phila Co attorny of the said JAMES WALLIS, RICHARD CROFLEY, CHARLES JONES Junr & THOMAS TAYLOR in their lifetime which JOSEPH CROWDEN conveyed to JAMES STEEL and THOMAS SHARP both of same co yeoman ... (pursuant to the order of the Court of Equity 16 May last past JAMES STEEL and THOMAS SHARP paid 159 pounds 7 shillings 9 pence 1/2 penny to the complainant JOSEPH CROWDEN and JOHN BRADSHAW) ... this indenture JOHN BRADSHAW sold to JAMES STEEL and THOMAS SHARP the afsd land ... Wit: EVAN JONES, JOHN COOK, ABSALOM CUFF, CHARLES HILLIARD, BENJAMIN SHURMER. Ackn 12 Nov 1719. (G:pg 107)

621. 10 May 1721. Bond of Conveyance. ANDREW CALDWELL of Kent Co yeoman am bound unto RICHARD JAMES of New Castle Co for 100 pounds ... ANDREW CALDWELL to render unto RICHARD JAMES one half of two parcells of land called Norringe & the other called Arundell excepting 440 a. ... Wit: RICHARD UNDERWOOD, ROBERT WILLSON,

WILLIAM MANLOVE Junr. Ackn 8 Apr 1727. RICHARD JAMES received of ANDREW CALDWELL 2 pounds 10 shillings 6 pence in full ... Wit: JOHN HOUSMAN, MARK GRIER. (G:pg 108)

622. 9 Oct 1722. Deed. FRANCIS HIRONS of Kent Co yeoman son and heir of SIMON HIRONS late of same place decd in consideration of a deed dated 17 Oct 1721 release unto BENJAMIN SHURMER of same place gentleman and JOHN HALL all his rights to 300 a. of land being pt/o a tr n side of Dover River called The Range (Book A folio 44) ... this indenture FRANCIS HIRONS for 10 pounds sold to BENJAMIN SHURMER afsd 300 a. ... Wit: JOHN CURTIS, ROBERT BYGRAVE. Ackn 11 Oct 1722. (G:pg 108)

623. 5 Oct 1722. Quit Claim. Whereas FRANCES HIRONS of Kent Co yeoman son and heir of SIMON HIRONS late of same place decd did by deed bearing date 17 Oct 1721 release and convey to BENJAMIN SHURMER of same place gentleman and JOHN HALL a tr of land called The Range 1000 a. n side of Dover River ... JOHN HALL by articles of agreement bearing date 19 Dec 1720 hath released and quit claimed to said BENJAMIN all his right and title to 300 a. ... BENJAMIN SHURMER for 10 shillings quit claims 300 a. unto SIMON HIRONS ... excepting all the land belonging to the 1000 a. called The Range ... Wit: JOHN CURTIS, ROBERT BYGRAVE. Ackn 11 Oct 1722. (G:pg 109)

624. 1 Oct 1722. Marriage. JOHN NEWTON and MARY ROGERS dau of JOSEPH ROGERS late of MD decd haveing lately published their intentions of marriage ... did at the dwelling house of THOMAS BERRY esqr sollomnize their marriage ... Wit: THOMAS BERRY, MOSES WHITTAKER, WILLIAM FINNE, JAMES KIRKHAM, JNO SLATER, WM DRISKELL, WILLIAM NEWELL, ANN WHITTAKER, MARY BUNN, JOSHUA CLARK, GEORGE GOULT, AARON PARROT, MARY LOVEDAY, EDWARD NEAL. (G:pg 110)

625. 1 Oct 1722. Marriage. JOHN SLATTER and SUSANNA PARROTT widow and relict of WILLIAM PARRATT late of Talbot Co MD decd haveing lately published their intentions of marriage ... did at the dwelling house of THOMAS BERRY solleminize their marriage ... Wit: THOMAS BERRY, THOMAS SELVESTER, WM DRISKELL, LYDIA KENTON, JAMES KIRKAM, EDWARD NEALL, AARON PARRATT, JOSHUA CLARK, GEORGE GOULT, TIMOTHY LANE, JOHN NEWTON, MICHALL CORDY. (G:pg 110)

626. 1 Mar 1722. Bill of Sale. MICHAEL DONOHO of Kent Co yeoman for 50 pounds sold to BENJAMIN SHURMER of same co gentleman ... one negro man named QUA aged 21 years or thereabouts ... Wit:

THOMAS WESTBERRY, JOHN RUSSELL. (G:pg 110)

627. 12 Apr 1722 at Phila. Bill. [amounts omitted] JAMES GUMLY to EDWARD CAROLTON: to ROBERT ELLIS for tools, to cash paid THOMAS SURVEY, to cash lent by mother on my account, to 1 quart of rum, to a small peace of gold, to paid MR. CADWALLADER, to cash, to cash for ELIZABETH FAGAN, to 2 1/2 gallon of rum, to paid WILLIAM BOYD, to sundrys, to your pt/o makeing the deeds, ... I was bound in behalf of THOMAS FLEMING ... ED CARLETON received of JAMES GUMLEY 14 pounds 2 shillings and 5 pence being the full contents of this bill and all amounts (except of a bond bearing date 6 Apr 1722) penalty 100 pounds condition that the said JAMES GUMLEY should make me a sufficient conveyance 80 a. of land ... Wit: JOSEPH STIRK, JOSHUA MADDOX. (G:pg 111)

628. 14 Nov 1710. Deed. THOMAS BEDWELL and HONOR his wife executrix of the will of WILLIAM CLARK late of Lewistown in Suss Co esqr decd for 40 pounds sold to JAMES BROOKS the elder of Murtherkill Hund Kent Co yeoman ... a tr of land called Brimley s side of Dover River formerly granted and laid out for WILLIAM DORRINGTON who sold the same to RICHARD MITCHELL who dyed intestate and by indenture bearing date 13 Jun 1700 WILLIAM DIXON one of the adminr sold to WILLIAM CLARK ... near the land called Amsterdam formerly surveyed and laid out for HENRY JOHNSON ... 549 a. ... Wit: MOSES BROOKS, DAVID ROWE, FRANCES ALLEN. (G:pg 111)

629. -- Oct 1722. Affidavit. MICHAEL LOWBER aged 45 years or thereabouts made oath that the above written deed is the very same to the best of his knowledge which he saw ackn in open Court of Common Pleas held at Dover about 12 years ago by THOMAS BEDWELL & HONOR his wife to JAMES BROOKS Senr. (G:pg 112)

630. 15 Aug 1722. Deed. There is a 300 a. tr of land n side of Mispillion Cr a deed executed by JOHN CURTIS late of same co decd unto MARK MANLOVE of same co also decd bearing date 5 Jan 1693 ... whereas MATHEW MANLOVE son and heir of MARK MANLOVE by deed the 13 Aug 1718 did sell unto WILLIAM MULRONY of Kent Co yeoman 100 a. pt/o afsd 300 a. ... at line of THOMAS FESTER's land ... to line of a tr of land called Maidens Plot ... this indenture WILLIAM MULRONY for 45 pounds sold afsd 100 a. to HENRY HALL of same co yeoman ... Wit: GEORGE ROBBISSON Junr, JOHN EDMUNDS, TABER JENKINS. Ackn 17 Aug 1722. (G:pg 112)

631. 18 Aug 1722. Deed. JOHN HILLYARD of Kent Co yeoman for 12 pounds sold to WILLIAM MULRONY of same co yeoman ... a 200 a. tr of

land n side of Mispillion Cr and buffing ne on a tr of land called Swamp Barron now in the tenour of said WILLIAM MULRONY being pt/o a 500 a. tr called Manloves Plott and is the lowermost 200 a. ... bounded to the n by land called Aberdeen in possession of JOHN HILLYARD ... Wit: JOHN HALL, JOHN PORPOLE, JOHN NOWELL. Ackn 18 Aug 1722. (G:pg 113)

632. 18 Mar 1722/3. Power of Atty. JOSHUA WHEELER of New London in New London Co CT in New England the only son of JOHN WHEELER late of same place decd have appointed my beloved friend SOLOMON COITS of same place to be my atty to request, recover, receive from all persons any lands which of right descendeth to me from my honoured father JOHN WHEELER decd and to demand any sums of money, debts, merchandise oweing to me ... Wit: JOHN PLUMBS, DANIEL COIT. Proved 18 Mar 1722/3 by GORDON SALTONSTALL. (G:pg 114)

633. 18 Mar 1722/3 at CT Collony. Affidavit. JONATHAN PRENTICE aged 60 years or thereabouts and JOHN PLUMB esqr aged 57 years both of New London CT in New England haveing been inhabitants in the said town of New London for divers years pass and was well acquainted with JOHN WHEELER late of New London decd merchant who was in profession called Quaker, we testify that JOSHUA WHEELER who is now living in said New London is the reputed son of said JOHN WHEELER decd and his only son that we know of living and further we know of no issue of any other son that is decd. (G:pg 114)

634. 19 Mar 1722/3. Deed. Whereas JOHN BLAND was seized of a tr of land called Doncaster 1025 a. by deed of sale by HUGH MACDERDNEND & ELLINOR his wife alias ELLENSWORTH only dau of WILLIAM ELLENSWORTH to whom the said tr of land was granted & surveyed the 18 Feb 1695 and deed of sale made to JOHN BLAND of Kent Co merchant ... this indenture JOHN BLAND for 50 pounds sold to HUGH MACDERMEND (MACDARMEND) of Talbot Co MD planter one half of afsd tr of land 500 a. ... n side of Little Duck Cr ... along the line of land called The Mill Range ... to tr of land called Doncaster ... Wit: ANDREW CALDWELL, JOHN READ. Ackn 21 Mar 1722. (G:pg 115)

635. 10 Mar 1679. Deed. RICHARD LEVERITT of St. Jones Cr Whorekills Co NY planter and MARY his wife for 6000 pounds of tobacco in casque sold to WALTER DICKINSON of Talbot Co MD planter ... a tr of land called Shrewsbury n side of St. Jones Cr ... bounded by land called Mulbery Swampe ... intersecting with the land of JOHN BURTON ... 400 a. ... Wit: J BARKSTEED, EVAN DAVIS, GRIFF JONES. Ackn 11 Mar 1679. (G:pg 115)

636. 3 May 1720. Power of Atty. MARY WARNER alias BURFORT of Dorchester Co MD heir of and executrix of DANIEL CLARK late of same place but formerly of Kent Co decd appoint my trusty and loveing friend ANDREW CALDWELL of Kent Co yeoman my atty to ask & demand, recover & receive all debts belonging to me ... particularly of DANIEL HUDSON of same co on his own or on account of his father ROBERT HUDSON decd ... Wit: NEHEMIAH BECKWITH, WILLIAM YEO, GRACE BRUFET, JOHN HUDSON. Proved 6 May 1720 by MARK MANLOVE. (G:pg 117)

637. 10 May 1723. CHARLES HILLYARD this is to acquaint you that as concerning JOHN SMALLCORN debt to me I am freely willing to acquitt and forgive him so if the Court and you acquit all charges he may have liberty and be discharged upon my own debt ... (signed) WILLIAM TURNER. Attest: JOHN WILLSON. (G:pg 118)

638. 10 Oct 1722. Deed. HENRY MOLLESTON son of HENRY MOLLESTON late of Kent Co gentleman decd ... whereas the tr of land s side of Fishing Br of Mispillion Cr ... to corner of REYNIER WILLIAMS ... 600 a. called Gooseberry being formerly surveyed and laid out to CORNELIOUS VERHOOFE by virtue of a warrant the 21 Dec 1680 was afterwards by writ of execution directed to GEORGE MARTIN high sherrife bearing date 28 Sep 1686 at the suit of RICHARD BUNDOCK levied and taken to satisfy the value of 5000 pounds of tobacco ... and on 27 Oct year last mentioned sold at publick vendue unto THOMAS STRETTON for 27 pounds being the highest bidder and by deed bearing date 16 Mar 1687 conveyed unto DANIEL JAMES who afterwards by deed bearing date 2 Nov 1688 conveyed land unto DAVID POWELL who afterwards by his deed 8 May 1697 did convey land unto HENRY MOLLESTON father to HENRY MOLLESTON the younger ... HENRY MOLLESTON in his lifetime did make his will barring date 17 Oct 1708 ... I bequeath to my loving wife ANN MOLLESTON my plantation whereon I now live 300 a. during the time of her natural life and after her decease said land and plantation to descend unto my son HENRY MOLLESTON ... I bequeath to my son HENRY MOLLESTON the other pt/o the afsd tr of land 158 a. and remaining pt/o the 600 a. tr ... HENRY MOLLESTON for 95 pounds sold all afsd parcells of land to WILLIAM MOLLESTON of same place gentleman ... Wit: WM RODENEY, JOHN HALL. Ackn 11 Oct 1722. (G:pg 118)

639. 12 Nov 1722. Deed of Gift. ANDREW CALDWELL of Kent Co yeoman and MARGARET his wife in consideration of fatherly love and tender respect I give to my beloved children ROBERT HODGSON and FRAIN his wife ... 200 a. of land being pt/o a tr called Roads Forest where ROBERT HODGSON and FRAIN his wife now dwells ... s side of Tidbury

Br ... Wit: RICHARD WEBSTER, JOHN GORDON. Ackn 20 Nov 1722. (G:pg 119)

640. 12 Nov 1722. Deed of Gift. ANDREW CALDWELL of Kent Co yeoman and MARGARET his wife in consideration of fatherly love and tender respect I give to my beloved children JOHN GORDON and ELIZABETH his wife ... 200 a. of land being pt/o a tr call Roads Forest ... Wit: RICHARD WEBSTER, ROBERT HODGSON. Ackn 20 Nov 1722. (G:pg 120)

641. 17 Nov --. Deed. MICHAEL (MIKEL) MASON of Kent Co and MARY his wife for 16 pounds sold to JOHN CHANCEY of same place yeoman ... 50 a. being the same which JOHN CHANCEY and MARY his wife executrix of the will of WILLIAM FREEMAN late of Kent Co decd formerly sold to MICHAEL MASON and is part of a tr of 200 a. upon Willsons Br in Little Cr Hund ... Wit: JAMES WORRELL, ROBERT HIRONS. Ackn 20 Nov 1722. (G:pg 120)

642. 20 Nov 1722. Deed. ROBERT DICKINSON of Kent Co PA wheelright sole son and heir of WALTER DICKINSON of same co gentleman decd for 300 pounds sold to SAMUEL DICKINSON of Talbot Co MD merchant ... a tr of land called Shewsberry [see #630] 400 a. ... and also one other tr being pt/o a tr called Mulberry Swamp ... at St. Jones Cr being the division between afsd ROBERT DICKINSON and SAMUEL DICKINSON ... to land of ROBERT DICKINSON called Whortons ... 100 a. and also the tr called Whartons ne side of St. Jones Cr ... to land called Mulberry Swamp ... 400 a. ... Wit: THOMAS ADAMS, NICHOLAS LOCKERMAN. Ackn 20 Nov 1722. (G:pg 121)

643. -- Jan 1722. Deed. ANDREW CALDWELL of Kent Co yeoman for 6 pounds sold to WILLIAM NICKELS of same co ... one half of a tr of land called Southhampton conveyed unto ANDREW CALDWELL from MICHAEL LOWBARE bearing date 10 Feb 1719 which said tr of land was conveyed unto MICHAEL LOWBARR by a deed of sale from DANIEL RUTTEY bearing date 13 Nov 1717 and was surveyed 22 Feb 1681 ... binding to e most line of land which said WILLIAM NICKELS father ROBERT NICKELS bought of JAMES BROOKS 100 a. and is pt/o a tr of land called Kingstown ... Wit: SAMUELL WILLSON, BENJAMIN TURBU. Ackn 14 Feb 1722. (G:pg 124)

644. 13 Feb 1722. Deed. FRANCES ALEXANDER of Kent Co cordwiner for 12 pounds 10 shillings sold to CHARLES MARTIN of same place planter ... a tr of land formerly laid out for SIMON HIRONS ... w end of Rich Ridge ... bounded by said HIRONS lands on one side and Black Swamp on the other ... 100 a. ... Wit: JOHN RAYNALLS, MARK

MANLOVE. Ackn 13 Feb 1722. (G:pg 124)

645. 29 Jan 1722/3. Deed. JOHN JONES & MARGARET his wife of Duck Cr Kent Co for 6 pounds sold to ROBERT BOARDMAN of same place plasterer ... a piece of ground being in the town of Salsbury beginning at the corner of WILLIAM HICKETS ground ... paying to the landlord for the time being 6 pence yearly every yearly on 23 Dec forever ... Wit: JOHN HOLLYDAY, ANTHONY RUTHERFORD, RICHARD CARPENTER, GEORGE HOPPER, CHRISTO PENROSE. (G:pg 125)

646. 9 Feb 1722/3. Receipt. JOHN JONES received 6 pounds from ROBERT BOARDMAN ... Memorandum that peaceable and quiet possession of the [above] lands was taken ... Wit: JOHN HOLLIDAY, ANTHONY RUTHERFORD, GEORGE HOPPER, RICHARD CARPENTER, CHRISTO PENROSE.

647. 14 Feb 1722. Deed. MARK MANLOVE of Kent Co yeoman for 25 pounds sold to WILLIAM DEAN taylor of same place ... a tr of land n side of Murderkill laid out 24 Nov 1717 for said MARK MANLOVE pursuant to a warrant granted 25 Mar in the year afsd ... to corner of tr formerly surveyed for BENONY BISHOP ... to Nicholas Br ... 60 a. ... Wit: DANIEL RODENEY, WILLIAM MANLOVE. Ackn 11 Feb 1722. (G:pg 126)

648. 21 Nov 1722. Deed. ANDREW CALDWELL of Kent Co yeoman for 10 pounds sold to WILLIAM MACADOE of same place nailmaker ... 100 a. s side of Hudsons Br of Murther Cr ... to line of land called Burberry Berry ... being pt/o a greater tr ANDREW CALDWELL did purch of PHILIP and ABRAHAM MORGAN of Talbot Co MD 12 Nov 1718 ... Wit: EPHRAIM EMERSON, MARY EMERSON, MARY PERNALL. Ackn 13 Feb 1722. (G:pg 127)

649. 12 Feb 1722. Deed. ROBERT MEREDITH Senr of Dorcester Co MD planter for 15 pounds sold to THOMAS PRAT of Talbot Co MD planter ... 200 a. of land laid out and surveyed by HUGH DURBOROW surveyor called The Addition in the forest of Murderkill Hund near the n side of land whereon ROBERT MEREDITH now liveth ... by Beaver Dam Br 15 Feb 1721 ... Wit: THOMAS BAYNARD, JOHN WILLSON. (G:pg 128)

650. 13 Feb 1722. Power of Atty. ROBERT MEREDITH hath appointed my trusty and well beloved friend THOMAS BARRY my atty to ackn the [above] deed in open court ... Wit: THOMAS BAYNARD, JOHN WILLSON. (G:pg 128)

651. 12 Feb 1722. Deed. BENJAMIN SHURMER, RICHARD

RICHARDSON and JOHN CURTIS all of Kent Co gentlemen for 55 pounds sold to JOHN LINSAY of town of Dover same co gentleman ... by act of assembly past at Newcastle in 1717 BENJAMIN SHURMER, RICHARD RICHARDSON together with WILLIAM BRINCKLE late of Kent Co gentleman decd or any two of them are impowered to sell lotts adj the court house town of Dover being pt/o a larger tr called Brothers Portion originally granted to JOHN & RICHARD WALKER and came to be in the possession of RICHARD WILSON late of same co decd and from him unto the inhabitants of the co ... 2 a. ... [remainder blank] (G:pg 128)

652. 9 Dec 1717. Lease. NATHAN STANBURY of Phila merchant lease to ABRAHAM EVANS (EVENS) late of City of Bristol in Great Brittain but now of Phila mariner ... a tr of land patent bearing date 13 Nov last past granted unto NATHAN STANBURY s side of Duck Cr ... at corner of ROBERT DRAUGHTON's land ... 500 a. ... for one whole year ... Wit: JAMES STEEL, JN TISOM, THOMAS STANBURY. Ackn 12 Feb --. (G:pg 130)

653. 10 Dec 1717. Deed. NATHAN STANBURY of Phila merchant sold to ABRAHAM EVANS late of City of Bristol in Great Brittain but now of Phila mariner ... [above] tr of land ... Wit: JAMES STEEL, JN TISOM, THOMAS STANBURY. (G:pg 130)

654. 15 May 1723. Deed. JOHN TURNER of Mispillion Hund Kent Co yeoman for 20 pounds sold to NICHOLAS GATTEAN of Phila and MARY his wife ... two parcells of land 200 a. ... 100 a. called Turners Hill in the forrest of Mispillion Hund ... by Browns Br ... the other 100 a. called The Oake Plaine between the head of Mispillion Cr and Marshahope ... Wit: TIMOTHY HANSON, JOHN HUTTON. Ackn 15 May 1723. (G:pg 131)

655. 26 Mar 1713. Bill of Sale. PETER ANDREWVIT boatman of Staten Island owner of the Good Sloop or vessell called the Three Brothers of the Burthen of 15 tons or thereabouts for 140 pounds sold to TIMOTHY TILLING of NY City boatman ... all that hull of said good sloop or vessell called the Three Brothers together with the mast, boom, bolt sprit and all other nessessaries ... Wit: JN HYATT, JACOB MONE. (G:pg 133)

656. 28 May 1723. Bill of Sale. TIMOTHY TILLY for 82 pounds 10 shillings sold to JOHN BLAND of Kent Co merchant ... the [above] mentioned sloop ... Wit: THOMAS FRENCH, JAMES MACKEY, ANDREW CALDWELL. (G:pg 133)

657. 28 May 1723. Writ of Execution. CHARLES HILLYARD sheriff by virtue of writt to me directed have levied of the goods & chattels of TIMOTHY TILLY late of NY City mariner the sum of 66 pounds of a

judgment for breach of covenant to JOHN BLAND as atty of THOMAS KEARNY of NY City merchant ... sold unto said JOHN BLAND one sloop called the Three Brothers ... Wit: THOMAS WARD, EDMOND BOWMAN. (G:pg 133)

658. [same as #650] (G:pg 133)

659. 27 Aug 1723. TIMOTHY TILLY late of NY City mariner do certify that the sloop The Three Brothers was sold at publick vendue by CHARLES HILLYARD esqr sheriff the 20 Aug 1723... Wit: THOMAS BURY, THOMAS CRAWFORD. Proved 27 Aug 1723 by BENJAMIN SHURMER. (G:pg 136)

660. 27 Apr 1722. Power of Atty. REBECAH KEARNY of Phila widow relict and adminr of PHILLIP KEARNY late of Phila merchant decd have made my trusty and loveing friend TIMOTHY HANSON of Kent Co esqr my atty to demand and receive all such sums of money, debts, goods and wares which shall be due me ... Wit: HENRY HODGE, SUSANAH KEARNY. Proved 1 May 1722. Attest: THOMAS FRENCH, BENJAMIN SHURMER.

661. 17 Apr 1704. Quit Claim. ROBERT BETTS & JOHN KING of MD yeomen a tr of land patent dated 15 May 1686 (Book A fol 194) w side of Jones Cr beginning at Tidbury Br near said BETTS house ... 1200 a. ... is now in the possession of LIONELL BRITTON of Phila ironmonger ... for 5 shillings JOHN BETTS & JOHN KING quitt claim afsd land to LIONELL BRITTON ... ROBERT BETTS and JOHN KING have made CAPT JOHN BRINCKLOE their atty to ackn & deliver these presents in open court ... Wit: DANIELL MAHANEN, RACHELL MANLOVE, WILLIAM WADDING, LIDIA ROBERSON. Ackn 8 Aug 170-. Certified by WM ANNAND Clerk. (G:pg 137)

662. Inventory of sundry goods, cattle, horses, sheep belonging to the estate of CAPT PHILIP KEARNY decd & now by order of REBECA KEARNY adminr to the estate delivered to JOHN BLAND merchant for the use of THOMAS KEARNY, the prises annexed to each article being the same as they were appraised by JOHN HALL & HUGH DURBOROW: looking glass & slate table, black walnut desk, walnut table ... [remainder of long list not included]. (G:pg 138-9)

663. 27 Jul 1722. These may certifie that I TIMOTHY HANSON atty to REBECA KEARNY of Phila adminr of estate of PHILLIP KEARNY esqr late of Kent Co decd pursuant to letter to me directed dated at Phila 16 Jul 1722 the other 18 Jul 1722 have delivered unto JOHN BLAND as atty to & for the use of THOMAS KEARNY merchant in NY all the goods in

[above] inventory and also the late dwelling plantation of PHILIP KEARNY decd ... thereon the agreement between REBECCA KEARNY & THOMAS KEARY ... Wit: ROBERT GORDON, THOMAS FRENCH.

664. 11 Aug 1722. REBECCA KEARNY of Phila widow & relict of PHILIP KEARNY late of same place merchant decd for 470 pounds 6 shillings 9 pence sold to THOMAS KEARNY of NY merchant ... all goods in inventory, estate real & personall ... Wit: PETER EVANS, JOHN BLAND. (G:pg 139)

-A-
ABERCONAWAY, 4
ABERCONDAY, 25
ABERDEANE, v
ABERDEEN, 48, 66, 86, 129
ABORDEEN, 48
ADAMS, Thomas, 48, 58, 68,
  69, 98, 112, 119, 131
ADDITION, THE, 132
ALBERSON, John, 44, 45
ALBERTSON, 30, 35
ALEN, Frances, 48
ALEXANDER, Frances, 41, 131
  Francis, 30, 36
  Spencer, 37
ALLAMS CABINES, 92
ALLEE, John, 44, 117, 119
ALLEI, John, 30
ALLEN, Frances, 42, 128
  Francis, 14, 15, 16, 19, 22, 25,
    26, 27, 28, 34, 55
  Mary, 26
  Thomas, 75
ALLEWAY, William, 89
ALLEXANDER, Abraham, 51
  Frances, 40
  Francis, 29, 110
ALLEY, John, 30, 119
ALLIN, Francis, 30
ALLOMS CABBINS, 60, 100
ALLSTON, Sarah, 74
  Thomas, 74
ALLTON, Thomas, 62
ALSON, Thomas, 102
ALSTON, Arthur, 74, 83, 87,
  109, 110
AMOS, Henry, 81, 82
AMPLUGH, Jacob, 49
  Nath, 49
AMSTERDAM, 128
ANAND, William, 4, 35
ANDRESS, Edmond, 78
ANDREWS, Edmond, 15, 111
  Hardin, 125
  John, 93

ANDREWVIT, Peter, 133
ANDROS, Edmund, 36
ANDROSS, Edmond, 26
ANNAN, William, 81
ANNAND, Elisabeth, 45
  Elizabeth, 30
  William, 1, 2, 4, 6, 8, 9, 10, 11,
    12, 13, 14, 17, 19, 22, 25, 28,
    29, 30, 32, 44, 51, 52, 62, 65,
    70, 71, 93, 94, 101, 111, 134
ANNITT, Richard, 70
ANTER, Alexander, 73
  Jane, 73
ARONDECK, 107
ARUNDELL, 126
ARYRES, Samuell, 52
ASHBERRY, Joseph, 5
ASHTON, Joseph, 109
ASKINS, Henry, 93
ASKWE, James, 13
ASTER, George, 64
ASTON, Joseph, 82
ATHOW, Thomas, 6

-B-
BACOME, Peter, 121
  Ruth, 121
BAILLIE, Jonathan, 117
BAILY, James, 24
  Jonathan, 24
  Sarah, 24
BAKER, Joseph, 9
BALL, James, 52
BANESES CHOICE, 7
BANISTER, Thomas, 107, 124
BARBADOES, 99
BARBADOS, 60
BARDEN, Mark, 28
BARDON, Mark, 15, 86, 117
BARKSTEAD, Joshua, 103
BARKSTEED, J., 129
  Joshua, 104
BARNES, Henry, 6
  Thomas, 35
BARNEY, Frances, 38

BARNS, John, 116
BAROM, Peter, 107
BARRAT, Benjaman, 50
  Humphry, 15
BARRATT, Ben, 87, 88, 105
BARRET, Benjamin, 78, 88
  Humphrey, 15
  Nicholas, 86
BARRETT, Ben, 87
  Humphrey, 23
BARRETTS LOTT, 86
BARRY, Thomas, 132
BARTER, William, 24
BARTLET, Nicklas, 91
BARTLETT, 121
BASNETT, Elizabeth, 91
  Richard, 91
BASSNETT, Richard, 15, 93
BASSONETT, William, 31
BAUCOM, Peter, v
BAYLY, Jonathan, 88
BAYNARD, Thomas, 68, 132
BECK, Robert, 36
BECKWITH, Henry, 110
  Nehemiah, 130
BEDSHOLD, Lawrence, 126
BEDWEL, Thomas, 6
BEDWELL, Elizabeth, 22, 27, 28
  Hannah, 19
  Henry, 4, 13, 28, 91, 107, 116
  Honor, 23, 24, 27, 128
  Honour, 26, 42
  James, 56, 96
  Mellecent, 37
  Robert, 4, 16, 22, 26, 27, 28, 56, 91, 96, 103, 105, 116
  Thomas, 4, 5, 7, 13, 16, 19, 22, 23, 24, 26, 27, 28, 34, 37, 39, 42, 45, 46, 89, 90, 91, 92, 116, 128
BEETLE, John, 83
BEETS, Elizabeth, 43
  Robert, 43
BENEFEILD, 59

BENEFIELD, 17, 99
BENYFIELD, 28
BERRY, John, 17, 51, 58, 68, 78, 98, 101
  Samuel, 3, 23, 29, 31, 32, 54, 64, 65, 68, 94
  Samuell, 2, 3, 5, 8, 15, 16, 23, 33, 40, 89, 97
  Thomas, 68, 77, 78, 79, 83, 86, 87, 88, 104, 120, 122, 126, 127
  William, 5, 11, 17, 30, 37, 52, 60, 68, 77, 92, 99, 112
BERRY FIELD, 78
BERRYS RANGE, 5, 17, 32, 108, 109
BERY, John, 61
  Samuell, 57
BETS ENDEAVOUR, 42, 45
BETTLE, John, 83
BETTS, John, 26, 50, 51, 55, 57, 61, 97, 115
  Mary, 25
  Robert, 2, 43, 56, 77, 121, 134
BETTS ENDEAVOUR, 35, 41, 50, 52
BETTY, Thomas, 111
BETTYES FORTUNE, 51, 94
BETTYS FORTUNE, 29
BIBBY, Edmund, 38, 40
BICKLEY, Abraham, 24, 25, 27, 28, 31, 34, 50
BICKNELL, Jury, 72
  William, 72
BIGNAL, Jury, 72
  William, 72
BIGNELL, William, 21
BIRKETT, William, 74, 105, 106, 107
BISALLION, Peter, 70
BISHOP, Benoni, 1, 5
  Benony, 39, 132
  Elizabeth, 1
  Margaret, 2, 85
  Margret, 1, 5

BISHOPP, Thomas, 104
BISHOPS CHOICE, 5
BISSALLION, Peter, 65
BLACK SWAMP, 131
BLACKSAW, 72
BLACKSHER, Robert, 108
BLACKTOIN, Ebenerer, 38
BLAND, John, 119, 129, 133, 134, 135
BLAUD, John, 118
BOACOMB, Peter, 121
 Ruth, 121
BOAK, Benjamin, 29
BOARDMAN, Robert, 132
BOLSTOCK, Ann, 110
 Thomas, 110
BONNER, Theodorus, 110
BOOKSTED, William, 24
BOOTH, Elinor, 83
 John, 84
 Joseph, 65, 71, 83, 86
 Margaret, 71
BOROIS, Da, 7
BORROWES, Edward, 8
BOURDET, Peter, 25
 Samuel, 25
 Samuell, 4
BOWERS, John, 36, 39, 41, 47, 64, 102, 103, 108
BOWES, George, 32
BOWMAN, Edmond, 119, 134
 James, 35, 64, 103
 John, 1, 2, 5
 Margaret, 2
 Margret, 1, 5
 Mary, 35
 Nathaniel, 119, 123, 124
 Thomas, 2
BOYD, William, 128
BOYDEN, James, 23, 24, 33
BOYDON, James, 25
 William, 99
BRADSHAW, 87
 Elizabeth, 52
 Francis, 119
 James, 50
 John, 4, 5, 6, 15, 17, 28, 29, 30, 34, 44, 45, 49, 52, 72, 73, 78, 85, 93, 95, 119, 122, 126
 Rachel, 29
BRADSHAWS CHANCE, 29, 30, 119
BRADY, Benjamin, 18, 23, 114, 115, 116
 Daniel, 115
 John, 115
 Mary, 18, 23
BRAIN, John, 126
BREWFORD, 99
BRIDGE TOWN, 82
BRIGGS, John, v, 15, 92, 93, vi, 124
BRIGS, John, 50
BRIMLEY, 128
BRINCKLE, John, 114
 William, 1, 2, 6, 7, 24, 35, 38, 41, 64, 65, 80, 133
BRINCKLEY, William, 24
BRINCKLO, William, 7, 11
BRINCKLOE, Elizabeth, 15
 John, 1, 4, 6, 7, 8, 10, 11, 13, 15, 17, 19, 38, 40, 58, 65, 92, 93, 134
 Peter, 40
 William, 38, 65, 92
BRINCKLOE HIS CHOICE, 15
BRINCKLOES RANGE, 21, 41
BRINCKLOW, William, 31, 32
BRINCLE, William, 36
BRINKLE, Elizabeth, 124
 John, 124
 William, 43, 65, 66, 67, 80
BRINKLO, John, 16
BRINKLOE, John, 72, 73, 88, 94, 95, 96, 98, vi, 103
 William, 95, 103
BRINKLOES RANGE, 72
BRISTERS DELIGHT, 21
BRISTOL, 114, 115
BRITTON, Lionell, 134

BROBSHAYS, 74
BROOK, Abraham, 86
  Samuel, 65, 80
  Samuell, 92
BROOKE, Arthur, 79
  Samuel, 81, 83
  Samuiell, 9
BROOKES, James, 48
BROOKHOSS, 36
BROOKS, Cherity, 117
  Elioner, 81
  James, 62, 102, 126, 128, 131
  Moses, 81, 128
  Rebecca, 62, 125
  Rebecka, 118
  Samuel, 38, 71
BROOKSHEAR, 52, 53
BROTHER'S PORTION, 67, 81
BROTHERS PORTION, 133
BROWN, Daniel, 47, 122
  George, 105
  James, 3
  John, 65, 70, 105
  William, 33
BRUCE, Allexander, 9
BRUFET, Grace, 130
BRULSHAW, 75
BRYANT, John, 55
BULKLEE, Samuell, 99
BULLER, John, 59
  Samuell, 60
BULLOCK, Rebecka, 94
BUNDELYN, ?, 123
BUNDOCK, Richard, 130
BUNN, Mary, 127
BURBARY, Samuel, 111
BURBERRY, Samuel, 121
  Samuell, 1, 4, 92, 104
BURBERRY BERRY, 132
BURBERRYS BERRY, 73, 104
BURBERY, Samuel, 2
  Samuell, 8, 11, 12, 16, 17
BURBURY, Samuel, 68
BURBURY'S BERRY, 68
BURBURY'S BURY, 68

BURBURYS LOTT, 68
BURDETT, Peter, 4
  Samuell, 4
BURFORT, Mary, 130
BURRAS, Thomas, 37
BURREY, Samuel, 43
BURTON, Elizabeth, 2, 93
  John, 1, 2, 7, 8, 22, 40, 47, 52,
    93, 111, 129
  William, 22
BURTONS CHANCE, 22
BURTON'S DELIGHT, 93
BURTONS DELIGHT, 2, 7, 93
BURTONS TRACT, 107
BURY, Thomas, 134
BUTTEN, John, 59, 78, 79
BUTTY, Daniel, 116
BYGRAVE, John Allee Robert,
  118
  Robert, 113, 116, 120, 121,
    126, 127

-C-
CABELLIS, John, 64
CABLEY, John, 103
CADWALDER, John, 85
CADWALLADER, Mr., 128
CAIN, John, 71
CALBELLES, John, 103
CALDWELL, Andrew, 58, 61,
  67, 68, 71, 72, 73, 74, 77, 80,
  82, 83, 87, 98, 101, 104, 107,
  108, 111, 113, 114, 116, 118,
  119, 120, 123, 124, 126, 127,
  129, 130, 131, 132, 133
  Joseph, 123
  Margaret, 130, 131
CALIB, Caleb, 63
CAMBLE, John, 35
CAMBRIDGE, 16, 77, 112
CANOAN MANNOR, 103
CANTERBURY, 80
CARDIFF, 85
CARDIN, William, 12
CARELES, Na., 88

141

CARILES, Wa, 63
CARLETON, Ed, 128
CARNNIFF, Jeremiah, 44
CARNY, Philip, 80
CAROLTON, Edward, 128
CARPENTER, Richard, 132
 Samuel, 10, 26, 46
 Samuell, 22
CARR, Joseph, 10
 Mary, 10
 Robert, 106, 125
CAVE, THE, 58
CAWDRY, John, 52
CEDER LANDING, 103
CHALKLEY, Thomas, 22
CHANCE, Allexander, 91
CHANCEY, John, 131
 Mary, 131
CHANCY, Allexander, 92
CHANSLEY, Allexander, 91
CHANTT, John, 49
CHAPPELL, Jo, 63
 Jo., 88
CHAUNT, John, 20
CHESTNUT LANDING, 117
CHIP NORTON, 75
CHIPENNORTON, 35
CHIPENORTON, 45
CHIPPANORTON, 87, 88
CHIPPENNORTON, 53
CHIPPENORTON, 18, 115
CHIPPING NORTON, 115
CHIPPINORTON, 23
CHIPPPING NORTON, 113
CITY OF BRISTOLL, 63
CLAFFORD, John, 20
CLAITON, James, 93
CLAPOLE, James, 19
CLARK, Daniel, 130
 John, 1, 3, 12, 39, 42, 43, 50, 56, 59, 75, 76, 77, 94, 99
 Joshua, 127
 William, 23, 24, 46, 56, 76, 77, 91, 104, 121, 128
CLARKE, Elizabeth, 38
 John, 38, 113, 114
 William, 42, 104
CLATON, Robert, 50
CLAYTON, James, 1, 64, 68, 103
 John, 8, 14, 18, 19, 21, 22, 23, 31, 33, 34, 37, 49, 52, 89, 90, 92, 109, 117, 120
 Josehua, 33
 Joseph, 114
 Joshua, 13, 14, 15, 18, 31, 33, 34, 50, 62, 66, 87, 101
 Mary, 107
 Sarah, 62, 101
CLEMISON, Elizabeth, 89
 Mathew, 89
CLIFFORD, Ann, 78
 John, 50, 78
 Thomas, 78, vi
CLIFFORTH, Ann, 105
 John, 104
 Thomas, 104, 105
CLIFFWORTH, Ann, 116
 John, 104, 116, 117
CLIFORD, Ann, 78
 John, 78
CLUFF, Edward, 55, 56, 57, 76, 97
CO. OF LINROTH, 63
COALI, Elizabeth, 2
COBLY, John, 64
COCA, William, 66
COE, John, 26, 39, 51
 Thomas, 53
 William, 51, 66
COGESHALL, Preserved, 88
COIT, Daniel, 129
COITS, Solomon, 129
COLEMAN, Joseph, 10
 Samuell, 56
COLLIER, John, 85
COLLINS, Jonathan, 29
 William, 64
COLMAN, Joseph, 10
CONTENT, 86, 88, 108, 109

CONVENTREE, 4
COOK, Arthur, 84
  Elizabeth, 84
  John, 20, 52, 53, 58, 98, 106, 126
COOL, Richard, 33, 34, 49, 63
COOLE, Richyate, 88
COOLI, Abraham, 63
  Richard, 63
COOPER, Thomas, 96
COPPERS, 44
COR, John, 107
CORDY, Michall, 127
COUNTRIE LAND, 11
COURDEME, John, 44
COURTNEY, John, 11, 94, 95, 104, 121
COUTTS, Hercules, 6, 9, 13
  James, 6, 13
COVENTREE, 25
COVENTRY, 28, 32, 84, 121
COVENTY, 95
COWGILL, 20
  John, 32, 125
CRAFORD, Thomas, 32, 40, 42
CRAP, John, 94
CRAWFORD, Elizabeth, 15, 16
  Thomas, 15, 16, 19, 22, 23, 27, 29, 62, 66, 80, 102, 118, 121, 134
CRIPPEN, John, 40
  William, 122
CROFLEY, Richard, 126
CROOKED BILLETT, 49
CROOKHILL, 49
CROSLEY, Mary, 87
CROWDEN, Joseph, 126
CT, New London, 129
  New London Co., 129
CUFF, Absalam, 57
  Absallum, 38
  Absalom, 20, 21, 36, 56, 57, 60, 64, 76, 77, 80, 96, 97, 100, 126
  Absalum, 55, 67

  Absolom, 32, 38, 52, 54
CULLEN, George, 116
CULLINGS PURCHASE, 116
CUMBERLAND, 90, 91
CUMING, Robard, 106
CUMMINGS, Robert, 119
CURTES, John, 39
CURTICE, John, 92
CURTIS, Caleb, 119, 124
  John, 64, 69, 83, 103, 105, 118, 121, 122, 124, 127, 128, 133
  Richard, 103
  Sarah, 118, 119, 124
CYPRESS NECK, 51

-D-
DABBS, Benjamin, 110
DAKEYNE, Thomas, 125
DANEY, Philip, 68
DARBY TOWN, 93
DARVAL, William, 111
DARVALL, William, 6, 103, 104
DARVELL, William, 104
DAVID, Evan, 129
  Owen, 40, 42, 43, 119
DAVIS, Evan, 88, 94
  Lewis, 107
  William, 88
DAWSON, John, 12, 44, 125
DE, Chester Co., 39
  Dover, 25, 26, 80, 102, 128, 133
  Kent Co., v, 104, 106
  Lewis, 18
  Lewis Town, 18
  Lewistown, 33, 128
  New Castle, 11, 14, 40, 51, 61, 66, 77, 88, 108
  New Castle Co., 19, 20, 29, 32, 36, 42, 49, 53, 55, 56, 58, 60, 62, 78, 86, 96, 107, 117, 124, 126
  Newcastle, 7, 16, 133
  Newcastle Co., 6, 8, 16, 17,

38, 61, 76, 95, 97, 99, 100, 125
Salesbery, 44, 56
Salesbury, 57
Salisburry, 106
Salisbury, 28, 42, 43, 60, 67, 76, 118
Salisbury Town, 125
Salsburry, 96
Salsbury, 97, 132
Saulesbury, 57
Saulsbury, 96
St. Jones Co., v
Sussex, 9, 77, 88, 99, 104
Sussex Co., 23, 24, 28, 42, 58, 62, 69, 70, 76, 78, 82, 104, 117, 123, 128
DEAN, William, 132
DEMBYTOUN, 12
DEMOCK, William, 26
DENBETOWN, 53
DENBY, 76, 118
DENBY TOWN, 5, 17, 53, 63, 66, 75, 95, 102, 111, 117, 125
DENHIGHTOURNE, 11
DENIFIELD, 28
DENNIS, Hanna, 10
  Hannah, 50, 58, 59, 75, 98
  John, 9, 10, 50
DENNUS, John, 9
DENNY, Phillip, 15, 28
DERBOROW, Hugh, 20
DERBUROW, Hugh, 45
DERIVALL, William, 47
DERVALL, William, 70
DESSEY, Solomon, 88
DICKENSON, Walter, 2, 7
DICKINSON, Jonathan, 33
  Robert, 131
  Samuel, 131
  Walter, 14, 70, 93, 129, 131
DICKISON, 73
DIFFY, Robert, 60
DIRK, 113

DIXON, William, 13, 22, 128
DONAHOE, Michaell, 5
  Michall, 8
DONCASTER, 16, 129
DONELSON, Alexander, 40
DONNAVAN, Randall, 119
DONNE, William, 33, 34, 49, 63, 88
DONOHO, Michael, 127
DONOVAN, Eelizabeth, 120
  Elizabeth, 120
  Randall, 68, 79
  Randol, 120
DORRINGTON, William, 128
DOSSY, Robert, 99
DOUGLAS, Elizabeth, 35
DOVER FARMES, 91
DOVER FARMS, 4, 47, 107, 111
DOVER HUNDRED, 49, 50
DOVER PEER, 35
DOWERY, 71
DOWNDEE, 43
DOWNHAM, Agnes, 107, 112
  Thomas, 107, 112
DOWNS, THE, 104
DRANGHTON, Robert, 43
DRASGATE, Richard, 103, 104
DRAUGHTON, Robert, 42, 133
DRISKELL, William, 127
DROUGHTON, Robert, 42
DUBROIS, John, 2, 96
DUBROIS PURCHASE, 2
DUCK CREEK, v
DUCKE CREEKE, v
DUCROIS, John, 3
DUGDALE, Thomas, 9
DUKE, Peter, 72
DUNCAN, David, 8
DUNDEE, 8, 12, 13, 76, 105, 113, 125
DUNSTON, John, 77
DUNSTONBY, John, 112
DURBEROW, Hugh, 23
DURBOREW, Hugh, 66

DURBOROUGH, Hugh, 27
DURBOROW, Hugh, 22, 57,
    62, 63, 72, 74, 75, 80, 82, 83,
    84, 86, 87, 88, 97, 98, 101,
    102, 108, 109, 110, 113, 117,
    118, 123, 125, 132, 134
  Sarah, 84
DURBORROW, Hugh, 51, 72,
    88, 107
DURBOVOW, Hugh, 58
DURTIS, John, 112
DUTTER, Thomas, 35
DWYER, Mary, 43
  Thomas, 43
DYER, Elizabeth, 94
  William, 41

-E-

EASTGATE, Frances, 40
  Francis, 91
  James, 40
EDINGTON, 106
EDINGTONS TRACT, 107
EDMONDS, Ann, 111
  John, 71, 83
  Prisala, 37
  Robert, 37, 65, 70, 111
EDMONDS CHANCE, 50, 75
EDMONDSON, James, 13, 14
  John, 13, 14, 16, 22, 60, 71,
    73, 77, 78, 79, 99, 112
  Mary, 71, 72, 77, 78, 79, 83,
    101
  Robert, 3, 39
  Sarah, 13, 14
  Thomas, 13, 16, 18, 58, 71, 77,
    78, 79, 83, 98, 101, 112
  William, 13, 14
EDMONDSONS CHOICE, 39
EDMONSON, John, 60, 77
  Mary, 61
  Thomas, 61
EDMUNDS, John, 71, 72, 128
EDVINTON, 43
EDWARDS, William, 5

EGMONDS CHANCE, 111
ELIZABETH'S CHANCE, 107
ELKES HORN, 95
ELLENSWORTH, Elinor, 129
  Elleanor, 59
  Sarah, 59
  William, 59, 129
ELLET, Isaac, 109
  Thomas, 76, 118
ELLETT, Thomas, 110
ELLICE, John, 17
ELLIOT, James, 31
ELLIOTT, Robert, 125
ELLIS, Benjamin, 21, 49, 125
  John, 34, 117
  Robert, 128
  William, 117, 125
ELLIT, Thomas, 73
ELLITS, Thomas, 9
ELLITT, Thomas, 110
ELLOIT, William, 101
ELLSWORTH, 16
ELMANA, William, 95
ELSTION, Ralp, 96
ELSWORTH, 122
EMERSON, ?, 64
  Eliz, 49
  Elizabeth, 53, 63, 102
  Epheram, 41, 42, 46
  Ephraim, 51, 63, 80, 85, 102,
    119, 120, 132
  Ephrain, 72
  Jacob, 1, 39
  John, 103
  Mary, 41, 46, 51, 63, 72, 86,
    102, 120, 132
  Philemon, 17, 58
  Richard, 100
  Thomas, 23, 42, 63, 102
  Vincent, 21, 22, 24, 41, 49, 51,
    52, 58, 62, 71, 81, 101
  Vineen, 40
  Vinson, 35, 41, 45
EMINS, Thomas, 9, 10
EMMERSON, Ephraim, 67, 81

EMMS, Thomas, 10
EMPSON, Corneess, 17
  Richard, 61
ENGLAND, County of North, 10
  Great Yarmouth, 9, 10
  Hall of Hertford, 14
  Joseph, 32
ENOIR, William, 62
EVAMS, John, 120
EVANS, Abraham, 133
  John, 5, 89, 90, 95
  Peter, 135
EVENS, Abraham, 133
  John, 2, 89, 90
EVERETT, Thomas, 13, 49, 89, 90
EXCHANGE, THE, 45, 46, 68, 69, 74, 79, 84, 123
EXECTER, 3

-F-
FAGAN, Elizabeth, 128
FAIR FIELD, 119
FAIRFIELD, 24, 42
FAIRFIELDS, 70
FARMER ELSWORTH, 57
FARMS ELSWORTH, 97
FARSON, William, 99
FEILDS, Abraham, 51
FERRY BRIDGES, 100
FERRY BRIGG, 109
FESTER, Thomas, 128
FIELD, Nehemiah, 6
FIELDS, Abraham, 29, 85
FILKIN, Henry, 45
FINNE, William, 127
FISHER, Adam, 4, 18, 24, 28, 32, 37, 44, 65, 72, 91, 94, 111, 116
  John, 24, 34, 44
  Margaret, 70
  Susanna, 94
  Susannah, 91
  Thomas, 70, 71

FISHERS DELIGHT, 4, 91, 94
FISHING POINT, 92
FITGARREL, Cathrine, 40
  James, 40
FITGARRELL, Frances, 40
FITZGARALD, Rowland, 88
FITZGARRALD, James, 91
FITZGARRALL, Ann, 110
  Edward, 110
  Mary, 110
FITZGERALD, James, 28, 73, 93
  Katharine, 28
FITZGERRALD, James, 19, 21
FITZJARRELL, Mary, 110
FITZJERALD, James, 52
FITZWATER, George, 84
FLEMING, Thomas, 128
FLOURS, John, 4
FLOWER FIELD, 77
FLOWERS, John, 4, 12, 13, 125
FOLKS, Thomas, 87
FOLLY NECK, 26
FOLLYNECK, 22
FORBES, William, 79
FORBUSH, William, 126
FORBY, Elizabeth, 37
FORD, William, v
FORELANDING, THE, 6
FORESTS LANDING, 7
FORSTER, Anne, 49
  John, 38, 43, 46, 49
FORSTERS PURCHASE, 45
FOSTER, Ann, 61, 100
  Anne, 49
  John, 1, 3, 12, 20, 28, 30, 31, 49, 61, 76, 84, 92, 100, 108, 115, 125
FOX, James, 89
FOX HALL, 40
FOYRE, Henry, 59
FRAMPTON, Thomas, 50
  William, 91, 93
FRAMTON, Elizabeth, 31

Thomas, 31
William, 31
FRANCES, Huber, 47
  Huberd, 47
FRANCIS, Hubert, 111
  Robert, v
FREAME, John, 96
FREELAND, Isaac, 13, 63, 102, 119
  Susanna, 15
  Susannah, 15
  William, 15, 90
FREEMAN, Elizabeth, 66, 125
  Mary, 86
  Moses, 71, 85, 109, 112
  Samuel, 63, 66, 102, 125
  Samuell, 53
  Susanna, 94
  William, 44, 60, 89, 92, 94, 99, 131
FREEMANS REST, 92
FRENCH, David, 86
  John, 9, 16, 20, 27, 29, 31, 51, 58, 76, 98, 114, 117
  Phillip, 7
  Robert, 2, 7, 8, 10, 11, 12, 13, 14, 17, 19, 29, 66, 87, 92, 93, 94, 95, 122
  Thomas, 6, 12, 23, 40, 44, 51, 65, 79, 80, 92, 95, 118, 133, 134, 135
FRETTWELL, Edward, 27
FRETWELL, Edward, 27
  Ralph, 60, 99
FURBER, Benjamin, 103
FURBY, Benjamin, 116
  Susanah, 116
FURBYS LOTT, 116

-G-
GAINSBROUGH, 110
GALAWAY, 100
GALE, John, 118
GALLOWAY, 60
GARDINER, Matthew, 31

GARINER, Anne, 10
  James, 10
GARLEN, Anne, 120
GARVEY, Owen, 38, 85
GARVIE, Elizabeth, 1
  Oven, 1
  Owen, 2
GARVIN, Thomas, vi
GARVIN'S, vi
GATTEAN, Mary, 133
  Nicholas, 133
GEMLEY, Benjamin, 19
GENDINGTON, 123
GENSELIN, Thomas, 20
GERALD, James Fitz, 1
GIBBONS, Edmond, 103, 111
  Francis, 111
GIBBSON, Frances, 47
GILFORD, 62, 101
GIVVSON, Edmond, 47
GLOUCESTER, 95
GLOVER, Elizabeth, 3
  John, 3, 119
  Richard, 3, 49
  Samuell, 49
GLOVERS NECK, 8
GOFFER, Zachariah, 36
  Zackeriah, 36
GOFFORTH, Zachirias, 56
GOFORTH, Zacariah, 44
  Zachariah, 80
GOGIN, David, 90
GOLDEN THICKET, THE, 46
GOLDEN THUBETT, THE, 124
GOLDNIS, Henry, 33
GONDWELL, Fr., 25
GONSEALA, Thomas, 108
GOODIN, Daniel, 126
  Daniell, 12
  Daninell, 12
  Elizabeth, 12
GOODSON, John, 22, 26, 46
GOOSBERRY, 2
GOOSEBERRY, 130

GORDEN, James, 95
GORDON, Elizabeth, 131
  James, 73, 81, 82, 90
  John, 124, 131
  Mary, 121
  Robert, 51, 65, 66, 86, 105, 108, 121, 135
GORLEAN, Ann, 120
GORLEN, Anne, 120
GOULD, James, 81
GOULDNEY, Henry, 96
GOULT, George, 127
GRAHAM, George, 53, 54, 55, 56, 57, 96, 97
GRAINGER, Joseph, 27
GRANGER, Joseph, 27
GRAVELLY RUN, 52
GRAVENRACH, Andries, 7
GRAVES END, 21, 38
GRAVES END, THE, 104
GRAVESEND, 20
GRAYHAM, George, 57
GREAT BRITAIN, Bristol, 26, 33
  City of Bristoll, 38, 49
  County of Norfolk, 58
  County of York, 27
  Great Yarmouth, 75
  Norfolk, 98
  Wickersley, 21
GREAT BRITTAIN, City of Bristol, 133
GREAT GENEVA, 77
GREAT PIPE ELM, 81
GREAT PIPE ELME, 12, 108, 111
GREAT YARMOUTH, 10, 58, 59
GREEN, George, 35, 45, 50, 51, 52, 58, 61, 76, 86, 97, 98, 100
  John, 35
  Mary, 20
  Mercy, 20, 38
  Rachell, 50
  Thomas, 68, 69
  William, 19, 38, 40, 95
GREEN HOOP, 95
GREEN HOPE, 96
GREEN OAK, 96
GREENAWAY, Nich, 119
  Nicholas, 115
  Nicolas, 119, 121
GREENWOOD, J., 103
  James, 73
  Johan, 6
  Jonas, 5, 6, 8, 9, 11, 12, 14, 17, 29, 33, 39, 41, 55, 63, 69, 92, 102
  Joshua, 64
  Phineas, 67, 68, 69, 72, 78
  Plineas, 67
  Samuel, 67, 80
  Samuell, 66
GRIER, Mark, 127
GRIFFETH, James, 37
  Marcy, 37
GRIFFING, Samuel, 49
  Samuell, 21
GRIFFITH, James, 25
GRIFING, Samuel, 54
GRIFTING, Samuell, 54
GRIGGES PURCHASE, 16
GROENENDIKE, Peter, vi
GROUNDICK, Peter, 68
GROUNDY, Robert, 16
GROWDEN, Joseph, 60, 99
GROWDON, Joseph, 14
GRUMLEY, John, 19
GRUNDEY, Robert, 79, 98
GRUNDY, Robert, 16, 18, 58, 74, 78, 79, 98
GUILFORD, 19, 22
GUMBEY, Benjamin, 42, 43
GUMBLEY, John, 19
GUMBLY, Benjamin, 95
GUMLEY, Benjamin, 19
  James, 128
  John, 29
GUMLY, James, 128

GURLEN, Anne, 120
  William, 120

-H-
HACKER, John, 78
HACKET, Thomas, 23
  William, 55
HACKETT, John, 60, 100
  Thomas, 20, 21, 34, 54, 99
  William, 54
HAEKEY, William, 30
HAILER, David, 46
HALL, Anna, 75, 107
  Annah, 88
  Anne, 46
  Hannah, 19
  Henry, 26, 56, 120, 121, 128
  Hugh, 13, 14
  John, 19, 22, 27, 29, 36, 41,
    42, 45, 46, 49, 50, 51, 53, 55,
    56, 66, 67, 72, 74, 75, 76, 77,
    86, 88, 96, 100, 106, 107,
    108, 109, 112, 113, 115, 118,
    120, 127, 129, 130, 134
  Nathan, 34
  Nathanial, 34
  Nathaniel, 34, 36
  Richard, 41
  Zodiack, 88
HAMBLETON, Walter, 44
  William, 35
HAMBLY, Richard, 11, 12
HAMELTON, A., 30, 31
  Andra, 27
  Andrew, 32
HAMILTON, A., 24, 69, 72, 115
  Andrew, 21, 25, 27, 28, 32, 67,
    69, 73, 78, 83, 84
  Ax, 27
  Springate, 104
HAMINERSMITH, 4
HAMLETON, Andrew, 39
HAMMOND, Daniel, 109
HANDSON, Timothy, 33
HANNAH, 113

HANSON, Peter, v
  Rimothy, 50
  Samuel, 69, 70, 84, 115
  Susanah, 41
  Susanna, 15
  Susannah, 39
  Tim, 67
  Timothy, 15, 20, 23, 24, 31,
    32, 36, 37, 38, 39, 41, 50, 53,
    58, 64, 65, 66, 67, 68, 69, 70,
    76, 79, 81, 82, 105, 113, 114,
    115, 117, 133, 134
HARBOT, Timothy, 106
HARBOTT, Thomas, 60
HARFORD, Charles, 49, 63, 88
  Charter, 33, 34
HARGROVE, Stephen, 105
HARGROW, Stephen, 46
HARMAN, Ephraim, 124
  Ephrim, 17
HARPER, Charles, 33, 36, 54,
    57, 106
  John, 61, 101
HARRAWAY, Samuell, 19
  William, 19
HARRIS, Charles, 112
HARRISON, Charles, 112
  Samuell, 94
HART, Anna, 29
  Georg, 90
  George, 19, 29, 40, 41, 52, 64,
    91, 93, 103, 116
  Henry, 52, 116
  John, 19, 107, 116
  Mary, 116, 119
  Robert, vi, 104
HARTE, John, 43
HARTT, George, 21
  John, 21, 119
HARWOOD, Jasper, 9, 109
HASTON, Anthoney, 31
HATHERDS ADVENTURE, 50
HATTWELL, Richard, 91
HAVOIER, John, 43
HAWKER, Ursula, 95

William, 95
HAWKETT, Thomas, 54
HAWKEY, William, 32, 54, 72, 83, 84
HAYPOLE, George, 117
HAYWOOD, Mary, 35
HEARGROW, Stephen, 46
HEARN, William, 50
HEARTT, John, 21
HEATERD, Thomas, 95
HEATH, Richard, 10, 14, 48
HEATHARD, Anne, 90
   Thomas, 3, 90, 111
HEATHERD, Thomas, 90, 91
HEATHERDS ADVENTURE, 75
HEATHERS, Thomas, 55
HENDRICKSON, Arnant, 76
HERCOMB, Baptista, 77
HERFORD, Charles, 49
HERN, William, 50
HERRYBRIDGE, 61
HETHARS, Thomas, 9
HETHERD, Thomas, 45
HEWHAT, Thomas, 4
HEWTHAT, Elenor, 37
   Mellecent, 37
   Prisala, 37
   Ralph, 37
   Thomas, 14, 18, 92
HEWTHATE, Anne, 37
   Elener, 38
   Elenor, 37, 38
   Thomas, 37, 38
HICKERSON, Jeremiah, 68
HICKETS, William, 132
HIGGINS, Patrick, 69
HIGH HOAK, 16
HIGHAM, John, 119
HIGHAM FERRY, 33, 62, 101
HIGHAMS, 87
HIGHAMS TRACE, 87
HIGHAN, John, 29
   Rachel, 29
HIGHMANS FERRY, 13, 90

HILL, Elizabeth, 69, 70
   John, 69
   Richard, 27, 33, 53, 58, 60, 83, 98
HILLIARD, Charles, 126
   John, 39
   Thomas, 21
   William, 39
HILLYARD, Charles, 10, 16, 45, 49, 65, 68, 69, 73, 79, 106, 108, 117, 121, 130, 133
   Elizabeth, 84
   John, 19, 21, 45, 68, 69, 72, 74, 76, 79, 84, 121, 128, 129
   Rachell, 68
   Thomas, 21, 45, 68, 69
   William, 109
HILLYARD BENLY, 68
HILLYARDS, Charles, 18
HILLYARDS ADVENTURE, 10, 12
HINMAN, Richard, 88
HIRONS, Elizabeth, 87, 114
   Fraancis, 87
   Frances, 10, 42, 43
   Francis, 8, 10, 12, 42, 87, 112, 113, 127
   John, 54, 73, 74, 75, 105
   Peirses, 37
   Perces, 52
   Perciss, 75
   Perses, 35, 45, 54
   Robert, 53, 54, 87, 88, 106, 131
   Simon, 10, 11, 12, 35, 37, 41, 45, 46, 50, 51, 52, 53, 54, 55, 58, 73, 74, 75, 79, 81, 85, 87, 105, 106, 107, 112, 114, 120, 127, 131
   Timothy, 107
   William, 20, 25, 26, 37, 39, 52, 53, 54, 74, 75, 114
HIRONS CHOICE, 74
HIRSON, Benjamin, 56
HIXON, Benjamine, 96, 97

HIXSON, Benjamin, 57
HODGE, Henry, 134
HODGES, Fustrum, 34
HODGKINS, Thomas, 123
HODGSIN, Robert, 124
HODGSON, Frain, 130
  Robert, 120, 122, 123, 130, 131
HODKINS CHOICE, 16
HOLE, THE, 16
HOLLIDAY, John, 64, 132
HOLLYDAY, John, 132
HOLY NECK, 90
HOPEWELL, v, 38
HOPPER, George, 132
HORN, William, 10
HORSTEAD, John, 7
HORTON, George, 61
HOSKINGS, Henry, 53
  Rachel, 53
HOSKINS, Henry, 5
  Rachell, 4
HOSTER, John, 60, 61
HOUSMAN, James, 100
  John, 127
HOWARD, James, 72, 85
  Robert, 72, 110, 123
HOWELL, James, 116
  Jane, 73
  William, 73
HUDLESTON, George, 9
HUDSON, Daniel, 24, 67, 71, 130
  Daniell, 22
  Elenor, 105
  Elenour, 105
  Elinor, 105
  Elioner, 105
  Eliounr, 105
  John, 16, 71, 123, 130
  Lenour, 105
  Richard, 105
  Robert, 5, 71, 130
  Thomas, 75, 104
HUDSON'S LOTT, 71

HUDSONS LOTT, 81, 82
HUGHS, Anne, 39
  Griffeth, 39
HUMPHRYS, Alexander, 86
HUMPLUGH, Nathaniel, 53
HUN, Nathaniel, 50
HUNN, Nathanial, 39
  Nathaniel, 39, 64, 90, 91, 102
  Nathaniell, 1
HURBER, Benjamin, 64
HURREY, Thomas, 10
HURY, Thomas, 9
HUSTON, Anthony, 31
HUSTONE, Anthony, 27
HUTTON, John, 133
HYATT, John, 133

-I-
ILLE OF AXOLIMI, 63
INDIAN FIELD, 106
INDIAN FIELDS, 1, 120
INDIAN FIELDS, THE, 48
INTOLLAHAY, 118
IRONS, Timothy, 107
ISAAC'S PURCH, 13
ISGATE, Caleb, 59
ISLAND OF BARBADOES, 13
ISLAND OF BARBADOS, 59, 98

-J-
JACKSON, Christopher, 24
  James, 30, 31, 32, 43, 49, 60, 61, 72, 84, 100, 109, 115
  John, 55
  Lyddea, 2
  Margaret, 61, 66, 72, 84, 100, 115
  Margarett, 60, 100
  Marget, 30
  Margit, 32
  Margret, 30
  Margrit, 31
  Richard, 2, 24, 51
  Stephen, 16

William, 105
JACOCK, William, 88
JACOKS, William, 46
JAMES, Daniel, 130
  Phillip, 95
  Richard, 107, 122, 124, 126, 127
  Ruth, 122
JANALLE, T., 32
JANSEN, Henrich, 91
JENINGS, Edward, 108, 110, 113, 121, 123
JENKINS, Jabez, 23
  Taber, 128
JENNINGS, Edward, 72, 79, 105, 108, 110, 126
JESTER, Thomas, 44, 69, 119, 124
JINKINS, Jaber, 52
JOANES, Evan, 55
  Griffith, 51
JOHN BETTS ENDEAVOR, 57, 97
JOHN BETTS ENDEAVOUR, 61, 100
JOHNSON, Elenor, 48
  Henry, 48, 128
  John, 20, 36, 42, 47
JOHNSTON, 93
JOILLSON, Thomas, 27
JONES, Charles, 126
  Daniel, 105, 108, 116
  Daniell, 2, 7, 23, 91, 93
  Evan, 1, 4, 6, 11, 14, 17, 24, 25, 27, 28, 30, 32, 45, 49, 65, 68, 69, 79, 84, 85, 89, 96, 106, 114, 118, 126
  Evans, 122
  Even, 30, 32
  Evin, 53
  Frances, 56, 57, 96, 97
  Francis, 20, 32
  Gabriel, 13, 73
  Gabriell, 16, 17
  Griff, 2, 4, 5, 24, 47, 71, 73, 76, 80, 82, 91, 92, 93, 105, 114, 129
  Griffen, 81
  Griffeth, 7, 29, 94, 95, 99
  Griffith, 11, 17, 21, 24, 25, 56, 60, 77, 78, 94, 108, 121, 122
  Grifith, 88
  Henry, 55, 56, 57, 97
  John, 73, 116, 118, 132
  Joseph, 21, 24, 25
  Margaret, 132
  Robert, 15, 31, 70, 91
  Sara, 99
  Walter, 30
JONES' CREEK, v
JONSON, William, 95
JOYCE, Henry, 36, 62, 71, 89, 101, 122
JUCH, Isabel, 112

-K-

KARR, Robert, 106
KEARNY, Phil, 87
  Philip, 113, 118, 134, 135
  Phillip, 134
  Rebeca, 134
  Rebecca, 135
  Susanah, 134
  Thomas, 134, 135
KEITH, William, 65, 88, 117
KELLY, John, 32, 60, 84
  WIlliam, 32
  William, 100, 115
KELPERS, John, 43
KENTON, Lydia, 127
KERNEY, Phillip, 48, 116
  Phillys, 19
KEYSAR, Deborah, 34, 35
  Derick, 34, 35
KICKMANS WORTH, 80
KILLINGSWORTH, Edward, 81
  John, 81
KING, John, 94, 134
  Richard, 9, 76

KINGSAILE, 92
KINGSALE, 30
KINGSGIL, 43
KINGSTON, 30, 96
KINGSTON UPON HULL, 27,
   31, 40, 50, 93, vi
KINGSTOWN, 131
KINGSTOWNE UPON HULL,
   91
KIPHAVEN, John, v
KIRKAM, James, 127
KIRKHAM, James, 127
KNIGHT, John, 96
KNOX, Thomas, 117

-L-
LALLOI, John, 44
LAMPLUGH, Nathaniel, 76
LANE, John, 14
   Timothy, 127
LARRANCE, William, 37
LATEHAM, Gabriel, 41
LATHAN, Adam, 23
LAUDE, John, 110
LAWRANCE, Joseph, 27
   William, 22, 23
LAWRENCE, Jo., 61
   To., 101
   William, 12, 34
LEASON, 29
LEATHERBURY, Thomas, 88,
   108, 109, 117
LEAVERPOOLE, 95
LEBITT, Richard, 91
LEDGAR, William, 82
LEESEN, 40
LEGRIER, Thomas, 98
LEGRIRE, Thomas, 58
LESSEN, 90
LESTER, George, 68, 73, 103
LESTERFIELD, 73
LETCHAM, Gabriel, 41
LEVERITT, Mary, 129
   Richard, 129
LEVICK, John, 112, 113, 116,
   118
   Mary, 113
   Richard, 29, 40, 69, 76, 85,
      113, 114, 120
   William, 113
LEVITTE, Richard, 106
LEWIS, John, 108, 109
   Lancelot, 49, 76, 108, 109
   Samuel, 88
LINSAY, John, 133
LISBON, 1, 4, 6, 11, 94
LISENBEY, Henry, 48
   John, 48
LISENBIE, Henry, 73
LISSEN, 80
LITTLE CREEK, v
LITTLE GENEVA, 16
LITTLE JANEWAY, 77
LITTLE PIPE ELME, 21, 22
LIVINFORD, 39
LLOYD, Abrah, 34
   Abraham, 33, 63, 88
   Caleb, 33, 34, 63, 88
   Edward, 33, 34, 63, 88
   Philemon, 77
LOBER, Michael, 24
LOCKERMAN, Nicholas, 131
LOCKHAIT, James, 37
LOGAN, James, 27, 33, 53, 58,
   60, 83
   Samuel, 98
LONDON, 10, 15, 89, 90, 105,
   116
LONG REACH, 4, 8, 28, 116
LONG TRACT, 110
LONGREACH, 16, 17
LONGROATH, 13
LOOCKERMAN, Nicholas, 112,
   120
LOVE, Samuel, 43
LOVEDAY, Mary, 127
LOVELACE, Francis, 119
   Governor, 70
LOW, Samuell, 7, 11
LOWBAR, Michael, 66, 82

Micheal, 116
Susanah, 116
LOWBARE, Michael, 131
LOWBER, Michael, 58, 98, 128
  Micheal, 116
  Susanah, 116
LOWDEN, Edward, 34
LOWDER, Edward, 76, 125
  Mary, 125
LOWMAN, Samuel, 117
LOWTHER, George, 5, 6, 13
LOYD, Abraham, 49
  David, 10
  Edward, 49
LOYED, Abraham, 49
  Caleb, 49
  Edward, 49
LUCAS, John, 62
  Rebecca, 62
LUCOS, John, 126
  Rebecca, 126
LUCUS, John, 102
  Rebecca, 102
LUFF, Nathaniel, 123
LUKE, Richard, 108
LUSHER, Anne, 49

-M-
MAC-QUEEN, Dav, 79
MACADOE, William, 132
MACBRIDE, D., 125
MCCLANEY, Thomas, 124
MACDARMEND, Hugh, 129
MACDERDNEND, Ellinor, 129
  Hugh, 129
MACDERMEND, Hugh, 129
MCDOWELL, John, 120
MACHAN, John, 113
MACK-QUEEN, Dav, 78, 79
MACKELANEY, Thomas, 124
MACKELANY, Thomas, 81
MACKEY, James, 133
MACKQUEEN, David, 83
MACKY, James, 107
MCLEARE, Robert, 3

MADDOX, Joshua, 128
MAGILL, An, 124
MAHAN, Eneas, 82, 119
  John, 110
  Orpha, 119
MAHANEN, Daniell, 134
MAHON, Aenes, 120
  John, 5, 51
MAIDENS PLOT, 128
MAIDENS PLOTT, 69
MAIDSTONE, 104
MALONEY, William, 56
MAMSON, Isaac, 71
MANFORD, Ayda, 44
  John, 44, 45
MANLOE, Mark, 100
MANLOV, Mark, 56, 57, 97
MANLOVE, Absalom, 72
  Ebenezer, 72
  Elizabeth, 43, 84
  Jonathan, 67
  Luke, 39, 41, 81, 92
  Mark, 31, 43, 47, 49, 56, 65,
    68, 69, 72, 75, 77, 80, 81, 92,
    106, 111, 115, 121, 122, 123,
    128, 130, 132
  Marke, 38
  Mathew, 1, 3, 31, 43, 68, 77,
    80, 85, 92, 120, 128
  Matthew, 91, 114, 116
  Rachel, 43, 72
  Rachell, 134
  Roger, 44
  Samuel, 32, 43, 61, 84, 86,
    100, 115
  Samuell, 49
  Susannah, 86
  William, 39, 46, 49, 72, 85, 86,
    92, 103, 106, 114, 122, 127,
    132
MANLOVES PLATT, 44
MANLOVES PLOTT, 129
MANNOR OF FEITH, 60
MARAM, Charles, 85, 86
  John, 86

MARIM, Charles, 85
MARIN, Charles, 43
MARKHAM, William, 26, 39, 46
MAROM, Frances, 106
　John, 106
MARON, John, 27, 28, 29
　Mary, 29
MARONEE, William, 126
MARSH, Charles, 104
MARTAIN, Elisabeth, 45
　George, 35, 45
　James, 36, 47
MARTIN, Charles, 131
　Georg, 91
　George, 30, 58, 61, 79, 85, 95,
　　98, 100, 101, 106, 118, 121,
　　122, 130
　John, 14, 43
MARUM, John, 21
MARUNS DELIGHT, 21
MASON, Isaac, 73, 83, 119
　Mary, 131
　Mathew, 92
　Michael, 131
　Mikel, 131
　Susanna, 119
MASONS LOTT, 71
MATHEWS, Mary, 3
　Samuel, 3
　Samuell, 2
　Susanna, 3
MATHON, John, 118
MAURITZ, Jacob, 6
MAXON, Nicholas, 46, 47, 48
　Nicklos, 45
MAXWELL, James, 5, 17, 47,
　　103, 109, 111, 119, 124
　Meliston, 109, 110
　Robert, 109, 110
　William, 5, 109, 110
MAXWILL, James, 32
MD, Annapolis, 16, 78
　Cecil Co., 100
　Cecle Co., 38
　Dorcester Co., 132

　Dorchester Co., 5, 89, 90, 110,
　　130
　Dorset, 10
　Dosset Co., 84
　Kent Co., 61, 81, 88, 113, 114,
　　117, 125
　Luel Co., 54
　Queen Ann Co., 77
　Queen Anne Co., 74, 77
　Queen Anns Co., 81, 113, 115,
　　118
　Summerset Co., 48, 76
　Talbert Co., 101
　Talbet Co., 5
　Talbot Co., 12, 13, 16, 18, 19,
　　22, 41, 58, 59, 68, 71, 73, 74,
　　77, 78, 79, 89, 98, 110, 112,
　　127, 129, 131, 132
　Talbott Co., 17, 68
　Talbut Co., 61
　White Marsh, 84
MEREDITH, Robert, 132
MERRITT, Thomas, 70, 119
MESSING, John, 99
MESTON, Arthur, 7, 8, 12, 13,
　　15, 48, 91, 93
METCALFE, George, 113
MICHOLDS, Thomas, 113
MIDDLE WICKS, 90
MIFFING, John, 60
MIFFLIN, John, 67, 71, 80, 81,
　　82, 83, 106
　Sarah, 82
MILL, David, 12
MILL NICK, THE, 36
MILL RANGE, 46
MILL RANGE, THE, 129
MILLES, Mary, 2
MILLS, Andrew, 93
　George, 72
　Jane, 93
　John, 38, 40, 114
MITCHELL, Richard, 22, 30,
　　68, 71, 104, 128
MODEUAMOTT, Elleanor, 59

155

Hugh, 59
MOIES, James, 36
MOIR, Isaac, 25
   James, 23, 31
MOLESTON, Henry, 2, 8, 9, 11, 65, 103
MOLESTONE, William, 43
MOLLESTON, Ann, 130
   Henry, 130
   John, 110
   William, 130
MOLLESTOON, Henry, 14
MOLTON, Susanah, 72
MONE, Jacob, 133
MONGER, Tron, 88
MONTGOMERY, Robert, 24, 25
MOOR, Henry, 29
   James, 20
MOORE, Christopher, 19, 22
   John, 96
   Stephen, 68
   William, 19
MORE, James, 37
MORGAN, Abraham, 73, 74, 132
   David, 33, 40, 53, 62, 67, 80, 81, 87, 101, 114
   George, 8, 14, 49, 89, 93
   James, 73
   John, v, 29, 48, 85
   Mathew, 78
   Phebe, 40
   Philip, 73, 74, 132
   Phillip, 58, 98
   Sarah, 62, 101
   William, 49
MORISSON, John, 106
MORLEY, Richard, 110
MORONY, John, 24
MORREY, Daniel, 37
MORRICE, James, 73
   John, 122
MORRIS, Anthony, 69
   Elizabeth, 69, 70
   Isaac, 83, 98
   James, 8, 23
   John, 42, 67, 106
MORRISS, John, 106
MORRY, Humphry, 30
   Rebeca, 30
MORTON, George, 100
   William, 5, 8, 9, 10, 11, 13, 20, 51, 76, 89, 90, 114, 121
MOTT, Samuel, 111
MOTTS, Samuell, 1
MOUNT PLEASANT, 1, 22, 43, 76, 77, 87, 121
MOUNT PLEASENT, 56
MOWBARR, Michael, 131
MULBERRY SWAMP, 131
MULBERRY POINT, 103
MULBERY SWAMPE, 129
MULLBERY POINT, 64
MULRONEY, William, 69
MULRONY, William, 64, 65, 103, 128, 129
MUNTFORD, Alburt, 95
MURREY, Rebacca, 35
   Rebeca, 30

-N-

NACARRO, John, 4
NACKARRA, Elinor, 25
   Helenor, 25
   John, 25
NASSON, F., 25
NAYLOR, Mary, 94
NEAL, Edward, 127
   Francis, v
NEALL, Edward, 127
NEEDHAM, Anna, 55, 90, 91
   Daniell, 7, 8, 9, 14, 15, 18
   Danill, 2
   Edmand, 33
   Edmond, 2, 3, 4, 9, 28, 55, 90, 91
   Edmund, 91
   Elizabeth, 14
   Ezekiel, 14, 23, 28, 55

Ezekiell, 4, 8, 13
Mary, 72
Ralph, 87, 88, 114
NEEDUM, Anne, 37
Edmond, 37
NELEY, John, 32
NEW ABERDEEN, 40
NEW BRISTER, 21
NEW BRISTOL, 64, 103
NEW DESIGNE, 11
NEW ENGLAND, Barnstable, 26
County of Barnstable, 34
NEW LINE, 16, 74
NEW SEVENHAVEN, vi
NEW WEST JERSEY, Burlington, 91
NEWELL, John, 24, 25, 117
Stephen, 91, 93
William, 18, 127
NEWELLE, William, 110
NEWIL, John, 79
William, 80
NEWILL, John, 86
NEWTON, John, 46, 127
Mary, 127
NICHOLLS, William, 5
NICHOLS, Robert, 96
Thomas, 7
NICKALSON, Jerimiah, 24
NICKARRA, Elinor, 25
NICKELS, Robert, 131
NICKELSON, John, 89
NICKERSON, Jeremiah, 120
Jerimiah, 24
Joseph, 71, 80
NICKLES, William, 131
NICKLSON, John, 41
NICKOL, John, 5
NICKOLDSON, Jeremiah, 79
NICKOLLAS, Thomas, 7
NICKOLLS, Thomas, 12
NICKOLLSON, Elizabeth, 14
John, 14
NICKOLS, Thomas, 43

William, 96
NICKOLSON, John, 8, 14, 89, 90
NICKSON, Nicholas, 73
NIXON, Elizabeth, 125, 126
Mary, 18, 23, 106, 114
Nicholas, 14, 50, 62, 74, 75, 102, 111, 125
Richard, 22
Thomas, 18, 23, 114
NIXONE, Nicholas, 8
NIXONS DELIGHT, 27
NIXSON, Richard, 27
NJ, Burlington Co., 17
Maidenhead, 2
NOCK, Thomas, 23, 24, 66, 117
NORRING, 107, 124
NORRINGE, 126
NORRIS, Isaac, 27, 33, 53, 58, 60
NORTH GREAT YARMOUTH, 10
NORTHAMPTON, 89
NORTHAMTOM, 14
NOVA COSEASIA, Esea Co., 44
Hackingsack, 35
NOWELL, George, 27, 31, 40, 50, 89, 122
John, 24, 129
Sarah, 89, 122
Stephen, 50, 92, 93
William, 24, 71
NUGAN, Christopher, 80
NY, 78
Island Nassaw, 35
Jamaica, 2
New York City, 6, 133
NY City, 18
Queene Co., 44
Queens Co., 2
Staten Island, 133
Whorekills Co., 129

-O-
OAKE PLAINE, THE, 133
OCHARON, Timothy, 2
ODOCHARTIE, Ferdinando, 105
ODOCKARTIE, Ferdinando, 43
ODONAHOE, Michael, 6
  Michaell, 51
ODONOHOE, Michaell, 5
ODOWGHERTY, Ferdinando, 105
ODUNUKER, Michel, 44
OFFLEY, Caleb, 32, 108
  Fafadiah, 45
OFLEY, Hoyidiah, 30
OGLETHE, John, 70
OHARAN, Timothy, 29
ONEAL, Bryan, 104
OPDEGRAFTE, Deborah, 34, 35
  Herman, 34
OPDEGRAVE, Herman, 35
  Isaac, 35
OSBORN, Joseph, 2, 7, 93
OUSBE, 92
OUSBEY, 3, 4, 9, 14, 18, 71, 90, 91
OUSBY, 37
OWEN, Robert, 70

-P-
PA, Bensalem, 126
  Burks Co., 126
  Chester Co., 9, 27
  Kent Co., 1, 2, 3, 5, 6, 10, 11, 12, 44, 45, 48, 60, 71, 81, 89, 90, 91, 93, 94, 95, 98, 99, 110, 114, 131
  New Castle, 60, 99
  New Castle Co., 11, 92
  Newcastle, 11, 95
  Newcastle Co., 95, 97
  Philadelphia, 9, 10, 12, 18, 21, 23, 24, 26, 37, 39, 42, 43, 44, 57, 58, 59, 61, 64, 65, 69, 72, 73, 74, 77, 80, 81, 83, 85, 87, 89, 94, 95, 97, 98, 99, 100, 102, 107, 110, 115, 121, 133, 134
  Philadelphia Co., 126
  St. Jones, 59
  Sussex, 90
  Sussex Co., 43, 59
PAIN, Elizabeth, 28
  Fletcher, 86
  Gletcher, 86
  John, 28, 46, 49, 71, 79, 106
PANNAND, William, 62
PARADDE, Staphen, 10
PARADDEE, Peter, 40
  Stephen, 89
PARADDENE, 10
PARADEE, Stephen, 4, 69, 107, 114
PARBO, Thomas, 110
PARIS, Edward, 72
  Susanah, 72
PARK, Thomas, 34
PARKE, Sarah, 34
  Thomas, 19, 21, 32, 34, 37, 52, 73, 119
PARKER, John, 76
  Richard, 104
  Thomas, 34
PARMAIN, Henry, 5
PARMAINS CHOICE, 5
PARNEL, Elizabeth, 107
PARNELL, Edward, 107
  Elizabeth, 107
PARRADEE, Margaret, 29, 107
  Stephen, 2, 27, 29, 107
PARRATT, Aaron, 127
  Susanna, 127
  William, 127
PARRISS, Robert, 22
PARROT, Aaron, 127
PARROTT, Susanna, 127
PARSON, John, 56, 76, 96
  William, 60
PARTENERSHIP, THE, 46

PARTNERS, THE, 92
PARTNERSHIP, THE, 11
PARVIS, Robert, 19
PARVISS, Robert, 61, 62, 101
PASTURE POINT, 64, 103
PATERSON, Andrew, 12
PEACH BLOSSOM, 59
PEACOCK, George, 4
PEARCE, D., 32
PEARMAIN, Henry, 32
PELLTON, 77
PEMBERTON, James, 77
PENDER, Alexander, 125
PENDOR, Alexander, 125
PENEFF, Henry, 33
PENENTON, Elizabeth, 105
PENN, William, 26, 27, 33, 37, 38, 55, 59, 99, 111
PENNENTON, Elizabeth, 105
  Henry, 105
PENNINGTON, Elizabeth, 105
  William, 19
PENOCK, Nathaniel, 37
PENROSE, Christo, 132
PENWELL, Marma Duke, 101
  Marmaduke, 61
PEPPER, Elizabeth, 125
PERMAIN, Henry, 5
PERMAINE, Henry, 95
PERNALL, Mary, 132
PERRY, Michajah, 96
PETERSON, Elizabeth, 52
  Thomas, 52
PETIPHER, Francis, 61
PHILADELPHIA, PA, 70
PHILIP, Thomas, v
PHILIPS, James, 86
PHILLIPP, Mary, 31
PHILLIPS, Hanah, 60
  Hannah, 99
  John, 20, 23, 53, 54, 60, 64, 99
  Mary, 50, vi
PHILLIS, 113
PHIPS, Joseph, 112

PICKERIL, William, 124
PICKERING, Charles, 60, 99
  William, 32
PIDGEON, Joseph, 94
PINER, Edward, 114
PLAINS, THE, 48, 62, 102, 126
PLEASANTINE, John, 85
PLESENTON, John, 105
PLUMBS, John, 129
PLUMSTED, Clem., 115
POPLAR HILL, 104
POPLAR NECK, 15
POPLAR RIDGE, 15, vi
PORPOLE, John, 129
PORTER, 93
  Ann, 111
  James, 85, 101
  Lawrence, 3
  Robert, 3, 15, 18, 31, 33, 50, 66, 101
PORTERS LODGE, 17
POTTER, James, 3, 37, 52, 54, 62, 73, 74, 75, 87, 89, 90, 94, 101, 109, 110
POTTERS LODGE, 93
POUND, John, 112
POUNDS, John, 49
  Samuel, 61, 100
POWELL, David, 2, 130
  John, 67, 72
PRAT, Thomas, 132
PREESTON, Samuell, 14
PRENTICE, Jonathan, 129
PRESTON, Samuell, 14
PRICE, Anna, 90
  Anne, 90
  John, 90
  Thomas, 90
PRIME, Ralph, 5
PRINER, Edward, 38
PRITCHARD'S, vi
PROVOST, Johanes, 7
PRSONSS, John, 89
PUGH, Ann, 67
  David, 67

-Q-
QUA, 127
QUEEN, Da Mack, 74
  Dav Mack, 73
  Dave Mack, 79
QUILLEN, Barberry, 54

-R-
RAMSEY, Charles, 41
  Mary, 41
RANDOLS, Benjamin, 48
RANGE, THE, 112, 113, 127
RAYNALLS, John, 131
RAYNOLDS, Benjamin, 48
  John, 113, 114
  Thomas, 113, 114
READ, John, 129
  Robert, 106
RECE, John, 42
REDING, 93
REDMAN, John, 18, 42, 55
REECE, John, 42
REES, John, 40
REESE, John, 42
  Reynolds, 42
REGESTER, Robert, 114
REGISTER, John, 72, 87, 108, 109
  Robert, 113
  Sarah, 108
  William, 114
REGISTOR, John, 72
REIGESTER, John, 32
RENALDS, John, 86
RENALLS, Francis, 1
  John, 13
RENNALLS, Benjamin, 86
  John, 52, 75
RENNALS, Benjamin, 85, 106
  Francis, 106
  John, 75, 85
RENOLLS, John, 39
RESERVE, THE, 118
REYNALLS, John, 44, 47, 86
  Mary, 47

REYNOLDS, 72
  John, 40, 42, 49, 55
  William, 40, 55, 85
REYNOLDS FARM, 49
REYNOLLS, John, 39, 44
REYNOLS, John, 47
  Mary, 47
RICHARDSON, 46
  Elizabeth, 48
  Frances, 35, 48
  Francis, 30, 61, 69, 70, 100, 101
  John, 113, 5, 10, 11, 12, 13, 15, 18, 31, 33, 38, 48, 52, 62, 66, 85, 89, 90, 94, 101, 112, 114, 115, 116, 118, 120
  Mary, 11, 18, 31, 33, 38, 39, 52, 66, 112, 113
  Rebacca, 35
  Rebeca, 30
  Rebecah, 48
  Rebecca, 30, 48
  Rebecka, 48
  Richard, 16, 18, 20, 23, 29, 31, 58, 64, 65, 66, 67, 76, 78, 80, 81, 82, 133
  Richardson, 18
RICHMANWORTH, 44
RICHMOND, Michaell, 120
RICOM, 73
RIDDICK, Robert, 19
RIDGEWAY, 99
RIDGWAY, 60
  William, 13
RIGHTS LOTT, 83
RIKY, Israel, 116
ROACH, Nathaniel, 53
ROAD, Charles, 34
ROADS, John, 123
ROADS CHOICE, 123
ROADS FOREST, 130
ROADS FORREST, 123
ROBBINSON, George, 73
ROBBISON, Ellinor, 92
  George, 74

John, 92
ROBBISSON, George, 119,
   123, 124, 128
ROBERSON, Lidia, 134
ROBERTSON, Elener, 38
   Elenor, 37
   George, 36, 44, 45
   John, 37
ROBESON, Andrew, 126
   Anna, 2
   Ellinor, 92
   George, 2, 3
   John, 3, 19, 90, 91, 92
   Sarai, 2
ROBESSON, John, 94
ROBINS, Thomas, 59
ROBINSON, Constance, 122
   Elin, 2
   George, 3, 55, 80, 98, 122
   John, 9
   Mary, 71
   Patrick, 59, 99
ROBISSON, Ann, 25
   Charity, 25, 59, 98
   Daniel, 26, 59, 98
   Daniell, 26, 59
   George, 25, 26, 59, 98, 99, 108
   John, 26
   Lawrence, 59, 98
   Samuel, 25
   Sarah, 26, 59, 99
ROCH, Deborah, 62, 63, 102
   Nathaniel, 54, 62, 63, 102
ROCK, Nathaniel, 102
   Thomas, 111
RODD, Berkley, 117
RODENEY, Caleb, 89
   Cesar, 122
   Daniel, 50, 83, 89, 122, 132
   Daniell, 19, 51, 52, 56, 96
   George, 89, 114
   Ruth, 46, 111, 112
   Sarah, 13, 23, 89, 122
   Thomas, 47, 111, 112
   William, 5, 6, 10, 11, 13, 14,
      17, 18, 20, 22, 24, 27, 34, 36,
      40, 45, 46, 47, 48, 49, 50, 51,
      52, 54, 55, 56, 62, 65, 67, 69,
      71, 74, 77, 79, 80, 82, 85, 89,
      90, 92, 93, 94, 96, 101, 102,
      103, 105, 107, 108, 109, 111,
      112, 122, 123, 124, 130
RODENY, Ruth, 105
   William, 67
RODGIERS, Thomas, 1
RODNEY, William, 47, 67, 107
ROE, Ann, 120
   Anne, 120
   David, 24, 70
   George, 115, 118
   John, 113, 115, 116, 118
   Judeth, 115
   Judith, 118
ROELOFF, Deborah, 35
   John, 35
ROGERS, Joseph, 127
   Mary, 127
   Thomas, 11
ROLEFF, Deborah, 35
   John, 35
ROODIN, 43
ROODING, 106
ROUSE, Hannah, 10, 58, 75, 98
   Mary, 9, 10, 50, 58, 75, 98
   Thomas, 9, 10, 39, 50, 58, 59,
      75, 98
ROW, David, 42
   George, 112
   John, 42, 43, 113
   Joseph, 42
   Judith, 112
ROWE, David, 24, 70, 128
   Joseph, 24
   Susannah, 70, 71
ROWLAND, John, 36
   Samuell, 43
ROXHALL, 42
ROYALL, Thomas, 58, 98
ROYDON, William, 60
RUDOLPH, John, 123

RUHMANS WOORTH, 36
RUMSEY, Charles, 51, 61, 97, 100
　Mary, 51, 61, 97, 100
RUMSY, Charles, 58
　Mary, 58
RUSSELL, John, 76, 128
RUTHERFORD, Anthony, 132
RUTHLEDGE, Edward, 105
RUTLEDGE, Edward, 83
RUTNER, John, 35
RUTTEY, Daniel, 66, 82, 123, 124, 131
RUTTINGTON, 123
RUTTY, Daniel, 46, 48
　Daniell, 24, 90
　Ellener, 90
　Ellinor, 90

-S-
SADDOCK, Zac, 34
SAINT ANDREWS, 23, 29
ST. ANDREWS, 16, 18, 89
SAINT COLLOM, 39
SALTONSTALL, Gordon, 129
SANDELAND, James, 14
SATERFIELD, James, 66, 72, 73, 109
　Mary, 66, 72
SAUNDERS, Elizabeth, 52
　John, 52
SCHARF, J. Thomas, v
SCHOOL HOUSE, 49
SCOT, John, 109
SEAT, John, 43
　Mary, 43
SEELY, Isaac, 59, 75, 98
　Joseph, 10
　Mary, 9, 10, 50, 58, 59, 75, 98
　Thomas, 58, 75, 98
SELVESTER, Thomas, 127
SEVEN HAVEN, 94
SHARP, George, 25, 32
　John, 71
　Sarah, 49

　Thomas, 1, 9, 14, 28, 45, 72, 84, 85, 93, 96, 126
　Thoms, 92
SHARPAS, Will, 7
SHARPE, William, v
SHAW, Henry, 63, 102
　Mary, 16, 17
　Thomas, 16
SHEPARD, Mary, 85
　Samuel, 85
SHEPARDS LOTT, 90
SHEPHARD, John, 40
SHEPHERD, John, 84
SHERER, Mary, 95
　William, 1, 95
SHERERS FORTUNE, 96
SHERRER, William, 52
SHERRITT, William, vi
SHERRITT'S CHOYCE, vi
SHERWOOD, Mary, 95
　William, 95
SHERWOODS FORTUNE, 95
SHEUSWORTH, 104
SHEWFORTH, 22
SHEWLY, Richard, 9
SHEWSBERRY, 131
SHIPPANORTON, 120
SHITEHART, Richard, 53
SHOEMAKERS HALL, 34, 37
SHORT ISLAND, 1, 52
SHOWFORTH, 19
SHREWSBURY, 94, 129
SHUMER, Benjamin, 23
SHURER, Benjamin, 100
SHURLEY, Rebaccah, 45
　Richard, 45, 55, 68
　Rodgeir, 3
SHURLEYS PURCH, 45
SHURMER, Ben, 20, 72, 76, 81, 85, 87, 98, 99, 114
　Benjaman, 53
　Benjamin, 20, 21, 23, 33, 34, 49, 50, 57, 60, 65, 66, 67, 68, 69, 77, 79, 80, 81, 82, 86, 99,

104, 105, 107, 112, 113, 115, 116, 117, 118, 119, 121, 126, 127, 132, 133, 134
  Benjamine, 97
  Sarah, 60, 99, 113
SIMKINS, Michael, 118
SIMON, Stephen, 38, 65
SIMONS, Stephen, 1, 3, 4, 9, 18, 90, 92, 95, 120
SIMONS FOLLY, 120
SIMPSON, William, v, 51, 94
SIMPSON'S CHOICE, v
SIMSON, William, 78
SIMSONS CHOICE, 3, 16, 29, 78, 108
SIMSONS CHOISE, 20
SIPEL, Waitman, 2
SIPELL, Garrett, 2
SIPLE, Christopher, 106
  John, 48
  Waitman, 47
  Wattman, 67
SIPPLE, ?fman, 44
  Christopher, 39, 106, 107
  John, 39, 106
  Lydia, 123
  Morriss, 107
  Waitman, 112
  Wateman, 44
  Waterman, 72, 81
SKETNDREWS, 18
SKIDMORE, 16
  Abraham, 25, 36, 43, 80
  Joseph, 4
  Thomas, 3, 4, 8, 35, 36, 44, 47, 48, 50, 65, 70, 82, 91, 107, 108
SKIDMORES FOLLY, 4, 14
SKIMORE, Thomas, 37
SKIPTOP, 105, 116
SLATER, John, 127
  Susanna, 127
SLAUGHTER, John, 5, 6
SLEEPS LOT, 37
SMALLCORN, John, 130

SMITH, Daniel, 121
  Daniell, 11
  Elizabeth, 11
  Henry, 65, 71, 80
  Jacob, 66, 89, 90
  John, 1, 3, 8, 12, 24, 36, 40, 91
  Joseph, 2
  Mary, 2
  Maurice, 93
  Morace, 3
  Morris, 48, 94
  Nathaniel, 74
  Richard, 46, 28, 35, 36, 45, 46, 48, 49, 50, 51, 55, 74, 114
  Sarah, 80
  Solomon, 48
  Susanna, 2
  Thomas, 2
SMOUT, Edward, 18
SNOW, Elisha, 25, 27, 28, 53, 75, 83, 118
  Isaac, 25, 27, 28, 49, 53, 55, 86, 87, 118
  Isack, 25
SOUTH HAMPTON, 66
SOUTHBE, William, 102
SOUTHBY, William, 60, 81, 99
SOUTHEBE, William, 17, 53, 63
SOUTHHAMPTON, 131
SOUTHHEMTON, 116
SOWELS POINT, 74
STANBURY, Nathan, 133
  Thomas, 133
STANDISHE, Daniel, 36
STANDLY, Christopher, 41, 45, 50, 51
  Mary, 41, 50
STANLEY, Christopher, 35, 57, 58, 97, 98, 100
  Mary, 57, 97
STANLY, Christopher, 52, 61
STARKEY, Ann, 111
  Edward, 63, 102

William, 21, 48, 63, 102, 111
STEALE, Frances, 8
  William, 8
STEAVENS, Elizabeth, 21
  John, 21, 49
  William, 51
STEEL, Arthur, 105
  James, 14, 17, 18, 19, 20, 23, 24, 25, 27, 28, 30, 31, 32, 33, 35, 38, 39, 40, 41, 46, 49, 53, 57, 58, 61, 65, 67, 68, 69, 70, 71, 72, 73, 76, 83, 84, 88, 97, 100, 108, 109, 115, 117, 118, 126, 133
  John, 71
  Martha, 18, 53, 83, 115
STEELE, Arthur, 105
STEELL, James, 42
  William, 12
STEELS LOT, 12
STEILL, Frances, 8
  William, 8
STEPHENS, Henry, 40
  William, 94
STEVENS, Elizabeth, 27, 28, 86
  Henry, 24, 29
  John, 55, v, 10, 15, 27, 28, 51, 86, 89, 90, 115
  Katharine, 29
  William, 5, v, 10, 85, 89, 90
STEVENSON, Henry, 1, 15, 52, 91
STIRK, Joseph, 128
STOLLGOFF, Garret, 45
STOOOPS, John, 60
STOOPS, John, 60, 99
STOTT, John, 74
STRALLOW, 92
STRATHCUM, 31
STRATON, Thomas, 122
STRAWHIN, David, 30
STRETTON, Thomas, 130
STUART, Michael, 34
STURGES, Jonathan, 48

STURGESS, Jonathan, 48
STURGIS, John, 66
  Jonathan, 63, 81, 86, 87, 102
STURKEY, William, 42
SULLIVAN, Cornelius, 44
SULLIVANT, Cornelius, 24
  Sarah, 24
SURGAN, 60
SURVEY, Thomas, 128
SWAMP BARRON, 129
SWAMPBORN, 39
SWIFT, John, 38, 54, 55, 56, 57, 97
SWILLIVANT, Cornellius, 44
  Sarah, 44
SYMKINS, Michel, 39
SYMONS, Mary, 35, 36
  Stephen, 35
SYMPSONS CHOYCE, 89
SYMSONS CHOYCE, 94

-T-

TALLMLUM, John, 72
TARRING, William, 75
TAYLER, Samuel, 33, 55, 56
  Samuell, 32
TAYLOR, Abraham, 22
  Jacob, 20, 28, 36, 60, 73, 99
  John, 34
  Samuel, 36, 38, 49, 54, 96, 97
  Samuell, 19, 20, 23, 53
  Thomas, 126
TEBOW, Andrew, 19
TESTER, Thomas, 116
THEROLD, Timothy, 12
THOMAS, James, 55, 60, 99
THOMAS HIS LOTT, 89
THOMPSON, Elizabeth, 52
  John, 51, 67
THOMSON, John, 111, 116, 126
  Mary, 47
THOROLD, Timothy, 7, 40, 91
THORP, George, 32
THROPP, John, 38

THYIEN, Joseph, 30
TILLING, Timothy, 133
TILLY, Timothy, 133, 134
TILTON, John, 28, 45, 118
TIPPEN, William, 41
TISOM, John, 133
TIVERTON, 89
TOAES, Daniell, 13
  John, 113, 114
TOAS, John, 113
TOBIAS, Mary, 43
  Tunas, 43
  Tunis, 45, 92
TOBITT, Cornelis, 54, 55
TODD, Abraham, 58, 75, 98
  Mary, 58, 75, 98
TOMBLIN, John, 119
TOMKINS, Joshua, 70
TOMPKINS, Anthony, 17
  Antony, 17
  Joshua, 17
  Joshuai, 17
TOMPSON, Urbanus, 31
TOMSON, John, 118
  Mary, 47, 92
  Samuell, 92
  Urbanus, 92
  William, 47
TONGE, William, 8, 9, 13
TOUNSEN, John, 2
TOUNSEND, John, 2, 3
TOUNZEN, John, 1
TOUNZENS FOLLY, 1
TOUNZIN, John, 106
TOWN OF DOVER, 67
TOWN POINT, 40
TOWN POINT, THE, 50
TOWNSEND, John, 75, 110
TOWNZIN, John, 110, 120
TRACY, Henry, 20, 34, 36, 38, 47, 76
TRAITT, James, 66
TRAVELLERS DELIGHT, 9
TREELAND, Isack, 12
TRIPET, William, 71, 107

TRIPINGTON, 108
TRIPIT, John, 71, 83
TRIPPET, William, 71, 83, 107, 108
TROY, 94
TUE, James, 89
TURBU, Benjamin, 131
TURNER, John, 35, 124, 133
  Richard, 1, 52, 95
  Robert, 19, 26, 46
  William, 130
TURNERS HILL, 133
TYRE, James, 122

-U-
UNDERWOOD, Richard, 83, 107, 126

-V-
VANBINGH, John, 7
VANDERFORD, John, 21, 25
VANNOY, Frances, 35
  Francis, 45, 51
  Kathrine, 45
VAXON, 32
VEFFEY, Robert, 63, 64
  Solomon, 64
VERHOOF, Cornelius, 123
VERHOOFE, Cornelious, 130
  Cornelius, 68
VICKERER, David, 53
VIRGIN CHANCE, 65, 103

-W-
WADDING, William, 134
WALKER, John, 2, 3, 4, 9, 11, 53, 55, 63, 67, 75, 81, 87, 102, 133
  Mary, 110
  Richard, 53, 73, 75, 109, 110, 118, 133
  Thomas, 53, 75
WALKER'S LANDING, 75, 83
WALLIS, Elston, 89
  James, 126

WALTER, Michel, 34
　Thomas, 83
WALTON, Michael, 12, 34
　Michall, 12
　William, 82
WAPPEN, 16
WARD, Thomas, 82, 113, 116, 118, 134
WARDELL, William, 3
WARNER, Mary, 130
WARRALL, Joseph, 27
WARRELL, Joseph, 27
WARTON, Walter, 70
WATERS, John, 32, 61, 100
WATKINS, Ann, 120
　Samuel, 106, 120
WATKINS DEAR PURCHASE, 120
WATTKINGS, Samuell, 48
WATTKINGS DEAR PURCH, 48
WAY, Richard, 7
WEAD, Thomas, 5
WEBB, Isaac, 34, 37, 43, 105, 122
　Mary, 34, 37
　Robert, 34, 37, 66
　William, 37
WEBSTER, Rachel, 43
　Richard, 131
　Samuel, 43, 77
WEDMORE, 56, 96
WEELS LOTT, 25
WELLDON, Joseph, 56, 96
WELLES PURCHASE, 116
WELLING BROOK, 13
WELLINGBROOK, 18, 90
WELLLINGBROOK, 114
WELLS, Ann, 123
　Catharine, 94
　James, 57, 94, 97, 108, 122, 123
　John, 18, 21, 23, 41, 45, 94
　Katharine, 94
　Mary, 94, 108

　Richard, 39
　Thomas, 29, 57, 90, 91, 94, 97, 116, 122, 123
　William, 40
WELLS PURCH, 91
WELLSWOOD, Francis, 19
WEMOIRE, 6
WESSEY, Solomon, 88
WESTBERRY, Thomas, 128
WESTWOOD, Francis, 1
WETTSWOOD, Francis, 1, 52, 95
WHALE, George, vi
WHARTON, Thomas, 71
　Walter, 70
WHARTONS, 131
WHEELER, John, 129
　Joshua, 129
WHITAKER, Moses, 116
WHITATEE, Moses, 84
WHITE, Benjamin, 4, 6, 44, 94
　James, 124
WHITE HALL, 21
WHITEHALL, 73
WHITEHART, James, 75, 83, 87
　Richard, 63, 66, 87, 93, 102
　Samuel, 63, 73, 87, 102, 117
WHITEHART NECK, 63
WHITEHARTS NECK, 102
WHITEHEAD, George, 33, 34, 49, 63, 88
　Isaiah, 47, 112
　Nathaniel, 119
WHITEHEART, James, 75
WHITEWELL, Frances, 99
　Francis, 30
WHITEWELL'S CHANCE, 73
WHITEWELLS CHANCE, 17, 28, 69
WHITEWELLS DELIGHT, 35, 59, 99, 103
WHITHALL, Francis, 36
WHITHART, Richard, 17
WHITHEAD, George, 63

WHITMAN, Samuel, 125
WHITTAKER, Ann, 127
  Moses, 127
WHITWELL, 46
  Francis, 17, 52, 53, 59, 60, 78, 81, 99, 118
WHITWELLS CHANCE, 126
WHITWELLS DELIGHT, 108
WHORTONS, 131
WILBEE, Samuel, 110
WILEMAN, H., 119
WILKINS, Richard, 72
WILLCOE, Barnabas, 99
WILLIAM BROOK, 101
WILLIAMS, Aaron, 43
  Alece, 47
  Edward, 24, 85
  Kathrine, 47
  Mary, 47
  Owen, 36, 47
  Reinier, 2
  Reynear, 39, 82
  Reynier, 130
  Richard, 44, 50, 57, 81, 97
  Rineer, 43
  Thomas, 51, 95, 103
  William, 92
WILLIAMS CHANCE, 103
WILLIAM'S CHOICE, 70
WILLIAMS CHOICE, 65, 105
WILLIAMS FANCY, 24
WILLIAMSON, John, 56, 96
WILLIBE, Samuel, 110
WILLINGBROOK, 33, 62, 115
WILLLIAMS, Reynor, 82
  William, 82
WILLOBE, Samuel, 110
WILLROE, Abraham, 60
WILLS, William, 20
WILLSON, 67
  Elizabeth, 46, 51
  James, 120
  Joannah, 124
  John, 19, 22, 68, 74, 102, 119, 123, 130, 132
  Mary, 46, 51, 120
  Mathew, 119, 12, 92, 111
  Matthew, 91
  Michel, 37
  Richard, 3, 33, 37, 45, 46, 51, 55, 58, 67, 73, 81, 101, 107, 115, 120, 123
  Robert, 107, 123, 126
  Samuel, 46, 124
  Samuell, 124, 131
  Thomas, 2, 5, 11, 17, 29, 53, 93, 95, 100, 102, 111, 125
  William, 2, 3, 6, 13, 17, 26, 80, 95, 112, 113, 114, 125
WILLSONS CHOICE, 41, 55
WILLSONS FANCY, 74
WILLSONS PURCHASE, 41
WILSON, Abel, 108
  Deborah, 63, 102
  John, 52, 62, 63, 101
  Mary, 72
  Richard, 51, 53, 62, 72, 107, 133
  Samuel, 107
  Samuell, 116
  Thomas, 53, 60, 62, 63, 83
  William, 77
WILSONS CHOISE, 51
WILSONS WILD, 9
WINDFORD, Alexander, 74, 84
WINDFORD'S DESIGN, 84
WINGATE, Mary, 12
WINSMORE, Thomas, 12
  William, 4, 6, 12, 16, 17, 24, 30, 81, 82, 105, 108, 111, 119
WISE, Abigail, 59
WITHERS, Thomas, 18, 23, 44
WITHOLL, Thomas, 76
WOOD, Joseph, 88
WOODSTOCK BOWER, 35, 44
WOODWARD, William, 20
WOOTTERS, John, 18
WORCESTER, 123
WORD, Margrit, 31

Patrick, 31, 43, 92
WORESTER, 16
WORRAL, James, 113
WORRALL, James, 108, 112, 118
Joseph, 112
WORRELL, James, 78, 109, 131
John, 78
Joseph, 39, 77, 78, 99
WRIGHT, Animadab, 71
F. Edward, vi

-Y-
YATES, Jasper, 91
YEATS, Jasper, 14, 88
YEO, William, 130
YORK, 5, 85, 114, 115
YORKE, v, 52
YOUNG, Thomas, 119
YOUNG HALL, 19